Fundamentals of Economics

Making Your Way in Our Economy

Second Edition

Daniel Francis Hess, NBCT

v2.1

Author

Daniel Francis Hess is a teacher with National Board Certification who teaches advanced placment economics, economics, and entreprenuer studies to high school students. He has written curricula as well as other topics in history and economics. He earned his MA from Cleveland State University.

For Sophia, Brendan, and Billy

Editorial Director: Dawn P. Dawson
Proofreader: Chris Moose
Editorial Assistant: Melissa R. R. Gutierrez
Graphic Designers: Joseph Diaz, Linda Deverich
Cover Illustration: Joseph Diaz

Printed in the United States of America

The Center for Learning
10200 Jefferson Boulevard, P.O. Box 802
Culver City, CA 90232-0802
United States of America

(310) 839-2436
(800) 421-4246

www.centerforlearning.org
access@socialstudies.com

This book replaces the *Fundamental Economics* curriculum unit published by The Center for Learning in 2001. This version contains 20 percent more content, updated statistics, and more than thirty new and revised worksheets.

ISBN: 978-1-56004-977-7
Product Code: CFL221 v2.1

Contents

Introduction

What a privilege it is to be an economics teacher. From the earliest class discussions to their final exam, students never need to be reminded of the importance of the subject. While it may not be their favorite class, most students will admit that it is their most *useful*.

Many people consider economics a dry, dull subject. In reality, it is the most current and vibrant offering of any social studies department. When taught well, students will find the material engaging, challenging, and illuminating.

This text condenses a great deal of material into easily learned segments. Six units fit easily into a standard-length semester, or units can be lifted and taught as components in other classes. Each unit begins with questions aimed toward promoting a lively, Socratic discussion. Reading sections are conveniently numbered and lettered (reading 1A connotes the first topic from the first unit). Worksheets, called *handouts*, are listed similarly, with the unit number first and the handout number second (Handout 1.1, for example). Each reading section builds off its predecessor, allowing for meaningful scaffolding of content. The handouts provide different ways to help teachers deliver content and assess student performance.

In this second edition, the amount of lessons, readings, and handouts has increased. Numerous Internet-based assignments teach students not only how to conduct research but also how to hone their critical thinking skills. Students are encouraged to evaluate the validity of information and consider the source.

This new edition also helps students satisfy the requirements of the Common Core State Standards. They will learn key ideas and details necessary for understanding economics. They will integrate concepts and ideas into their own unique worldviews. They will use their acquired skills and knowledge on their paths to becoming well-informed and responsible citizens.

This textbook is a broad survey. The six units follow a logical order from simple to complex and local to global. Students will study markets and basic economics first. The microeconomics of business and labor follow in Unit 2. The macroeconomics of money, monetary policy, and fiscal policy are covered in Units 3 and 4. Leave the most time for the fifth unit on personal finance. It covers many essential life skills and includes new sections and handouts on cyber threats and identity theft. Last, the book concludes with an exploration of globalization and technology.

Unit 1
Basic Economics

Questions to Consider

1. What do you consume in an average day?
2. What is the difference between a "good" and a "service"?
3. What is the difference between a good and a bad economy?
4. How is our economy doing now?
5. How do consumers decide what they want to buy?
6. How can an economy grow?
7. How are our lives affected by a bad economy?
8. Who is in charge of our economy?
9. What do we produce in the United States?

Terms You Need in Order to Read

Demand
Economics
Economy
Market
Recession
Scarcity
Supply

Basic Economics

1A. What Is the Economy?

At its heart, economics is about *happiness*. People may not know much about economics, but they know about the economy. We are all a part of it, and we have a sense of how it is doing. We are all aware of our own financial well-being, our employment status, and the prospects for the future. We also try to make decisions that we believe are in our own best interests. People make decisions attempting to maximize their own satisfaction. In fact, economists try to understand how people satisfy their wants and needs. We all make decisions, buy products, switch jobs, or start businesses in order to maximize our happiness.

How many times have you heard people discussing the economy? Sometimes you overhear the news as you ride in the back of your parent's car. Adults often talk about situations at work, how their business is doing, or changes in the economy. Maybe you had a relative out of work. These conversations can bore you to tears, but there are a great many reasons the economy is on their minds. It affects each one of us. They might say that the economy is "bad right now," or that economic conditions are such that "unemployment is rising." You may have heard on the news that the economy is "doing very well" or "heating up." Young adults usually become aware of the economy in their late teens, soon after they get their first jobs.

Think about the 1930s Great Depression from your history class. It is safe to say that it was the worst economy of the last one hundred years. Somewhere around 30 percent of our workers did not have jobs. It started with a 90 percent drop in the stock market and a wave of bank failures. Many families lost their life savings. People were scared. They bought fewer goods, and businesses slowed production. If fewer people are working, then fewer goods are being produced. The cycle continued (graphic 1.1). In other words, there was little consumption and little production of goods and services. It took people a long time to get over the shock. Eventually, World War II provided enough demand for goods to kick-start production and hiring.

GRAPHIC 1.1

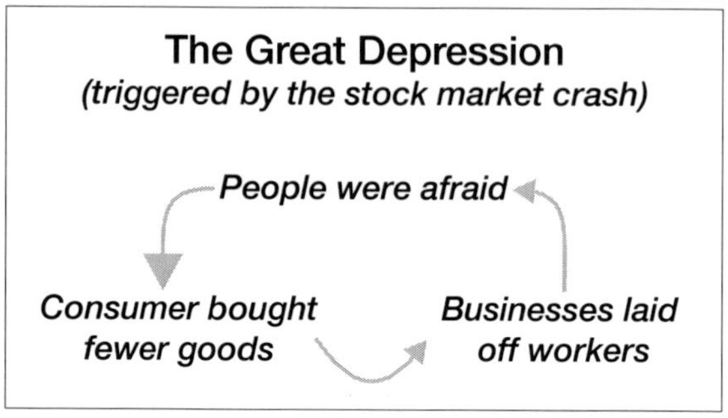

The Great Depression
(triggered by the stock market crash)

People were afraid

Consumer bought fewer goods

Businesses laid off workers

Simply put, an **economy** is a system of consuming and producing. To fight in World War II, our government needed businesses to produce many **goods**. Today, material goods are not the only things that people can produce and consume. **Services** (80 percent of our entire economy) are actions or activities that are done for others for a fee. While Ford and Apple make goods, lawyers and accountants provide services.

GRAPHIC 1.2

When an economy produces and consumes at a high rate, it allows some people to spend extra cash on luxuries.

A dairy produces milk, but the store provides the service of putting it on shelves for retail sale. No matter what we do for a living, we are all subject to the swings in the economy.

Every person in the United States has a lot at stake when it comes to the health of our economy. Economists tell us how things are going and where we might be headed. Their predictions are used by businesses that might want to buy new equipment or used by a government that wants to provide social services. Economists are highly trained and educated. **Economics** is a social science: the study of the production, consumption, and distribution of society's scarce resources. It is relatively young compared to other areas of study, only about two hundred years old. Its most useful ideas are even newer, and we will learn more about them later in section 1E.

Since the Great Depression, our economy has grown steadily (about 2 percent) each year. It doubles in size about every thirty-five years. There have also been times when it has not done well. Year after year, however, and on average, this growth means that we have higher and more disposable incomes, more great things to buy, and a higher standard of living than in previous years.

Pressing Question

- How has our economy changed in the last fifty years?

1B. Scarcity and Opportunity

The fundamental problem of economics is **scarcity**. In our world, people have unlimited desires and wants, but our resources are too limited to satisfy them. People must decide how to allocate time, money, and resources. We also often want multiple things at once. Some decisions we make without much thought, while others are more difficult. If you decide to hang out with friends, then you may not have time to study for your math test. If you spend your twenty dollars to see a film, then you cannot also get a burrito on the way home. These choices are the very heart of economics.

We all have **wants** and **needs**. Our needs include things like food and shelter. They are necessary to our survival. Jewelry and a new dining room set are wants. They are not vital to life, but we desire them just the same. Based on our resources, we must make decisions about how to satisfy our wants and needs.

As a result of both your limitless wants and limited resources, if you decide to buy a new smartphone it may mean you will not have enough money for homecoming. You must choose. If you spend money on one thing, it will not be available for another. This dilemma is fundamental to the study of economics. You have to weigh the benefit of owning a phone versus a night out with your friends at a dance. How much additional benefit (**marginal benefit**) will the phone give you? How much would it hurt (**marginal cost**) not to go to the dance? The deliberation is what we call **marginal analysis**, and the choice with the higher marginal benefit wins (see graphic 1.3).

GRAPHIC 1.3

Marginal Analysis			
Your decisions	marginal cost	versus	marginal utility
Business	marginal cost	versus	marginal revenue
Government	marginal social cost	versus	marginal social benefit

The scarcity of our resources also leads to **competition** for those resources. For instance, how does the movie theater get you to buy a ticket and not buy that delicious burrito? Is there a way the burrito restaurant could get you to choose food over entertainment? Those businesses know you have only so much money. They have to compete in order to get you to make a choice that benefits them.

Consider another business example. A dentist faces a difficult decision. Some other local dentists bought a machine that takes 3D images of patients' teeth instead of the old fashioned X-ray films. The machine costs $125,000. How does the dentist make such a huge financial decision? She will make a **cost-benefit analysis** (graphic 1.4). This is when a person assesses how much a decision will cost and weighs it against benefits gained.

If that new machine generates more profits and business than what it costs, she will buy it. She has to predict how much extra money will come into her practice if she buys the machine.

Businesses, governments, and individuals are confronted with choices all the time. A **choice** is an act of selecting or making a decision when faced with two or more possibilities. In economics, a choice between two alternatives is called a **trade-off**. Economists do not consider every available choice; that would be impossible. Instead, we only consider the *next best* alternative. In your case, you were confronted with the choice of a film or a burrito. You love burritos, but you really wanted to see the film. Each of those options is the next best alternative to the other. Let us say you choose the film. The benefits you give up by making a decision are called **opportunity costs**. In this case, the film cost you the enjoyment of eating a burrito.

Economists analyze not only what you do but what you do not do. They really want to know if our decisions create the most satisfaction and efficiency for ourselves and our society. No matter how good the news is, you can always find an economist who can point out the downside. This is why economics is sometimes referred to as "the dismal science."

GRAPHIC 1.4

Cost-Benefit Analysis
marginal benefit (MB)
marginal cost (MC)

If MC < MB, make that choice
If MC > MB, don't make that choice

Choosing between food and a film is a simple example, but what if the decision involves millions or billions of dollars? What if the wrong decision could ruin your company or cost thousands of jobs? A trade-off becomes more serious when the costs are much higher. Businesses and governments seek guidance from economists who can help predict what the costs of decisions will be. They can help weigh alternatives and provide insight on the benefits. Whether it is going to see a film or building a billion-dollar factory, economists study choices.

Because economists are concerned about each person's happiness, they want people to have the freedom to make their own choices. They want business owners to decide on how to conduct their affairs most efficiently. They want governments to interfere with these decisions as little as possible. Economics studies how our systems are imperfect and how sometimes situations can take away some of our happiness. For instance, if a government overtaxes its people, its people will get less satisfaction out of the money they earned. If a monopoly raises prices above a fair market value, it reallocates money that should be spent by those consumers into its own bank account. Economics is really the study of efficiency, so economists dislike wasteful and inefficient behavior. The more efficient our economy, the more happiness it can produce.

Pressing Question

- Name one trade-off decision you had to make in the last couple of days. How did you come to that decision? What were the benefits and costs?

1C. Life on the Margins

Scarcity, trade-offs, and opportunity costs are vital concepts in economics. To analyze how businesses and individuals make decisions, however, economists use marginal analysis. In economics, marginal means "one additional." Whether an economist is studying individuals, businesses, or governments, the most efficient place for them to make a decision is where the cost of that choice equals the benefit.

As an individual, you make these decisions all the time. You are concerned with the utility of a product, service, or decision. **Utility**, or satisfaction (and happiness), is the perceived ability of something to satisfy our wants and needs. Consider a simple example. You are taking a very restful nap on the couch. Your phone is across the room. It signals that a text message has just come in.

To sleep, or not to sleep, that is the question. Which decision will bring you more utility? If you keep napping, then you will get the benefit of that extra sleep (but then you might miss an important text). If you get up, it will cost you that rest you need.

Let us consider a business next. Your favorite pizzeria is considering staying open later. The owner estimates that he could sell $600 more of pizza. He knows that the extra labor, utility bills, and supplies would cost him $500. Should he do it? Economically, staying open a little longer makes sense. He would increase his profits by $100 per night. If he goes ahead with his decision only to find out he's making $400 per night, then he will quickly realize that he made the wrong decision.

Governments use the same calculus to decide whether to commence a public works project. A local government is considering building a bridge over a river valley. Local engineers estimate it will cost $100 million. Citizens must pay higher taxes to fund the bridge. Economists estimate that the bridge will save commuters thousands of hours in travel time to work. Time sitting in a car is not productive. If people get to work more quickly, then they can make more money. They spend less money on gas and get bigger paychecks. Therefore, if the taxes (marginal social cost) are less than the increased earnings and quality of life (marginal social benefit), then the community should build the bridge.

No matter the circumstance, economists know that the most people benefit when those people make rational decisions that they consider to be in their best self-interest. In addition, if there are no barriers to consumers and producers interacting, then society can reach **allocative efficiency**. This is a situation in which consumers are all paying the lowest prices possible and all the producers capable of supplying at that price are doing so. This means that nobody has an advantage in the market to raise prices, no consumer or producer is forced out, and all resources get allocated in a way that maximizes society's utility.

Pressing Question

- How many pieces of pizza can you eat before the marginal utility begins to fall?

1D. Types of Economies

Modern humans appeared on Earth about 150,000 years ago. For most of that time, people survived by hunting and gathering. As farming developed, communities formed alongside rivers. From these earliest civilizations, almost everybody worked on farms. They plowed fields with their own strength and tools. Eventually, they domesticated animals, which made farming somewhat easier. Even though their techniques were primitive compared with today's methods, at times they produced surplus food. This excess of energy not spent on farming allowed others to specialize in different occupations like masonry or pottery. People then desired these goods and began to trade. They wanted to maximize their utility.

There are a variety of basic decisions that must be made when it comes to running a society's economy. First, leaders must decide on how much freedom to give citizens. Second, they must decide what goods will be produced. Third, the difficult question of how the goods are to be distributed must be answered. An **economic system** is an organized set of procedures and practices that a society follows in the production and distribution of goods and services. It answers three basic questions: What gets produced? Who produces it? and who gets the product? In essence, *Who gets what and why*? Economists have identified four types:

- **Traditional economy**—Older systems like these rely on customs and past practices to answer these questions. Religion and culture aid in the passing of skills from parent to child. Change happens slowly because people are reluctant to move away from how things were done in the past. This system is rare today, existing in only the most isolated parts of the world.
- **Command economy**—This kind of economy relies on powerful government officials using

central planning to make economic decisions. They decide on how goods will be produced, how many are made, and how they are distributed. The individual plays little or no role in economic decisions. In ancient Egypt, the Pharaoh exerted considerable control over the economy. In medieval feudal societies, manor lords exercised similar power. North Korea is still attempting to enact this model.

GRAPHIC 1.5

Even ancient civilizations like Egypt had vibrant economies. Pharaohs wielded great influence on what was produced and consumed, marshaling society's resources for elaborate burial rites.

- **Market economy**—This system relies on individuals to make all economic decisions. The government has little or no say in what is produced, sold, or consumed. Consumers buy what they believe will maximize their utility. Producers produce only what they believe will maximize their profits. A **market** is a place or venue where goods and services are exchanged. People are motivated by self-interest. Producers strive to maximize profit while consumers look for lower prices. In the end, markets, more than any other economic model, tend to serve a society's needs best.
- **Mixed economy**—This classification occurs when it combines aspects of the market and command systems. Most economies today can be classified as mixed. In a modern economy, as in the United States today, individuals own and control the resources. The government does have some control of the economy through taxation and regulations. Our system favors the individual's freedom in the market-place and is sometimes referred to as capitalist. Nations like North Korea that are closer to the command-style economy are known as authoritarian socialist or communist. The government controls most of the resources and makes most economic decisions.

One final note: People often confuse communism and socialism. For example, a country like Sweden has a mixed economy that has many socialist aspects. The government levies high taxes for which the citizens receive a great many social programs, such as state-provided medical care and higher education. However, as in other modern democracies, the people still elect a government.

Examine graphic 1.6. The horizontal line shows a spectrum of economies. The vertical line shows a range of different political systems. Notice that Sweden is farther right along the market—command economy line. It is also a democracy, placing it farther up the politics line. We call their society democratic socialist (a system discussed in Unit 6). The United States is more market oriented, as is China. The United States and China have very different political systems. Hence, the two societies occupy different spots on the political and economic spectra in graphic 1.6.

Pressing Question

- A warlord in western Afghanistan controls the opium trade and shipments of foreign aid. What type of economy is it?

GRAPHIC 1.6

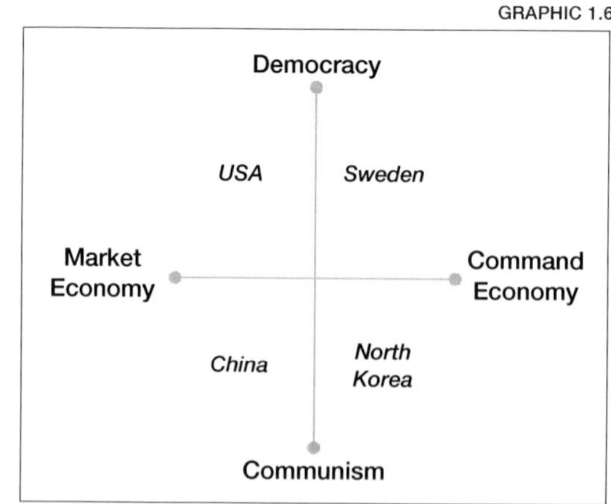

1E. Studying Economics

Something might have occurred to you as you read the last section. Each of the four systems addressed in the previous section answers the question, "Who gets what and why?" While that question puts it rather simply, it captures the essence of what economics is all about. Economists study how people deal with the fact that goods and services are inherently scarce.

Businesses have scarce resources, because time, money, and labor are finite. Economists take a careful look at businesses and their productive efficiency and study the markets in which consumers interact with producers. They want to know what people buy. They study trends in business and consumer behavior. These topics and the study of economics on a smaller scale are known as **microeconomics**.

Economists also study how resources are allocated nationally and globally. For example, while the United States has more than 4 percent of the world's population, we produce 22 percent of the world's goods and services. How did we gain such prominence? In what ways do we interact with other countries? The economic subject that focuses on international trade issues and national topics is called **macroeconomics**.

As our world has become increasingly complex, professions and careers have become increasingly specialized. Generally accepted views in one decade have been altered or cast aside by the next generation. Current major schools of economic thought include:

- **Classical**—The classical school of thought dominated economics through much of the 1800s and 1900s. It primarily holds that markets and economies self-regulate and that individuals make rational decisions based on what they believe to be in their best self-interest. Its prominent thinkers include Adam Smith, David Ricardo, and Milton Friedman.
- **Marxist**—This school of thought bears the name of its creator, Karl Marx. He is considered the father of modern socialism. His book, *The Communist Manifesto*, attests that history is a story of class struggle between owners and laborers. His book predicts a worldwide revolution in which workers would become the owners of the means and production and would distribute resources more equally.
- **Keynesian**—Named for British economist John Maynard Keynes, these ideas offer an antidote to the boom and bust cycles that occur in unregulated economies. Keynesians advocate the use of government involvement to alleviate the unwelcome social and economic effects of recessions. Their ideas are in direct contrast to those of the classical school.
- **Behavioral**—This is the youngest of the four schools of thought. Its ideas first appeared in the 1960s. This field combines psychology and neurology with economics and challenges the idea that people are always rational. Consumers often make decisions that go against the classical model. These economists try to show how human behavior affects the overall economy.

Regardless of the economist's viewpoint, each tries to explain how an economy can more efficiently distribute its resources.

Pressing Question

- What circumstances have led to the dominant position of the United States in the global economy?

1F. The Factors of Production

Think about a car that you might want to buy sometime in the future. How did the company actually produce it? They needed steel, rubber, and land. Workers labored on assembly lines to put it together. Computers, robots, and other advanced technology made the production process more efficient and cost-effective. The owners of the company risked their own time and money on the success of the venture. If any of these factors are missing, the car cannot be produced. This is the reason these features are called the **factors of production**. Also sometimes called the *means of production*, they are as follows:

- **Labor**—The application of human physical and mental talent to the production process.
- **Natural resources**—Items provided by Mother Nature. Remember that coal, oil, and natural gas often help produce electricity. Anything that is harvested off the land (graphic 1.7) or taken from the earth is included. This includes the land itself.

GRAPHIC 1.7

Even though agriculture accounts for less than 2 percent of the US economy (by dollar product), it is still vital to our society. In ancient civilizations, farming was the majority of the economy.

- **Capital**—This is the term for the tools, equipment, and machinery needed in the production process. New scientific methods improve products, invent new products, and increase efficiency. These new technologies, methods, and applications also fit under this category.
- **Entrepreneurs**—Finally, you need someone to put it all together. Someone has to risk time and money. A person's creativity, capital, know-how, and personal drive are instrumental to success.

Without all four of the factors of production, it is impossible to provide a good or service. Consider anything that you consume. Try to name the factors of production that brought it to you. In addition, remember that each factor of production is scarce.

Economists have ideas about how efficiently we can produce the goods and services we consume. They know that rarely are we completely efficient. They also know that, in order to keep the economy growing, we need to buy machines, build new roads, and invent new technologies. These **capital goods**, as they are called, will allow us to become more efficient in the future. More capital in place can help produce more consumer goods in the long run.

To illustrate all the possible combinations or capital and consumer goods, economists use

GRAPHIC 1.8

Course	Section	Instructor	Time	Room
ECN 201, Principles of Macroeconomics, 3 credit hours:				
	Section 1	Hess	T/Th 10:00-11:15 am	MC 106
	Section 2	Cicetti	MWF 11:00-11:50 am	MC 101
ECN 202, Principles of Microeconomics, 3 credit hours:				
	Section 1	Evans	T/Th 8:30-9:45 am	MC 106
	Section 2	Pecot	MWF 9:45-10:35 am	MC 104
ECN 301, Global Economics, 3 credit hours:				
	Section 1	Wimbo	MWF 1:30-2:20 pm	MC 105
ECN 302, Monetary Policy, 3 credit hours:				
	Section 1	Howard	MWF 9:45-10:35 am	MC 322
	Section 2	Caliguire	T/Th 10:00-11:15 am	MC 322
ECN 333, Fiscal Policy, 4 credit hours:				
	Section 1	Ober, SJ	MWF 9:45-10:50 am	RT 337
ECN 350, Economics of Crime & Punishment, 4 credit hours:				
	Section 1	Masterson	MWF 11:00-12:05 pm	MC 322
ECN 433, Industrial Organization, 4 credit hours:				
	Section 1	Corrigan	T/Th 1:00-2:50 pm	MC 311

Here is an example of a college's offering of economics coursework. Notice that the topics get more specific as you go through college.

a curve called a **production possibilities frontier**. Each point along the curve (graphic 1.9) represents a different mix of capital and consumer goods. As society makes more consumer goods, it must make fewer capital goods, and vice versa.

GRAPHIC 1.9

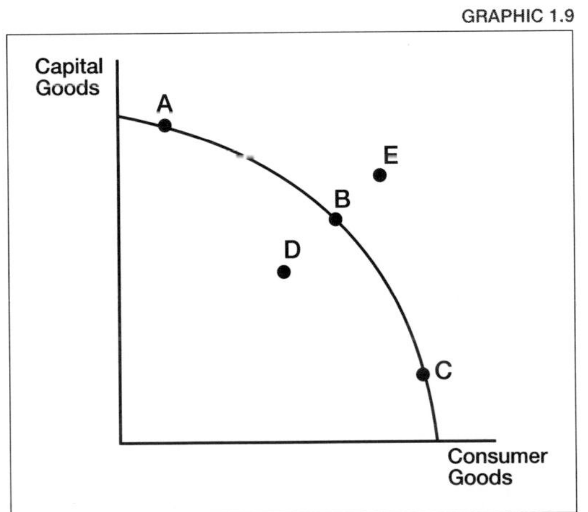

- **Point A**—Mostly capital goods being made.
- **Point B**—Capital and consumer goods created in relatively equal numbers.
- **Point C**—Mostly consumer goods being made.
- **Point D**—A point of inefficiency. Society is, for some reason, not producing these two goods efficiently. The line of the curve represents full capacity.
- **Point E**—Represents an amount of capital and consumer goods that society cannot reach yet.

Economists like to see our businesses and governments investing in capital. This allows us to become more productive in the future. We will be able to produce more goods more efficiently because of the money that we invest today. If society must allocate resources to particular goods, some should help ensure our future prosperity.

Pressing Question

- What factors of production were used to produce your family car?

1G. Markets and Their Behavior

Over the years as a species, we have developed economic systems in which we produce and consume. Throughout history, people have become more and more specialized in their trades, skills, and knowledge. Farmers would seek out goods to improve their lives and exchange their produce for products that would increase their overall utility. For instance, a farmer, busy in his fields, does not have time to make his own plow. He could, however, seek out a blacksmith with whom he could trade wheat for a plow. Often, this transaction would take place in a market. While today's exchanges are usually more complex, the idea behind them is the same.

Recall from section 1D, a market is any venue in which consumers and producers meet to exchange goods and/or services. Sometimes these resemble flea markets and other open-air exchanges. The New York Stock Exchange is a market that relies on human beings and computers to see that stock is traded from one investor to another. An example of a web-based market is eBay, which relies on the Internet to link suppliers with consumers. Markets take many different forms, but in the end their purpose is to exchange something to each party's mutual benefit (graphic 1.10).

GRAPHIC 1.10

Two Sides to a Market

Consumers	***Producers***
Want the lowest price	*Want the highest price*

Do markets need help in order to maximize the benefits to those who use them? That is an excellent question. Many economists subscribe to the idea that all markets, big and small, should be free of any interference, taxation, and regulation. They believe that a free market is most efficient in the absence of any government interference. In a completely free market, people demand goods and services to satisfy their wants and needs, and businesses and individuals are given free rein to attempt to supply those needs.

However, other economists believe that markets do fail to be efficient from time to time. These occurrences are called **market failures**. For instance, if a manufacturer makes a profit one month because she saved money by dumping chemicals in a river, society must bear some of her production costs when it cleans up the mess. Her business was not profitable after all, and her product should be priced higher. Another market failure might include a business that has the ability to dictate prices. Markets that have only one producer will have inflated prices. These monopolies produce less and charge more to inflate their own revenue. In essence, this transfers money from consumers' pockets to that of the monopolist. Economists do not consider that efficient.

The US economy is known for its steady growth, relative efficiency, and business freedom. It is made up of innumerable markets—local, regional, national, and global. Free markets are indeed more efficient, but markets are not perfect. They are made up of human beings who can sometimes abuse their market position.

One positive fact remains. Markets, on a simple level, can be modeled and can be predicted. Keep reading and you will learn how.

Pressing Question

- Define the following terms: *marketing*, *market research*, and *test marketing*.

1H. The Law of Demand

When you first chose to take economics, you probably thought very little of the prospect. What may have come to mind, though, are the words *supply* and *demand*. We need to look at these concepts very closely. As you are going to realize, they are very different.

Demand is the amount of a good or service that consumers are *willing* and *able* to buy at a given price. You have been a consumer your entire life. You cannot even count all the goods you have purchased over the years, although you know a good deal when you see one. You know how to use technology to find the lowest prices. Additionally, if you find something you normally buy available at a lower price, then you might buy more of it.

With this in mind, who do you think are the consumers in a market? Businesses need accurate figures to plan on how much to produce. For example, you may want to buy a Lexus when you get out of college, but that will probably not be an option. You desire the car, but you will not have the money or the credit. You are willing to buy a Lexus, but you are not able. Hence, you are not a consumer in the luxury car market.

The **law of demand** states that an increase in price will bring a decrease in quantity demanded, while a decrease in price will cause an increase in quantity demanded. This is common sense to us. Let us talk lunch. Your favorite burrito joint sells them at $7.50. Somebody at school hears that there is a sale, and the vendor has reduced prices to $5.00. What would happen? After school, a large throng of your classmates will descend on the restaurant to get the good deal. When the price decreased, the quantity demanded increased.

In this law, there is an inverse relationship between price and quantity. If you plot all the possible combinations of price and quantity, it will yield a curve (straight lines in our class) with a *negative* slope.

Price always goes on the y-axis and Quantity always goes on the x-axis. Examine graphic 1.11. At point A, the price is high, so fewer consumers are willing and able to pay at that level. Notice how the quantity demanded is low. As the price drops, every point on the line represents another possible combination of price and quantity. At point B, the price has decreased. This brings more consumers into the market to get that bargain. The people at that end of the curve will be the ones who drop out when prices rise.

GRAPHIC 1.11

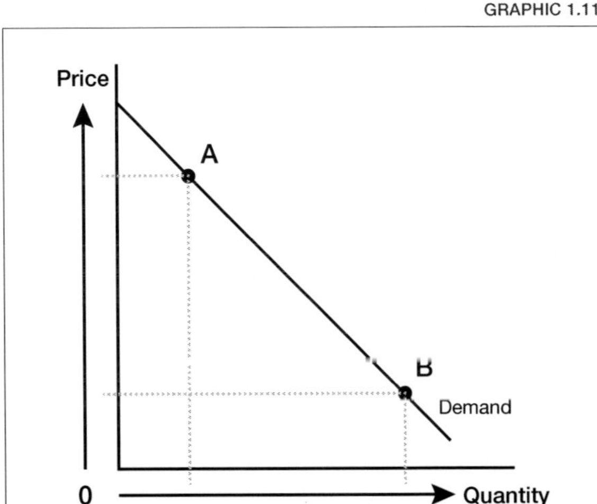

GRAPHIC 1.12

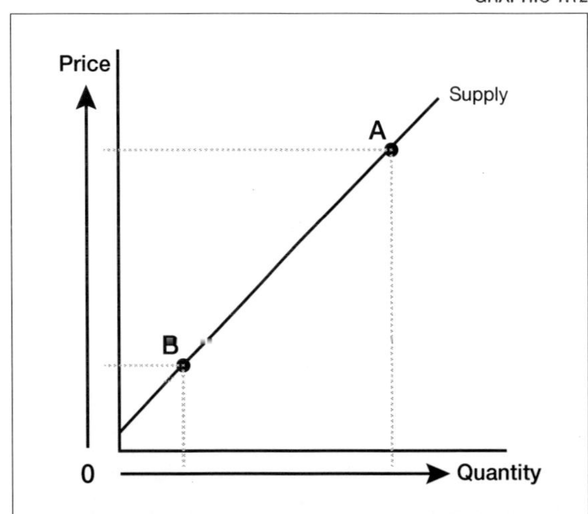

Pressing Question

- When was the last time you bought something on sale? Why did the business reduce its price?

11. The Law of Supply

Unlike the law of demand, the law of supply can be a little tricky. It is time to think like a *producer* (seller of products or services). People go into business to make a **profit**, the amount of money that a business owner can keep once all expenses are paid. However, running a business can be difficult. Satisfying customers can prove challenging, and other businesses want to take more market share. Markets are competitive and consumers demand quality at a low price.

After all of the expenses have been paid, one hopes to have money left over. When consumers want a product at certain price, a good business will do what it can to fill that demand. If the price in a market rises, firms will produce more so they can boost revenue. New businesses will join the market to make money as well. Thus, the **law of supply** states that an *increase* in price will result in an *increase* in the quantity supplied, while a *decrease* in price will cause a *decrease* in the amount supplied.

In the law of supply, the relationship between price and quantity is positive. When graphed, the line depicting producers' reactions to an increase in market price has an upward slope. Examine graphic 1.12. At point A, the price is high. Many producers have increased their production while many new firms have joined the market. An increase in price might mean an increase in profits if other costs stay the same. Conversely, as the price drops, producers will scale back their output. Some companies are not as efficient as others and will drop out of the market, because they cannot make a profit at the lower price. At point B, only the biggest and most efficient firms will remain.

Consider the global oil market when prices are $120 per barrel (point A). New wells are tapped all over Canada and the United States. They can get oil to market at $65 per barrel. For a variety of reasons, oil prices can drop. If they fall below $65, many North American firms will cap their wells rather than take a loss on each barrel. Foreign producers like Saudi Arabia can bring oil to market at $8 per barrel. At point B, they will be one of the few producers who can make money in the oil market.

It is important to think like a producer when considering supply. The object of business is to make a profit. So, if the market is offering a higher price, you will increase production. This could mean higher profits for you. If you choose not to increase production, then *others will step in to provide the product.* They might take your market share. Free markets do that.

Pressing Question

- How does the law of supply differ from the law of demand?

1J. Markets at Equilibrium

Supply and demand graphs are models of reality, like a model airplane. We cannot fly in a model airplane, because it is *just a model* (not to mention very small). These graphs are very handy ways of looking at human behavior. However, they work on the assumption that everything makes sense and runs logically. Humans are not always logical. The behavior of an individual human being is hard to predict, but when we are all together in a market, we can figure out what will happen if things should change.

The good news is that you do not have to consider a bunch of variables at once. Our markets will change in simple and predictable ways. For example, consider the world oil market again. Suppose another country discovers oil. That means there is more oil in the market, right? End of discussion. We do not have to worry if the tankers got lost at sea, or if there was a terrorist attack. Only one thing will happen at a time.

The **price system** is the means by which the price of a good or service is determined in a market economy. When a business produces something, it hopes to find a customer, retrieve the money spent in production, and make a profit. When businesses approach the marketplace, they post a price that says to customers, "If you want my product, you'll have to give me this much." Consumers also approach the market with something to say. If they choose to buy, then they signal to the business that they consider the price fair. If they forgo the purchase, the producer is being told that the price is not acceptable. The firms will respond by lowering prices until people start to buy.

When you are asked to "draw a supply and demand graph," graphic 1.13 is what you should duplicate. On a graph like this, the two opposing motivations, suppliers going for the highest price and consumers vying for the lowest price, come into balance at point A.

GRAPHIC 1.13

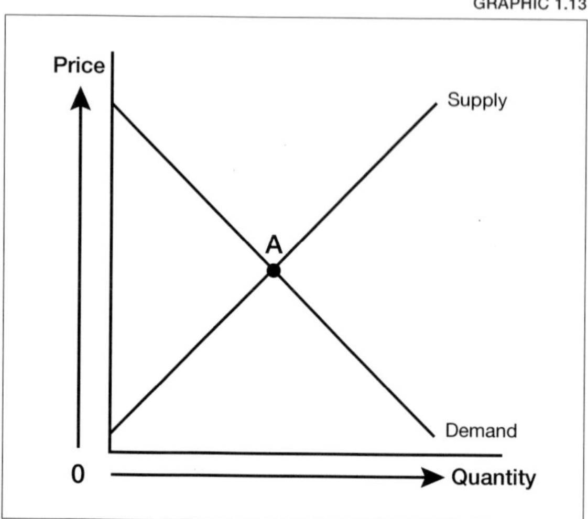

As you may have guessed, market price and market quantity are determined graphically at the point where the supply and demand curves meet. This point is called **equilibrium** (point A). It occurs when the supply for a product matches the demand for a product.

Pressing Question

- Consider your favorite sports team. What do you suppose the equilibrium price and quantity are for a regular season game?

1K. Markets Change—Demand

The simple demand curves that we have been studying may shift from left to right. Now, this does not mean a move in price along the demand curve. Rather, the entire demand curve will move left or right. This happens because all the possible prices and quantities that consumers would be willing and able to accept have changed.

For example, every summer, many Americans take to the road on summer vacations. This means that the demand for gasoline increases. Every possible combination of price and quantity along the first demand curve no longer makes sense. More cars will be on the road, and people will want that gas. If supply stays the same, this shift in demand means that consumers will want a higher quantity of gas and are willing and able to pay a higher price.

Examine graphic 1.14. There are two demand curves. The first one represents the usual market for gasoline. Demand 2 shows a new set of price and quantity combinations brought about by the increased demand of the driving season. Point B on the graph *shows what the market wants*. Consumers are willing and able to pay a higher price.

GRAPHIC 1.14

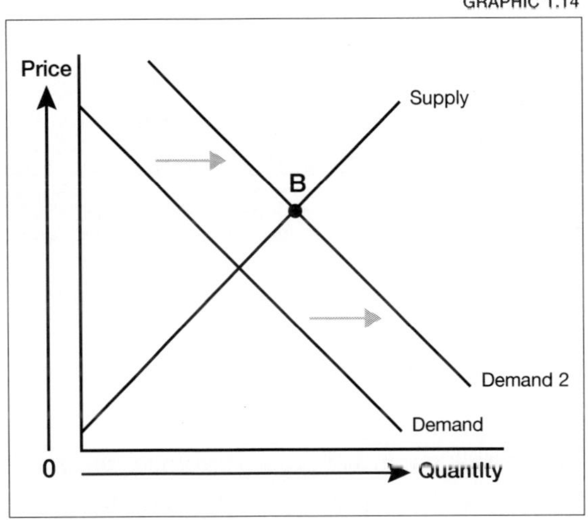

Any action that moves an entire demand curve is called a **determinant of demand**. These actions can make the curve move left or right. There are five of them:

- **Consumer preferences**—Shifting tastes can increase or decrease the demand for a product. For example, as more people prefer to use their cell phones as a primary means of telecommunication, the demand for landlines has decreased.
- **Market size**—The number of consumers joining or leaving a market can move the demand curve. If there is a baby boom in the United States, the demand for diapers will increase.
- **Income**—How much money consumers have to spend can alter their demand for goods and services. If the average income in the United States increases, then the demand for vacation rentals will increase.
- **Prices of related goods**—Many products are used in place of one another. They are called **substitutes**. When the price of beef doubles, the demand for pork will increase. On the other hand, many products are used together. We call them **complements**. If the price of gasoline falls, then the demand for cars will increase.
- **Consumer confidence**—Adults are aware of the state of the economy. If businesses are laying off people as a result of a slowing economy, it can make everyone feel nervous and unsure of their future. This will decrease the demand for many goods and services.

GRAPHIC 1.15

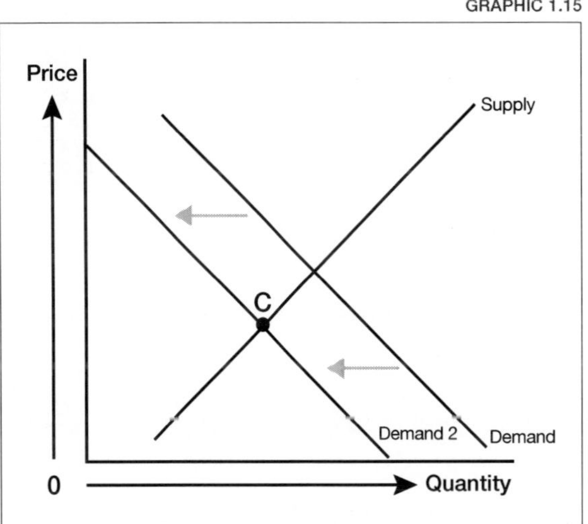

Examine graphic 1.15. How does it differ from graphic 1.14? In this graph, the demand curve shifted to the left. This can happen for many reasons. If people notice that a lot of coworkers and neighbors are losing their jobs, those who are still employed will tend to be slightly more careful with their money. They will not go out to eat as much. They will stay home instead of going on vacation. This dim outlook on their economic future will decrease the demand for restaurant meals and vacation rentals. Point C in graphic 1.15 shows the new equilibrium point brought about by the new demand curve, Demand 2. In this case, the market will only bear a lower price and a lower quantity.

Pressing Question

- List three things that could change the demand for cafeteria food at your school.

1L. Supply Curves Move Too

In the previous section, demand curves shifted to the left or right when market conditions changed the way consumers interacted with the market. On the other side of the market, producers will react to market changes by altering their willingness and ability to supply a certain amount of goods at a given price. These occurrences that move supply curves left and right are called **determinants of supply**. There are four:

- **Technological improvement**—Firms are always on the lookout for computer software, robots or other technology that can help them make more product more quickly and at a lower price. **Technology** is any process, machine, or application of scientific knowledge that increases productivity.
- **Resource prices**—Also known as "input prices," the price of these factors refers to anything needed to make a product or provide a service. Soda makers will alter their supply if the price of sugar changes. Car manufacturers will change production if the price of steel doubles.
- **Taxes and subsidies**—Government action can affect markets. A per-unit **tax** on a product will move the supply curve to the right. On the other hand, a **subsidy** is a payment to a business to help it lower costs or develop new products. Taxes reduce supply and subsidies increase supply.

GRAPHIC 1.16

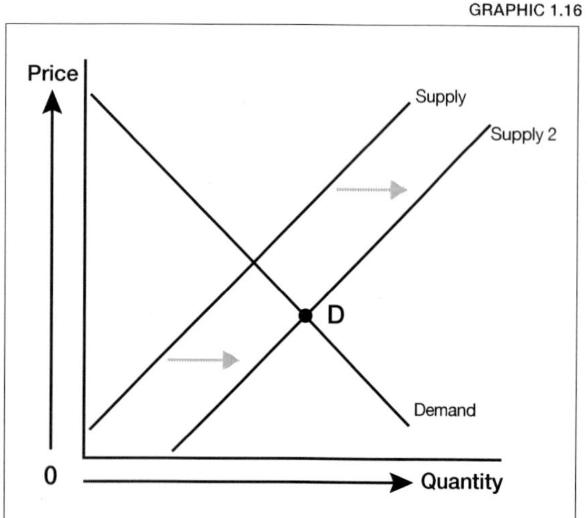

- **Competition**—If any business makes large profits selling a new product, then more firms will try to join that market. If more companies start delivering more products into the market, the quantity supplied will increase and prices will go down. Examine graphic 1.16. With more companies supplying more products, a new equilibrium point is created at point D.

A trick to remembering which way a curve should move is to pay attention to the quantity axis. Ask yourself, "Will this scenario increase quantity or decrease quantity?" If more companies join the market, it makes sense that more products will be supplied. That means the supply curve will have to move to the right. If it goes the other way, the quantity supplied would decrease.

This trick will help you in scenarios in which supply decreases. Consider the market for gasoline in the United States. We produce about one-half the oil we consume and import the other half. Gas is a by-product of crude oil. Oil must be refined to extract the gas. What if a hurricane disables many refineries along the coast of Texas? Would there be more gas or less gas in the market? Logically, there would be less, because the refineries would not be in place to keep supplying gas.

Consider graphic 1.17. The supply curve moved to the left, indicating less gas in the market at a higher price located at point E. This is what the model of the gasoline market would look like if a hurricane disrupts refinery capacity in the United States. This shift will make price increase and the quantity supplied decrease.

When trying to determine if a scenario will move the demand or the supply curve, ask yourself, "Which side of the market will be affected first, consumers or producers?" In the car market, producers watch the price of steel. A change in its price will affect supply. If people begin to prefer biking, the demand for cars will be affected. There is no shortcut to determining whether the market will have a shifting supply or demand. A young, budding economist must use intuition.

Pressing Question

- Will supply or demand move in the market for honey if (a) bee colonies collapse, (b) the news reports that honey prevents aging, and (c) scientists cure the disease that is causing bee colonies to collapse?

GRAPHIC 1.17

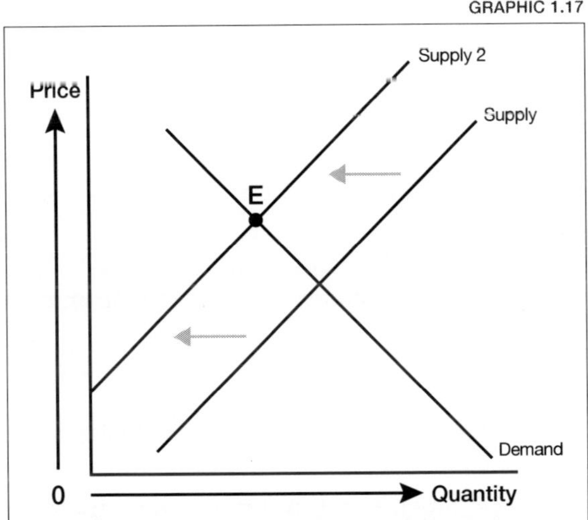

1M. Shortages and Surpluses

Businesses are constantly challenged to find out exactly what price to charge consumers. Furthermore, they must try to gauge how much of their product the consumer will be willing to buy. Because of this uncertainty, markets are rarely static, as the price system fluctuates in order to find a true resting point. In a market, consumers and producers settle on a quantity and a price. Let us use the volatile world oil market as an example.

Prices in markets tend to be "sticky." Producers are reluctant to move their prices quickly with every shift of supply and demand. Examine graphic 1.18. Demand increased in this market. The new equilibrium point shows that the market wants a higher price and a higher quantity (point A). At the original price, however, something different has happened. At that price, the quantity demanded exceeds the quantity supplied. Locate the two diamonds along that price (points B to C). Find where the price hits the demand curve and where it hits the supply curve. Because consumers want more than suppliers will supply at that price, there is a **shortage**, a situation where quantity demanded exceeds quantity supplied.

GRAPHIC 1.18

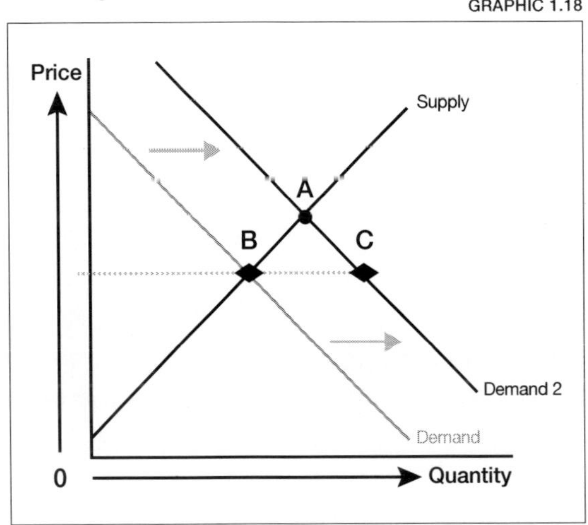

Similarly, a shift in the supply curve will cause a market imbalance (graphic 1.19). Let us assume the oil market is at an original market price of $80. That price hits the old supply curve (faded) at point A. Suppose geologists discover oil under Lake Erie. This oil is recovered and quickly finds its way to market. A new equilibrium price and quantity (what the market wants) will appear at

GRAPHIC 1.19

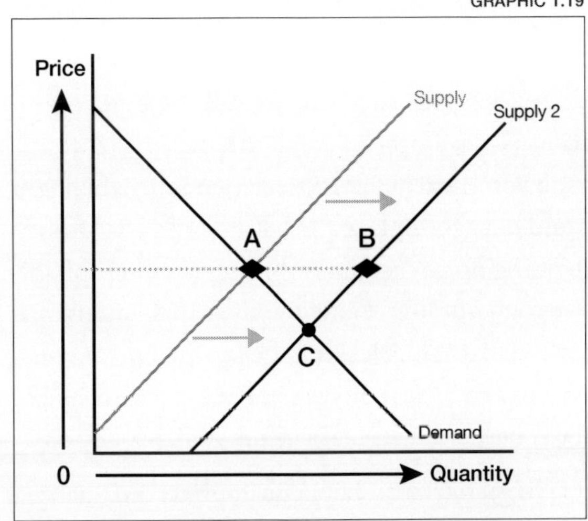

point C between points A and B would indicate that the quantity supplied exceeds the quantity demanded. This is known as a **surplus**.

Pressing Questions

- What happens to prices eventually when there is a shortage?
- What happens to prices when there is a surplus?

1N. Price Elasticity

Think about a rubber band. The more elastic it is, the more it can stretch. If a market price changes, there will usually be a change in the quantity demanded. How much will quantity change, however? Economists call the degree of that change a product's **elasticity**.

GRAPHIC 1.20

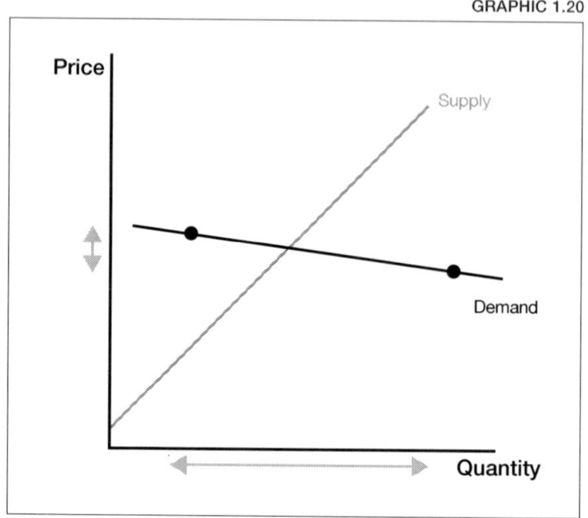

Examine graphic 1.20. When the price changed only a little, the quantity demanded changed to a much greater degree. Economists would say that this product has an **elastic demand**. A product like a candy bar would have a demand curve that looks like that. This occurrence happens because people know that they can live without the products, so they are more sensitive to price changes. Therefore, when price changes by a small percentage, sales will fall dramatically. We call products like candy bars **luxuries**. As a result of people feeling they do not need luxuries to survive, they will react to a higher price by doing without the product altogether.

On the other hand, there are products that are necessary to our survival. We call these **necessities**. For example, if you had a pacemaker that made your heart beat more dependably, then you would have to replace the battery every so often. Deciding not to get a new battery would probably cost you your life. You would buy that battery no matter what the price. A huge jump in price will not keep you from buying it. Paying a lot for a battery is better than a massive heart attack any day.

No matter what happens to price, the quantity demanded will remain rather constant. Look at graphic 1.21. Notice that when the price increases or decreases on the y-axis, the quantity on the x-axis hardly moves. Economists would say that pacemaker battery sales have an **inelastic demand**. How inelastic the demand for a certain product is depends greatly upon how much people need or want the product. Recall from section 1C that utility is the satisfaction people get from a good or service. For example, coffee in the morning might have a high utility, but late at night the same coffee has no utility. A bottle of water has utility in normal circumstances equal to about a dollar. Stand in line at an amusement park for a few hours, and the utility of that water will jump to a much higher level. The demand for water is much more inelastic when you are thirsty.

GRAPHIC 1.21

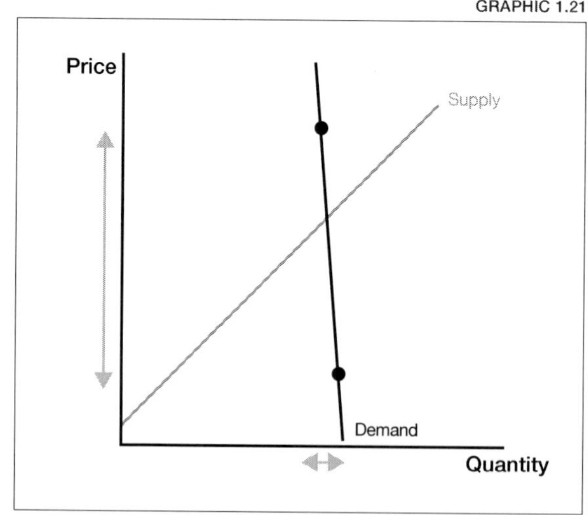

Last, when you venture out on your own into the "real world," what do you suppose you will eat? Many college students living on a shoestring budget eat generic goods and inexpensive foods like ramen noodles. They dream of the day when their budgets no longer constrain their diets. When they get a job and make more money, they will buy less of those cheaper foods. Products that one buys less of when one's income rises are called **inferior**. As people make more money, there are some products they tend to buy more often. These are called **normal goods**. Most students do not have money for luxurious items like steak and shrimp, but once they graduate and begin collecting a paycheck, their budgets may permit these purchases.

Pressing Question

- Think of two products that you buy that have an inelastic demand and an elastic demand, respectively.

GRAPHIC 1.22

Diamond/Water Paradox

Why do people pay so much for diamonds, but not a lot of water? After all, water is a necessity, and diamonds are a luxury. The reason behind this paradox is found in marginal utility.

Drink a bottle of water. If you are thirsty, that water has great utility. But your thirst is quickly quenched. A second bottle of water has far less utility, practically none.

If you get a diamond as a gift, it too has a high utility. But its utility does not diminish over time. It tends to remain high.

10. Elasticity of Supply

Changes in the price offered by the market will affect the amount of goods and services produced by businesses. The degree to which a product's supply is affected by price is called the **elasticity of supply**. The issue is not one of choice. If the price that consumers are offering for a product goes up, producers will usually make more. However, *can* they make more? The key phrase to remember in this tricky area of economics is "ease of production," or how easily a good or service can be produced and provided.

Let us compare two different products. First, say there is a factory that makes T-shirts with funny slogans. If the market price of the product increases, then the firm responds to the higher price by a relatively large increase in production. The shirts are relatively cheap and easy to make. We could say that they have an elastic supply. Consider graphic 1.23. Notice how the supply curve allows the quantity to stretch from point A to point B with a very small increase in price. That flexibility is why T-shirts are considered a product with an elastic supply.

GRAPHIC 1.23

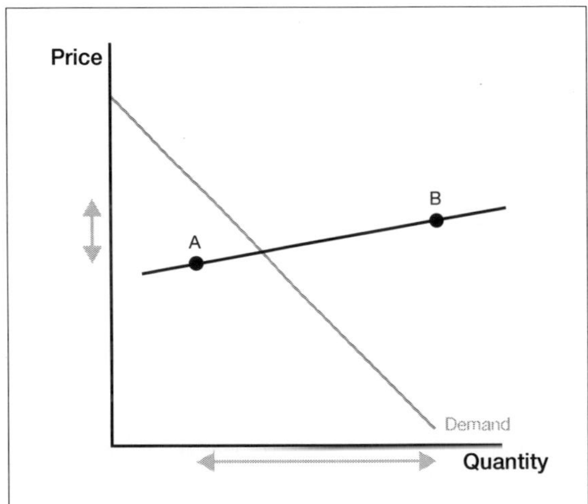

Second, let us consider the Boeing 787 (see graphic 1.24). A dictator in the developing world promises to pay triple the sticker price to buy airplanes for his country. He is angered when Boeing turns down his offer to buy twenty planes at $600 million apiece, especially when they cost only $225 million to begin with. Go back to the "ease of production" phrase that was mentioned previously. Jets are not something quickly or easily constructed. They are massive pieces of intricate machinery and technology. No matter what you offer, Boeing simply cannot make more. See graphic 1.24. The quantity does not stretch very much from left to right. Hence, economists refer to a product like a jet as having an **inelastic supply**.

Pressing Question

- Why do tickets to a school football game have a perfectly inelastic supply?

GRAPHIC 1.24

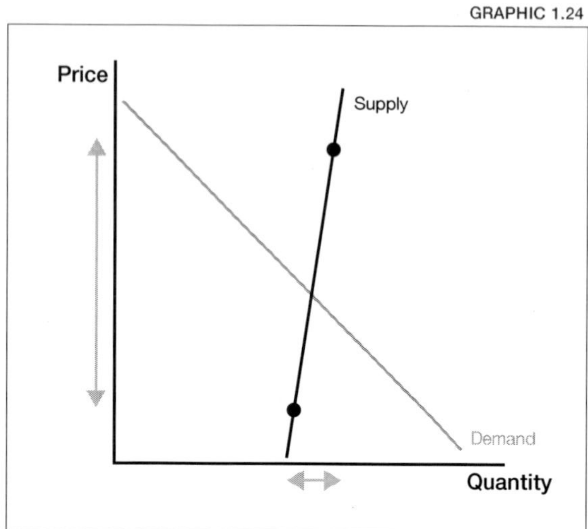

GRAPHIC 1.25

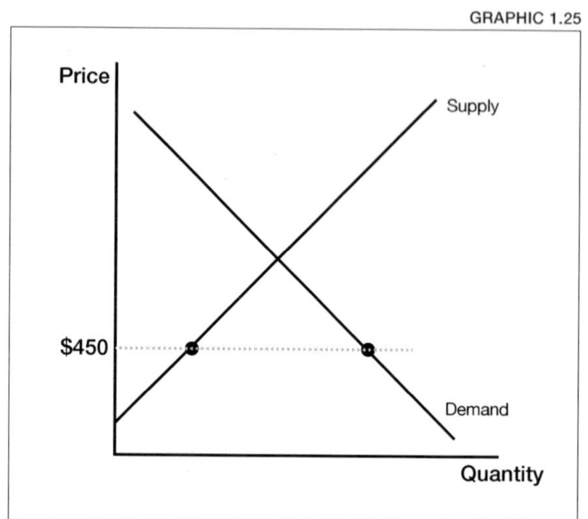

1P. Floors and Ceilings

After World War II, many veterans came home and decided to start families. There was a great demand for housing in American cities, because of this phenomenon. As soldiers moved back into cities, there was a strain on the housing market. There were not enough places to live for all the people who wanted them. This elevated demand created a spike in prices. Many veterans could not find affordable housing. To bring prices down, some local governments decided to impose rent control on apartments. In other words, according to their own beliefs, housing prices were too high, so they decided to set a maximum price that landlords could charge. We call that a **price ceiling**. See if you can notice the problem that arises when rent controls are imposed in graphic 1.25.

At $450, the supply of apartments will be very low, as landlords cannot afford to pay their house payment if they have to charge low rent. Consumers love the idea of the low rent and rush into the market. Because of the low price, everyone wants to move to the city. The quantity demanded will outstrip the quantity supplied. Many people want to move, but the shortage will leave many people without a place to live.

On the other hand, some American prices are set by the federal government. Imagine that the labor market and unions appeal to the government for higher wages to keep up with cost-of-living increases. Because people believe that the minimum wage is too low, the government will set a higher one. Examine graphic 1.26.

If the wage is set far above the true market equilibrium, many unemployed people will rush into the labor market to find a job. The quantity demanded for workers at $18 per hour is lower than the quantity supplied. There will be a surplus of workers (also known as unemployment). A minimum price for a product is called a **price floor.**

Setting a minimum wage, or any price control for that matter, can be troublesome. Legislators

GRAPHIC 1.26

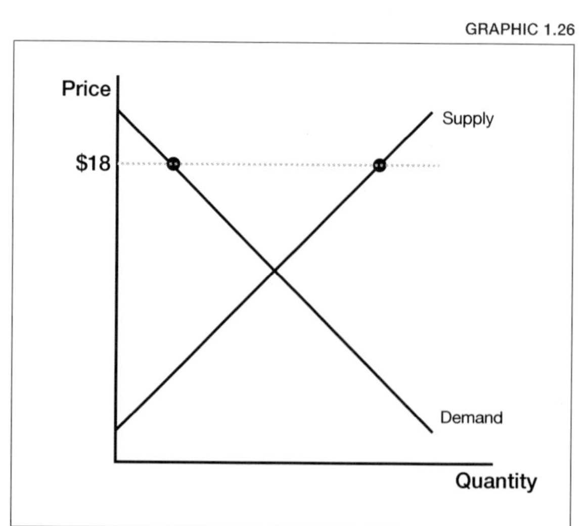

are, in essence, saying that they can predict what the market will bear. If they overshoot the actual market wage, then people will lose their jobs.

Proponents of this type of policy will say that it is a matter of justice for low-wage workers. They maintain that the current minimum wage is lower than the true equilibrium price. Raising it simply brings us up to equilibrium. Opponents of minimum wage argue that the government should not set prices and that markets should be the arbiter of what people earn. So what is the true minimum wage? What is the answer? This is a matter of much political debate.

Nevertheless, price floors will usually result in a surplus, and price ceilings will usually result in a shortage.

Pressing Question

- Consider graphics 1.25 and 1.26. Why do students typically get confused when graphing a price floor and a price ceiling?

Name:

Vocabulary Activity

Directions: Find the words from your reading that fit the blanks. Then unscramble the message at the bottom from letters that you placed in the boxes to answer the question, "How big is our economy?"

1. A system of production and consumption _ _ ☐ _ _ _ _
2. The study of the distribution of scarce resources _ _ _ _ _ _ _ _ _
3. The type of economy we have in the United States _ _ _ ☐ _
4. An economic system in which the factors of production are held in private hands _ _ _ _ _ _ _ _ _ _
5. A good that is commonly used in conjunction with another good _ ☐ _ _ _ _ _ _ _ _ _ _
6. A market in which supply cannot meet the demand _ ☐ _ _ _ _ ☐ _
7. A good that is commonly used to replace another good _ _ _ _ _ _ _ _ _ _
8. People try to satisfy their wants and ___________. _ _ _ _ _
9. The price of making an economic decision is called the _______ cost. _ _ _ _ _ _ _ _ _ _ _
10. A maximum price set for a product _ _ ☐ _ _ _ _
11. A person who risks capital to start a new business venture _ _ _ ☐ _ _ _ _ _ _ _ _ _
12. Another word for money or things bought with money _ ☐ _ _ _ _ _
13. Supply that exceeds the demand for a product _ ☐ _ _ _ _ _
14. The human element in the process of production _ _ _ ☐ _
15. New methods and innovations of production _ _ _ _ ☐ _ _ _ _ _
16. The usefulness or satisfaction one gets from using a product _ _ _ _ _ _ _

 Name:

17. The study of economics on a smaller scale _ _ _ _ _ □ _ _ _ _ _ _ _ _ _ _

18. The relationship between price and quantity _ _ _ □ _ _ _ _ _ _ _ _

19. A minimum price set for a product _ □ _ _ _

20. When price goes up, quantity goes down. This is the law of ________. _ □ □ _ _ _

21. When price goes up, quantity goes up. This is the law of __________. _ _ _ _ _ _

22. A type of economy in which custom decides who gets what and why _ □ _ _ _ _ _ _ _ _ _ _

How big is our economy?

_ _ _ _ C _ _ _ _ _ Y _ _ _ _ _ _ L _ Y _ U _ _.

Name:

Life on the Margins

Part 1

Directions: Fill in the blanks below using words from the Unit 1 readings.

The fundamental problem of economics is ________________ (1). People have unlimited wants and ________________ (2). Often times, we do not have enough time or money to satisfy all them. We must make ________________ (3). A choice between alternatives is called a ________________ (4), and every time we are forced to choose, there is an ________________ (5) cost. Therefore hundreds of times per day, without thinking about it, we make a ________________ (6)-benefit analysis. The additional happiness we get from a decision is called our marginal ________________ (7). We calculate how much a decision will cost us and how much it will benefit us. Our personal benefit or happiness is called ________________ (8). It is important to remember, that every time we have a trade-off, we will have to pay an opportunity cost. Such is the nature of scarcity.

Part 2

Directions: Review reading 1F. Using your own habits as your guide, try to answer the questions about the production possibilities graph on the right. Let us assume you have seven hours of free time every night when you get home. Let us also assume that you will spend that time doing homework or engaging with your friends on social media. Try to explain what is happening at each of the points.

- Circle the point at which you do seven hours of homework.
- Circle the point at which you do seven hour of online chat.
- Estimate the time spent on each activity (homework and social media) at points:

	Homework Time	Social Media Time
Point A		
Point B		
Point C		
Point D		
Point E		

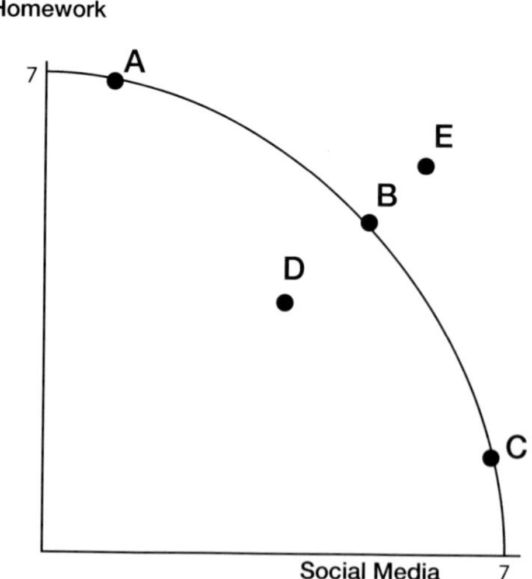

Name:

Economic Systems

Part 1

Directions: Fill in the table below with help from your reading.

What are the three questions a society must ask about its economy?

1.

2.

3.

	Pure Command	Mixed	Pure Market
1. Who gets to answer those questions?			
2. How much freedom do citizens have?			
3. What are some benefits of this economy?			
4. What is a downside of this economy?			

Part 2

Directions: Review reading 1D. Place the words in Box 1 on the ends of the grid in Box 2.

Box 1
market economy
dictatorship
command economy
democracy

Box 2

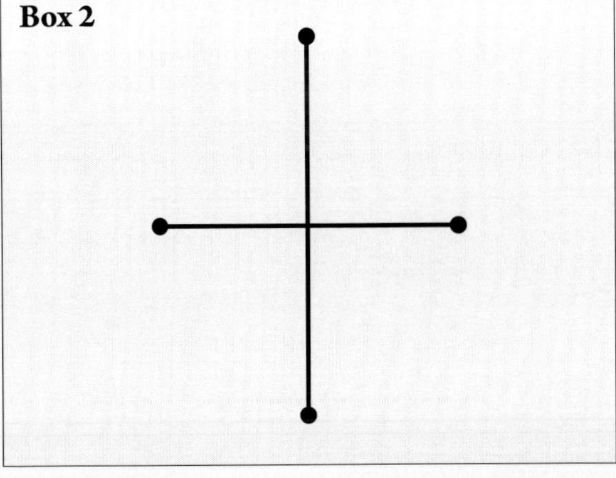

Part 3

Directions: Place the following countries on your grid in Box 2.

Hesstonia
A capitalist country with economic freedom, easy business start-up, and general political freedoms. Economic growth is dependable.

North Oppressionville
This reclusive regime uses communist central planning to control its economy. People have no political rights. Repression is brutal.

Socialtopia
People here pay high taxes in return for cradle-to-grave social care. They have full political rights.

Rising Star
This former communist country is using market reforms to grow economically. People have few political rights but can own property.

Name:

Production and Consumption

Part 1

Directions: Choose four products or services and fill in the chart with each of the factors of production needed to manufacture or provide them. Write the product in the first column.

Product	Labor	Natural Resources	Capital
1.			
2.			
3.			
4.			

Part 2

Directions: Consider the electric car industry. For each of the following factors of production, describe a change that could help increase/decrease the supply of electric cars.

Electric Car Market			
Factors of Production	**Make Supply Increase**	**Factors of Production**	**Make Supply Decrease**
Labor		Labor	
Natural resources		Natural resources	
Entrepreneurship		Entrepreneurship	
Capital		Capital	

1. What happens to price and quantity when supply increases? Decreases?

Name: ____________________

Supply and Demand Intro

Part 1

Directions: Fill in the blank to finish all of the following sentences:

1. Demand is the amount of goods or services that ________________ are willing and ________________ to buy at a given ________________.

2. The ______________ of demand states that as price increases, consumers will buy a ______________ quantity.

3. Supply is the amount of goods and services that _____________ are willing and able to ______________ at a given price.

4. The law of supply states that as price decreases, producers will produce a ______________ quantity.

5. The supply curve has a _____________ slope while the demand curve has a ___________ slope.

Part 2

Directions: Label the graph axes and "curves." Then answer the questions.

1. Some producers of oil can get product to market at very low prices. Where are they on the graph?

2. Other oil producers are less efficient and will only enter the market when prices are very high. Where are they on the graph?

3. Certain consumers are willing and able to pay a high price for steak, no matter what. Where are they on the graph?

4. Other consumers will buy steak only when prices are low. Where are they on the graph?

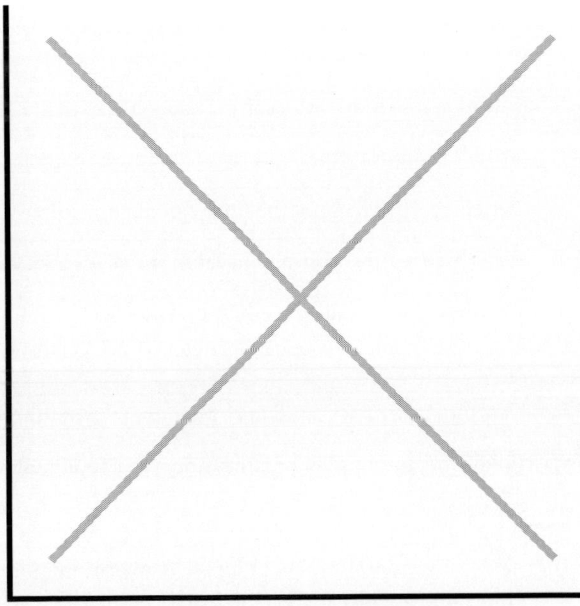

Name:

Supply and Demand in Action

Part 1

Directions: Use your reading to list the determinants of demand and supply in the table below.

Determinants (instances that make markets change; scenarios that shift curves)	
Demand	**Supply**
1.	1.
2.	2.
3.	3.
4.	4.
5.	

Part 2

Finish the sentence and put your answer in the blank.

1. ______________ Increasing demand for a product should make prices go…
2. ______________ Increasing supply for a product should make prices go…
3. ______________ Decreasing demand for a product should make prices go…
4. ______________ Decreasing supply for a product should make prices go…

Part 3

Check the box to indicate that the scenario is an issue of supply or demand for the market in parentheses.

Issue of supply or demand?		
	Demand	**Supply**
1. More people move into a city. (restaurant market)		
2. More restaurants open in a city. (restaurant market)		
3. People feel good about the future of the economy. (car market)		
4. Health-conscious consumers eat more salads. (lettuce market)		
5. Beehives die in California. (almond market)		
6. People switch from coffee to tea. (tea market)		
7. The auto industry uses 3D printing to make dashboards. (car market)		
8. People begin to prefer organic food. (fast-food market)		
9. A new study states that sun exposure causes more cancer than ever. (hat market)		
10. Watching entertainment online becomes more popular. (Internet-provider market)		

Name:

Supply and Demand Shifts

Part 1

Directions: Properly label all the graphs below. Following the prompt underneath each one, alter the graph accordingly.

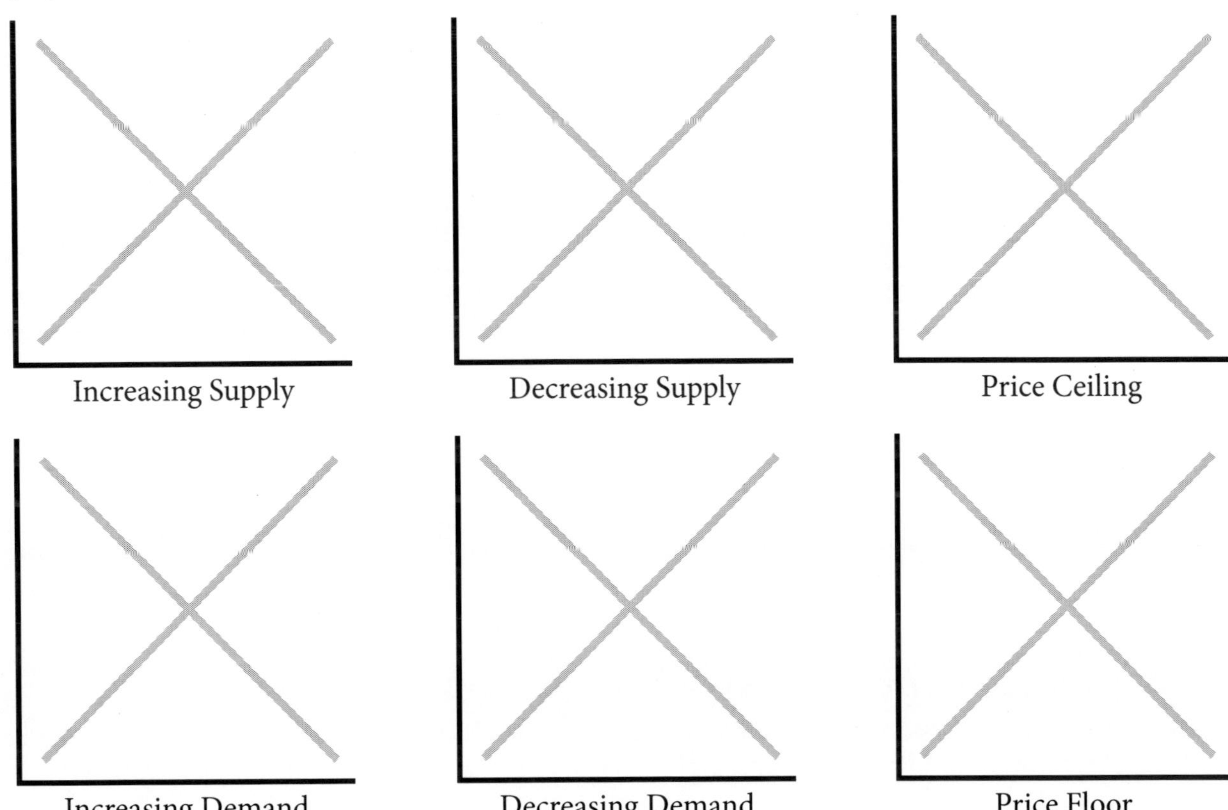

Part 2

Directions: In each of the markets for the products listed below, a new, less expensive battery has been invented. As a result consumers will prefer electric cars over gas-powered cars. This change will impact many markets. Circle the arrow that accurately describes what will happen in the market to demand, equilibrium price, and equilibrium quantity.

Scenario—a new, less expensive battery is invented				
	Electric Cars	**Gas-Powered Cars**	**Steel**	**Car-Building Robots**
Demand	↑ ↓	↑ ↓	↑ ↓	↑ ↓
Equilibrium price	↑ ↓	↑ ↓	↑ ↓	↑ ↓
Equilibrium quantity	↑ ↓	↑ ↓	↑ ↓	↑ ↓

Name:

Starting to Graph

Step 1: Draw a bigger version of what you see below in the space provided. It is best if you do this in PENCIL.

Step 2: Mark the x-axis "price" and the y-axis "quantity." Label the supply curve *S* and the demand curve *D*.

Step 3: Circle the equilibrium point.

Step 4: Indicate the price of that equilibrium point with a faint, dashed line that moves horizontally across the graph.

Step 5: Choose a market that you want to analyze (e.g., cars). Write the word below the graph.

Step 6: Come up with a scenario in which the market changes (determinants).

a. Is that an issue of supply or demand?

b. Would that increase or decrease the *quantity that the* market would see?

Step 7: Draw a new supply or demand curve that is parallel to the one you drew in Step 1.

Step 8: Circle the new equilibrium point. What happened to price and quantity that the market will bear?

Step 9: Lightly erase the first curve (supply or demand depending on your scenario).

Market Analysis and Graphing

Directions: For each of the following scenarios, the market is indicated in parentheses. The scenarios are given in the following sentence. On a separate paper, create twenty graphs that follow the model below. Draw your graphs in pencil and follow the format carefully. Make sure everything gets labeled correctly. Indicate what happened to price and quantity, and then circle the shortage or surplus.

Example: (electric cars) The government gives a subsidy to manufacturers.

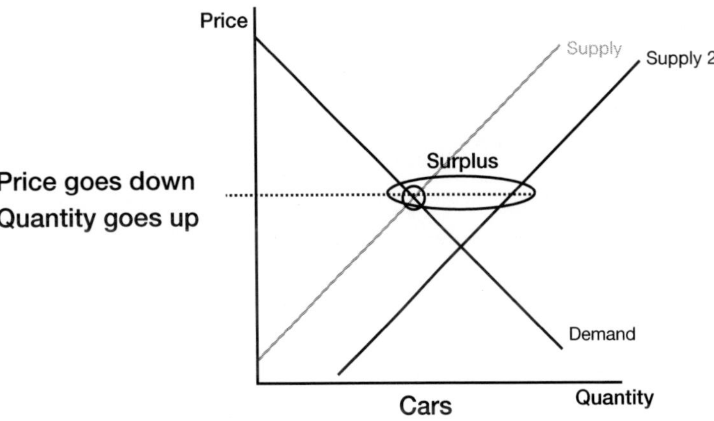

1. (oil) There is a terrorist attack on the Alaska pipeline.
2. (bread) A fad diet where people eat nothing but protein becomes popular.
3. (cars) There is a steel shortage in the United States.
4. (oil) The government opens up drilling in the Arctic National Wildlife Refuge.
5. (hard drives) Memory chips are being used for memory storage in computers.
6. (soda) The public rediscovers that tap water is good and practically free.
7. (satellite radio) Eight new companies join this market.
8. (compact discs) MP3 players and formats become more popular and affordable.
9. (diapers) The United States experiences a baby boom.
10. (hamburgers) Mad cow disease is discovered in the United States.
11. (electric cars) The US government promises a $2 billion subsidy.
12. (peanut butter) Bad fruit crops cause the price of jelly to climb.
13. (airline tickets) Another terrorist attack on the United States uses a plane.
14. (cable TV) Americans cut back on TV cable service because of a severe recession.
15. (land downtown) Your city announces that fifteen new businesses will be moving in.
16. (nurses) Half of the working nurses are expected to retire in the next ten years.
17. (home health care) Baby boomers are entering their elderly years.
18. (water in the Southwest) Another year of severe drought grips the region.
19. (health insurance) Congress mandates that all citizens have health insurance.
20. (garden supplies) Cost-conscious Americans plant vegetable gardens.

Name:

Primary Fieldwork

Part 1

Directions: Using an Internet search engine as a guide, fill in the tables and charts below. Choose an all-purpose financial site (make sure it is affiliated with a credible news agency).

Name of your site	
How did you find it?	
What are four features it has that should come in handy in this class?	1. 2. 3. 4.

Part 2

Directions: Choose a current event/news story to follow. In the table below, fill in the information using the Internet and TV news. Find an article about the same story from different sources.

THE MAIN STORY:

Site/Source	Title of Article	Gist of the Story/Differing Bias/Angle

 Name:

Final Questions for Thought

Directions: For each of the following questions, provide answers with the help of your book, outside sources, or adults. Each answer will need one to three complete sentences.

1. An economy is defined as "a system of producing and consuming." What could happen if there is too much consumption for the stuff that is produced?

2. If consumers do not consume all that is produced, what happens next?

3. How do we know if we are experiencing a bad economy? Give an example.

4. When VCRs first appeared in the late 1970s, they cost thousands of dollars. Why did they become so affordable in the 1990s? Where did they go?

5. What new technologies radically transformed our economy in the 1800s?

6. What new technologies are radically transforming our economy now?

7. In 1800, the United States was an agricultural/rural society. What are we today?

8. What benefits come from having a very productive society? What technologies have faded in your lifetime?

9. What technologies have faded in your lifetime?

10. Where does the United States stand in the world economically?

11. How is the job market changing in reaction to our changing economy?

12. Why are there still poor people in the United States if we have so much money?

13. Give examples of an inelastic supply and inelastic demand.

14. What prevents a stranger from entering your home and taking your possessions?

15. List five ways that our government is involved with our economy:

16. If the economy gets bad, list five negative effects that we would notice.

17. What is utility and how does it relate to pizza? Describe the utility of the first piece.

18. What do you suppose are the three most important ways to keep track of the economy?

19. Create a timeline of the two-hundred-year existence of the United States that details some of the major economic and technological phases or innovations of our history. Provide some descriptions of changing technology, labor, and demographics.

20. Why do stores have sales? What does that say about supply and demand?

21. What makes our standard of living better than other countries? How does the economy affect your standard of living?

Unit 2

Business and Labor

Questions to Consider

1. How does a business make money?
2. What gives a successful business its value?
3. What are the differences between big and small businesses?
4. What makes IBM and the American Red Cross different?
5. Why do people form their own businesses?
6. What power does a monopoly have in a market?
7. On what do workers and employers often disagree?
8. How has the job market changed in the last twenty years?
9. What rights do you have as a worker?

Terms You Need in Order to Read

Corporation
Merger
Monopoly
Product
Profit
Strike
Union
Wage

Business and Labor

2A. The Dream of Your Own Business

If you have already held a job in your lifetime, chances are you worked for a business. Think about the nature of that business. In other words:

- What does the business provide?
- Who owns it?
- How much money do you think it earns per year?
- What are its operating costs?

Just thinking about it for a minute can help you gain a new level of respect for the owners of that business. Starting a business can be extraordinarily difficult. Businesses are expensive, risky, and time-consuming. Remember the concept of opportunity cost from Unit 1. If you spend money on a new business, it cannot be spent elsewhere. If you spend time running your firm, then you cannot go on vacation. On the other hand, the satisfaction that comes from creating a successful venture is quite rewarding.

GRAPHIC 2.1

After years of working in a professional kitchen, Jill believes she has the energy, expertise, and creativity to open her own successful restaurant. To follow her vision, she will need money and hard work.

GRAPHIC 2.2

Gross Revenue - Expenses
= Net Revenue (Profits)

Many people at some point in their lives dream of owning their own business. Perhaps they believe they have found a niche in the marketplace that has not yet been tapped. Maybe they think that they have invented a device that could be useful to consumers or to industry. Sometimes the reason is even simpler: They just want to be their own boss.

Jill is just such a person. She has been a cook for five years, and she understands how to run a restaurant. She believes in her own talent and notices that her town does not have a higher-end, gourmet restaurant. There is a hospital in her city, and she believes that the professionals who work there could provide a steady stream of customers.

Jill spends a lot of time thinking about her idea. She pays attention to how her boss keeps track of money, orders food, and deals with employees. Sometimes she is intimidated by the idea of being in charge of an entire restaurant and of being responsible for the livelihoods of dozens of people, but the more she feels unsure, the more something inside her pushes her on. She sees herself as the next great local chef. She is willing to work hard and do what it takes. Jill is a true **entrepreneur**, a person who risks time and money to start a new business (venture).

There are three keys that make new businesses a success or failure. First, the idea behind the business, or **vision**, must be a good one. A terrible idea is destined to lose before the business ever opens. Second, the entrepreneur must work hard. Jill will be in charge of production, accounting, management, and marketing. Starting a business can be a twenty-four-hour-a-day job. Third, a new firm will need capital. When Jill begins the preparation to open her restaurant, she is shocked to find out how much everything costs. Despite all these challenges, Jill is going to move forward with her new business.

GRAPHIC 2.3

Parts of a Business Plan

- *Executive Summary*
  a description of who you are and what you want to do
- *Opportunity and Market Research*
  what makes you different, how you fit in the market
- *Market Plan*
  how will you let customers know about you?
- *Start-up Costs*
  how much money do you need to open?
- *Three-Year Cost Projection*
  how much money will you spend month to month?

According to Bloomberg Business, eight out of ten businesses fail in the first eighteen months of opening. That is a whopping 80 percent. So why on earth would anyone want to face those odds? In point of fact, thousands of organizations across the United States actively encourage entrepreneurs. These *incubators*, as they are called, provide mentors, guidance, and sometimes money to help start new businesses. The United States has an economic system that rewards good ideas and encourages entrepreneurs by letting them earn and keep most of the profits they acquire.

Pressing Question

- Jill can either start her restaurant or keep her current job as a cook. How does an entrepreneur make the decision to start a business?

2B. Challenges That Face Small Businesses

Before Jill does anything, she decides to write a **business plan** (graphic 2.3). This document will provide an introduction to the business, a description of the market, an analysis of the start-up costs, and a prediction of when the business hopes to break even. This plan will help her stay focused on her goals and keep her expenses down. She hopes to present the plan to a **venture capitalist**, a person who lends money to help businesses get started. However, venture capitalists can be hard to find. She crossed the first hurdle a small business must face: She had a vision. Now she must face the next big obstacle, finding money.

She knows other local restaurateurs. After she talks to people she knows and is introduced to others, a local venture capital group expresses interest in her business. They have agreed to meet with her. They give her a ten-minute appointment to make her presentation. She has to make a **pitch** (convince the capitalists verbally) in a very short amount of time. In the business world, it is called an "elevator pitch," as if an entrepreneur only has time equal to an elevator ride to describe the idea.

If the venture capitalists decline, Jill has other options. In the United States, access to capital (money) can be found in myriad places. For instance:

- **Bank**—We know that people put their money here and that banks lend it out. They are very cautious about business loans, however. Jill will have to offer **collateral**, or property offered in good faith, if the loan goes unpaid.
- **Personal funds**—Jill considers selling her car to help start the business. She quickly finds out she needs way more than that will provide.
- **Partners**—Jill knows people who love her food. She can offer them a share in the business, known as **equity**, if they are willing to put up some money.
- **Crowdfunding**—The newest of all the options, with dozens of websites that sell

products or offer special deals to the public in exchange for a special deal in the future. Some websites even allow entrepreneurs to sell actual shares in the business. People who sign up and send in money become partners in that business.

So, Jill manages to find her money. While the venture capitalists passed on her ideas, she takes in several partners. She also uses a crowdfunding website (like kickstarter.com, a site where businesses offer special deals in exchange for start-up money) to find other interested, local investors. Her new restaurant will cost more than $600,000 to open. No kidding.

Immediately, Jill makes decisions and faces challenges. All of the following parts of a business have to be addressed:

- **Accounting**—Businesses need to keep track of money that is coming in (**revenue**) and money that is going out (**expenses**). They also track things they own (**assets**) and debts that they owe (**liabilities**). Most important, Jill must stay on budget.
- **Marketing**—Even if Jill's restaurant serves the most delicious food in the world, it will not matter if consumers do not know it exists. Advertising, public relations, and promotion are needed to help the business begin to generate a cash flow.
- **Management**—Almost every day while she fixes up her space, Jill interviews potential employees. After she does, she needs to make sure they get paid and do their jobs well. Some businesses have whole departments called human resources to manage employees. For now, Jill must do this herself.
- **Legal**—Jill talks to a lawyer when she is making deals with investors. She also files a corporate charter for her business with the state. This makes her firm a separate entity from herself.
- **Government**—Her town and county want Jill to apply for the proper licenses, especially since she will sell alcohol with her food. Food safety laws dictate how she stores and prepares the food. Last, the government wants her to get an **employer identification number** (**EIN**). This step ensures that the Internal Revenue Service (IRS) can track the earnings of the restaurant and its employees.

While this seems like it might be too much to handle, Jill works day and night to open her business on time. Remember, her partners will also be paying attention. They want to make a return on their investment.

Pressing Question

- If you started your own business, what do you think you could do well? What are some areas in which you would need help?

2C. Being Cost Efficient

Just like in Jill's case, all businesses must track the money that comes in and the money that goes out. If more revenue comes in than expenses that must be paid, a for-profit company makes a profit. In microeconomics, students learn to break costs into several categories. Some costs are predictable for a year or two, while others can change from month to month. They are called:

- **Fixed costs**—These are expenses that do not change from one month to the next. Debt payments, insurance premiums, and rent have extended contracts that require equal payments. If for some reason a firm produces nothing, fixed costs must be still be paid.
- **Variable costs**—Labor costs and input costs (**inputs** are things that are physically necessary to produce your good, like wood in a furniture factory). Utility bills, like electricity, water, and gas, can vary greatly from one month to the next.
- **Total costs**—This amount is calculated by adding variable costs and fixed costs together.
- **Average total cost** (**ATC**)—A *very* important number found by dividing your total cost by the number of units you produce or provide.
- **Marginal cost** (**MC**)—Another important number, this is the cost of producing one additional unit. Remember from Unit 1 that economics really studies the margins.

Businesses pay close attention to average total cost. If a furniture company produces only one table, all its fixed and variable costs went into

GRAPHIC 2.4

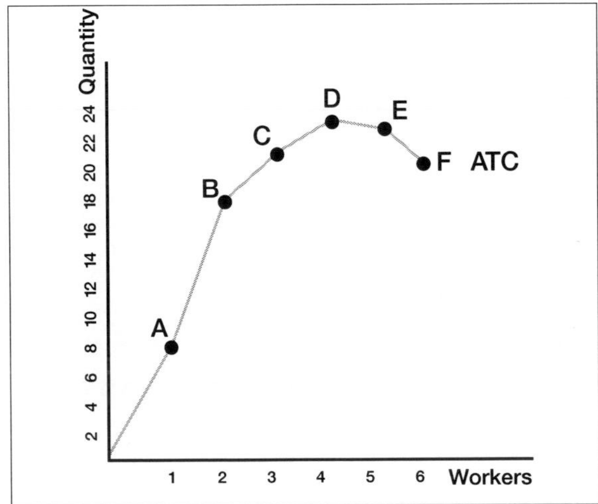

making that one unit. That is an expensive table. Most consumers would never pay that high a price. If it the company produces one more, then the two tables cost about half of what the first cost to make. As the firm makes more, the ATC and MC will continue to fall. Something will start to happen eventually, however. At some point, the cost of making one more table will be higher than the cost of the previous one, and the average cost of each unit produced will begin to increase.

Why would this happen? This occurs because of the **law of diminishing returns**, which states:

GRAPHIC 2.5

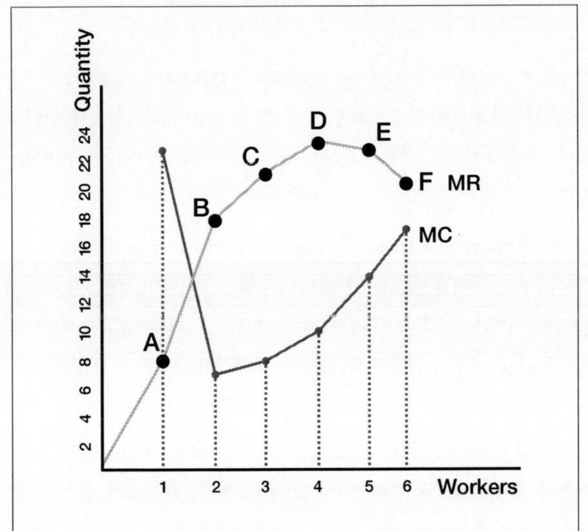

Given a fixed set of productive resources, adding one factor of production (like a worker) will result in an increase in output. As more of these factors are added, eventually, output will diminish.

Consider the furniture factory. They have one lathe and one table saw. Refer to graphic 2.4. With one worker, at point A, the factory can make eight tables per month. Given the business's success, the entrepreneur hires one more worker. The marginal product (benefit) of hiring that one extra worker (point B) will be ten more tables. The total output moved from eight to eighteen. When a third worker is hired, the workers have to take turns on the machines. The owner notices them standing around every so often. The total output increased from eighteen to twenty-two tables, so the marginal return of having a third worker is only four tables. Thus, the benefit of hiring workers begins to diminish after the second worker. Moving on, the benefit of a fourth worker (point D) will further diminish to two tables. There is just not enough space for the workers to produce efficiently. In fact, after four workers, they will produce fewer tables if more labor is hired. This would be a negative marginal return.

How does each marginal product relate to the costs of production? Graphic 2.5 has the marginal cost curve (MC) added to it. At one worker, the eight tables that are produced have the highest per-unit cost. With two laborers, they become so efficient when they work together that the cost per table plummets. However, because the factory has reached its point of diminishing return (the marginal product went down), the marginal cost of producing more tables will increase.

So where does a business decide to produce? Recall from Unit 1 that people will consume a product when the marginal utility equals the marginal cost. So it is with a business. A business will maximize its efficiency and profit if it can produce where the marginal cost equals the marginal revenue. How do we measure benefit in a market? In a perfectly competitive market, firms will produce the number of units where MC = MR. Why would the furniture factory sell one more table for $80 when it will cost $90 to make? This would not make economic sense.

GRAPHIC 2.6

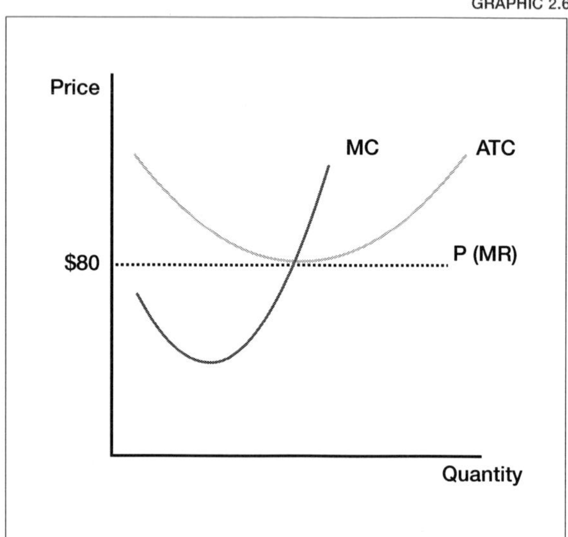

Remember that the total cost is a firm's fixed costs plus variable costs. If this number is divided by the number of units produced, it is called the average total cost (ATC). This curve in graphic 2.6 is bowl-shaped. Think about it. If the furniture factory makes more tables, each subsequent table should become cheaper to make. In the first half of the ATC curve, the average price steadily decreases. Also in this graph is the marginal cost curve (MC). Remember that it bottoms out when the law of diminishing returns occurs on the factory floor. When the MC curve crosses the ATC curve, each table that is made costs more than the average. That means that the average will have to rise with it.

So where will this firm produce? Notice the dotted line drawn across the graph emanating from the price axis. This is the price the market is offering for tables. It is also the marginal revenue curve for the firm. All other things being equal, this firm will have to take whatever price it gets. If it sells ten, then it will get $80 per table. If it sells one more, then it will increase its revenue by $80.

By looking at graphic 2.6, there is a way to tell what a table bought in this free market costs to make. The answer is $80, because a perfectly competitive business will always produce where MR = MC. Actually, this makes perfect sense. If the company's MC is less than $80, it can still bring in more money if it produces another unit. On the other hand, if the MC is $88, then the firm would lose money with each table sold.

Pressing Question

- What are some ways a furniture business can lower its ATC and its MC?

2D. Numbers to Watch

Good business owners watch every penny. They do not like waste or inefficiency, because these can eat away profits or build losses. Entrepreneurs are also aware of their personal alternatives. When they start a business, they too have trade-offs. Consider a teacher who wants to leave the classroom to start a pizza shop. If he opens the shop and makes more profit than he did on his teacher's salary, then he is making an **economic profit**. That is, he makes more money cooking pizza than his next best alternative, teaching.

GRAPHIC 2.7

Net Income / Sales = Profit Margin

If this teacher does open for business, he will think about the $200,000 of his own money he used for start-up costs. If he pays himself a salary, then he still needs to make more than $200,000 in profit to get back his initial investment. If his shop does very well, he will be making a **return on investment (ROI)**. Entrepreneurs look to make back their own money, but also that of their investors. People invest money in the hope of getting more in return.

The entrepreneur likes the idea of starting a pizzeria, because he believes the product to be more profitable than most. When comparing the cost of producing a pizza to the sales price, he believes his profit margin will be 70 percent. If each pizza sells for $10, and it costs the firm $3 to make, then each unit has $7 of profit (7/10 = 70 percent).

GRAPHIC 2.8

Many streets in the United States look like this. The United States is home to almost 30 million small businesses. Americans have the freedom and the access to capital necessary to start a new business.

To keep track of his monthly expenses, the pizza man uses a personal computer and finance website to track all the money coming in and going out. Other businesses hire accountants. The former teacher knows that his start-up money will not last very long, so he wants to sell enough pizza every month to cover his operating costs (fixed plus variable costs). If the shop sells 800 pizzas per month, it will **break even**. The store can keep going as long as it breaks even in the first few months of operation. You should know that most businesses do not break even for some time after starting (months or even years). It is up to the entrepreneur to decide how long the business operates with losses before it shuts down.

What causes a business to shut down? It happens when monthly losses become too much to bear for the operator. Specifically, a business that cannot cover its variable costs has to borrow money to keep operating. This borrowing adds to debt payments, which fall into the fixed-cost category. This elevates the average total cost, making it even harder for the business to break even. When a business closes or is bought, it is called an "exit" from the market. Many entrepreneurs suffer multiple business failures. The trick is to know when to get out. Some entrepreneurs waste too much money and time trying to make a bad business vision successful.

Pressing Question

- Name two businesses you know that have shut down. What factors led to the failure of those businesses?

2E. Types of Businesses

As you get older, you will begin to see that the world is more complex than you ever imagined. In opening a business, entrepreneurs have flexibility when it comes to the legal formation of their firms. Each one is structured to best suit its function, owner, and product. Each type will have advantages and disadvantages.

A new business owner has to decide what sort of business formation best suits his or her needs:

- **Sole proprietorship**—A business owned and controlled by one person or family. While these businesses are the riskiest to own, sole proprietorships are the most common business found in the United States today. Owners of these "mom and pop" establishments keep all the profits and declare them as income to the government. On the other hand, they assume full financial responsibility, or **liability**, for what happens with the business. If they are sued, personal assets (like a house or savings) may be forfeited.
- **Corporation**—A business that has filed a corporate charter with its state of origin. In legal terms, the business becomes a separate entity from the owner or owners. If the business gets sued, only the assets of the firm can be taken. This allows the owner to operate the business without the fear of losing personal assets. Without this protection, many people would avoid owning a business. Corporations come in many different shapes and sizes. A sole proprietor can incorporate a small business. It is merely a legal designation. Corporations are not all big companies, although large corporations do share a similar structure.

Any of the following categories can be registered as corporations:

- **Partnership**—A business with two or more people sharing responsibility in the funding or operation of a business. Partners can split the burden of day-to-day operations, pool talents, and share ideas. Many doctors, lawyers, and other professionals form partnerships. A medical practice can have several partners who see one another's patients while splitting the cost of their office space and employees. Young lawyers and accountants work long hours in hopes of one day "making partner." In essence, they then become part owner of the business and share in the profits. Partnerships typically work well if the business is profitable. If there are losses, disagreements can become problematic.

- **Nonprofit**—This is a company that tries to serve a public need. Charities, schools, and hospitals are examples. Because the government wants certain services to be provided to citizens, nonprofits do *not* pay tax on their revenue. As the name suggests, any surplus income is not shared by owners, but put back into the business. While its tax exemption is an advantage, the missing profit motive lends itself to a lack of efficiency. For this reason, it is common practice for a nonprofit to have a board of directors.
- **Cooperative**—This is a business that provides a service to a group of members. Sometimes requiring a fee, the co-op, as it is known, helps its membership perform a task too expensive for any one member to afford. For example, a local farmers' group may provide grain storage and distribution. Trade associations market the group's products on a larger scale. If you see a commercial for milk, it was most likely paid for by a co-op. Because co-ops are not for profit, they too can suffer inefficiency.
- **Franchise**—This is a business that comes from a parent company. This larger company (franchisor) gives the owner (franchisee) license to sell its products. In return for an initial fee, the business owner gets help from the franchisor in buying equipment and supplies. The franchisor provides training, marketing, and distribution channels. The owner will usually pay the franchisor a percentage of the new business's profits. Franchises are attractive not only because the franchisee has help starting up but also because the product in question has a proven track record.

Pressing Question

- If you are a sole proprietor, how can you protect yourself from the liability of owning your business?

GRAPHIC 2.9

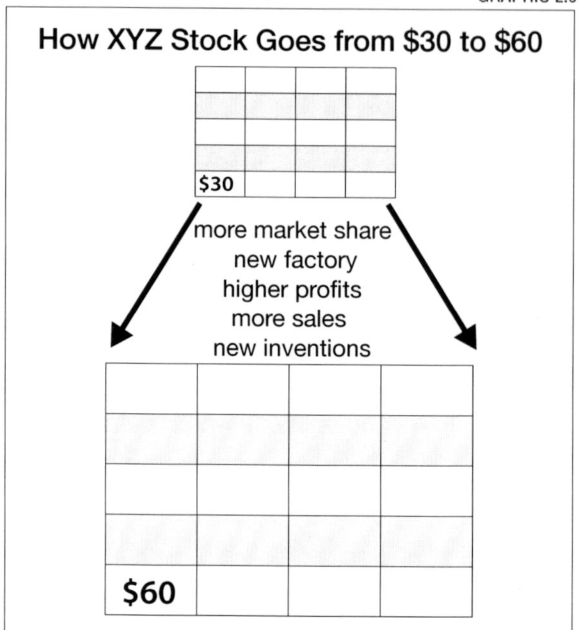

2F. Going Public

Sometimes a successful company wants to grow from a medium size to a large business. This process requires cash. Factories, distribution networks, technology, and labor can cost tens of millions of dollars. XYZ Corp., a new online social network, is in such a position. Its owners are discussing bringing in another investor, but there are few people willing to risk $30 million. XYZ's service is widely known and popular. So there are probably at least 1 million people willing to risk $30 each.

Going public is the process by which a corporation sells pieces of itself to the general public in order to raise money for expansion. XYZ meets with **investment bankers**, people who specialize in helping companies to raise capital. After a series of meetings and audits, they add up all the firm's assets, sales, and intellectual property. They even consider the company's anticipated future growth in their calculations. They advise XYZ on how many pieces of the company should be sold and at what price.

With a course of action decided, XYZ notifies the Securities and Exchange Commission (this agency will also be discussed in Units 4 and 5) that it will sell 1 million shares of stock at $30 a piece on a particular date. If this **initial public offering** (or **IPO**) is successful, XYZ will get its asking price of $30 (or more) depending on how the stock buyers feel about the company. Over time, if XYZ accumulates assets, sells increasing amounts of product, and gains market share against its competitors, then it will be a more valuable company. Each share of stock will increase in value commensurate with the overall value of the company. Consider graphic 2.9. XYZ sells more product than its competitors, expands its ability to produce new goods, remains popular with the public, and earns high profits. Stock investors notice how the company is doing and believe that the trend will continue. As more people buy the stock, the price goes up. We will learn more about stock investing in Unit 5.

After going public, shareholders in the company may have a say in how the firm is run. Additionally, for each share of stock owned, the holder may get a **dividend**, or share of the profits. As XYZ grows, much of its profit will be kept within the company to pay for new capital and develop new products. This is known as **internal financing**.

A major advantage of owning stock in a corporation is the stockholder's separation of ownership. If the business fails, then the investor can only lose the amount of the original investment. Furthermore, if the business is sued, stockholders are free from losing their personal assets and property. Stockholders can invest in companies that they know nothing about, while experts in what the company produces deal with all the management issues. Stockholders may get big returns on their investment while the company does all the work.

Despite the advantages, there are some drawbacks to larger corporations. They are often slow to make decisions because of the many people involved in the running of the company. Proposals must run through a complicated chain of command where disagreements may arise. Graphic 2.10 shows a typical corporate structure. While shareholders ultimately own the business, management must run the day-to-day operations. Employees may never meet or see the **chief executive officer** (**CEO**), a common title for the top administrator of a company (other titles include "president").

GRAPHIC 2.10

Corporations also get taxed twice. The business must pay a tax on its profits before it pays the dividends to stockholders. Once dividends are received, the shareholders must pay a tax on the dividends as well. This is a dilemma known as **double taxation**. Furthermore, if the value of the stock goes up, then the investor must pay a **capital gains tax** on the money made.

Despite the disadvantages, millions of people invest in corporations every year. Furthermore, while large corporations constitute only 20 percent of the businesses in the United States, they account for more than 90 percent of the total sales in the country. In fact, many of our top companies produce more goods in a year than most small countries around the world. Entrepreneurs who form a corporation must decide on how they want to pay taxes. Graphic 2.11 explains the difference between an S-type and C-type corporation. Typically, larger corporations tend to be C-type and smaller businesses, S-type.

GRAPHIC 2.11

Types of Corporations	
S-Type	The business's profits are the income of the propietor and taxed as income—there are limits to who can form these. Must be a citizen, and no more than 75 can be stockholders.
C-Type	Most common form of corporation. Unlimited amounts of stockholders, usually for companies that have public offerings of their stock. Has the problem of double taxation (corporate tax, then salaries are taxed).
LLC Limited Liability Company	More flexible in ownership. Non-residents can be stockholders and there is no limit to the number of owners. Owners can more easily drop in or out of the corporate charter.

Pressing Question

- What would you want to know about a business before investing in it?

2G. The Urge to Merge

Large corporations sometimes have the capability of raising large amounts of capital. At times, they might decide to buy a competitor to gain a greater share of a particular market. They could buy a business that is in trouble in hopes of getting a bargain and turning it around. They also can buy a company that has nothing to do with what they produce. Regardless, whenever one company absorbs another it is called a **merger**. Depending upon the situation, the bought company may keep its name or lose its identity altogether.

There are three types of mergers:

- **Horizontal combination**—A merger of two companies that offer the same good or service. For example, if Verizon and T-Mobile merged, that would be a horizontal merger.
- **Vertical combination**—This occurs when two companies at different phases of the production of the same good or service merge. For example, Andrew Carnegie's steel company bought a coal mine and railroad so he could control every phase of the production of his steel.
- **Conglomerates**—A merger of two or more companies that offer different goods or services. For example, if GE were to buy a hotel chain and a phone company, then it would be building a conglomerate.

Depending upon the economist you talk to, mergers can be both a positive and a negative occurrence. Merged companies can improve their decision-making process, combine capital resources, and expand production potential by utilizing already existing factories. Mergers are especially appreciated by the stockholders of the acquired company. The value of their stock may climb when another company attempts to buy them.

Consolidation, or the reduction in number of firms, happens in a market as companies go out of business and other businesses merge. It is natural that when a new technology, service, or product is developed, a great number of competitors enter the field. As time goes on, many businesses fail to compete effectively. Larger companies buy smaller companies or simply make better decisions. Either way, most markets seem to head in one direction—from many companies to one. Consider graphic 2.12.

GRAPHIC 2.12

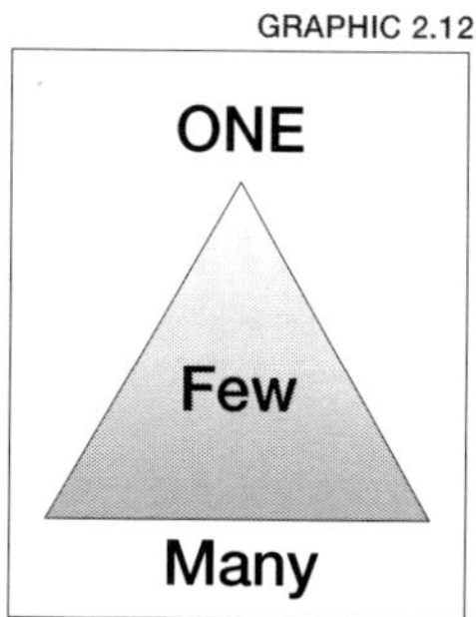

Pressing Question

- Which do you think is more important, the right to own a business that monopolizes a market, or the protection of consumers from a monopoly's unfair pricing?

2H. Competition and Market Structure

Economists closely watch how businesses interact with one another. Rivalry occurs when businesses compete for a greater share of the market. Each market has a limited amount of customers at any given time, and it is vital for a business's survival to compete. The market structure describes how a particular group of businesses compete with one another.

- **Perfect competition**—This is the most ideal market situation for consumers and the economy. A good example would be the market for corn. Three conditions must exist for such a market to exist. First, there should be a large number of buyers and sellers. Each seller must account for only a small part of the market. Second, firms are "price takers." They have to accept whatever price the market consumers will pay. No firm has an advantage in setting price. Third, there must be easy entry into and exit out of the market. Entrepreneurs can start a business in this market easily.
- **Monopolistic competition**—This market has many producers who all produce slightly differentiated products. Fast-food burger businesses fit under this category. Unlike perfectly competitive firms, they can move their prices up or down and still sell their product. Burgers will be different from one place to the next but not by much. These businesses try to stand out from their competitors and need to advertise heavily.
- **Oligopoly**—Sometimes, only a few companies exist in a market. These firms together behave like a monopoly in that they have great control over prices. They watch one another's prices very closely. If one raises a price, the other will follow suit. This is a behavior called **price leadership**. Companies that provide cell phone service fall into this category. There is little difference in their product, but they advertise heavily. Prices in this market from one company to the next do not differ all that much.
- **Perfect monopoly**—Monopolies have total control over price and quantity in a market. A company chooses to produce where it maximizes its profit, not its efficiency. There are no substitutes. Furthermore, because information is controlled by the monopoly, it can use advertising to mask the actual quantity of its product. A monopoly may cause great inefficiency in an economy. It takes money from consumers that they want to spend somewhere else, and it restricts competition from entering the market.

GRAPHIC 2.13

The market for corn is close to perfect competition. One farmer's corn is identical to everyone else's, and no producer can dictate price.

Despite the inefficiency that a monopoly can cause in an economy, the government allows monopolies to exist legally in certain unique situations:

- **Natural monopoly**—In some markets, it is impractical to start a new business. For instance, your gas company enjoys a monopoly in your area, because it is simply too expensive and impractical for another business to dig out the streets and lay new pipe. Therefore, the government gives a natural monopoly the right to operate and regulate the price. While competition is being introduced in certain areas, states use public utility commissions to set a fair price. Your electric company and water company are most likely monopolies as well.
- **Technological monopoly**—If you invent a new product, then you may apply for a patent from the United States Patent and Trademark Office. If it is approved, then you will have exclusive rights to produce that item for twenty years. Without this protection, pharmaceutical companies would not spend billions of dollars trying to develop new drugs. To be approved for sale to the public, the drug must clear eight to ten years of testing. That leaves the company only ten years to be the exclusive seller of the product.

GRAPHIC 2.14

This picture shows an African diamond mine. De Beers, a South African company, dominated the world diamond market for decades. To this day, most people do not know that diamonds are, indeed, not rare. They are overpriced. This effect shows the destructive power of a monopoly. Economists believe that the high prices decrease total utility in our society.

- **Geographic monopoly**—When a supplier is isolated, it may have little or no competition. Sometimes, an area does not have enough consumers to support more than one store. It would not make economic sense to have several stores in an area where there are very few people. You may notice in small towns that there is only one gas station. It may charge high prices.
- **Governmental monopoly**—Certain services have been determined to be best controlled by governments. The establishment of the United States Postal Service is provided for in the Constitution. Your local city government probably controls your water and sewer service, and the state is in charge of the maintenance of its highways. Many of these public goods would not be profitable to private enterprise.

Pressing Question

- In your opinion, when does it make sense to have a monopoly in a market?

21. The United States versus a Monopoly

In the late 1800s, industrialists combined their companies in efforts to create monopolies or combinations in multiple industries. Their behavior in doing so caught the attention of the public and the federal government. They felt that these mergers and market dominations would result in unfair prices for American consumers. Many businesses had unfair pricing strategies. Some people thought it was time for the government to break up monopolies or punish them in court. Others, usually the business owners, strongly opposed government interference. This attitude of laissez-faire (a French phrase for "leave it be") dominated the thinking of prominent industrialists and politicians.

This conflict reveals a fundamental question about which is better, freedom to own a business or fair competition. Even today, businesses engage in unfair trade practices using their market advantage. For instance, a large realtor moves into a midwestern city. In an effort to run the smaller firms out of business, it entices their agents away with signing bonuses. Then, once they are hired, the big firm uses information about the smaller brokers to outcompete them. In other cases, large box stores that move into small towns have been accused of using their market power unfairly. In one case a large retailer lowered the price of bicycles below cost (a price that the small shop in town could never match). In time, the local store had to close. Business can be tough. Some say, "it is a jungle out there . . . kill or be killed." But is it in the interest of that little town to have one retailer?

Congress thinks that competition is good for the economy, and "restraint of trade" harms consumers and producers. While some monopolies are considered legal by the government, it was determined in the late1800s that some monopolies were harmful to the public interest. Congress decided to make it illegal for companies to merge with one another if it meant that the market moved too close to monopoly. Congress began to pass legislation in the late 1800s and early 1900s. Here are three of the more important laws:

- **Sherman Antitrust Act** (1890)—Also called the Sherman Act, it is the true cornerstone of US free trade legislation. It prohibited any contract, combination, or conspiracy that resulted in the "restraint of trade." This act is the cornerstone of American anti-monopoly law. Congress believed that competition brings innovation and low prices.

GRAPHIC 2.15

A federal judge found Microsoft guilty of violating antitrust law and ordered the company split up. On appeal, the company was allowed to stay intact, although it had to modify its operating system to avoid putting Internet-service provider Netscape out of business.

- **Clayton Antitrust Act** (1914)—Strengthened the Sherman Act by prohibiting price discrimination, exclusive contracts, local pricing, and interlocking directorates.
- **Federal Trade Commission Act** (1914)—The act that created the **Federal Trade Commission (FTC)**, which is an agency that investigates charges of unfair trade practices and violations of the law.

Anyone who has a complaint about a business's behavior can complain to the FTC, which may conduct an investigation. If there is a case, the antitrust division of the Justice Department will have its lawyers bring a case to federal court. At that time, they will attempt to prove that the company's behavior violated antitrust law in some way. Remember, it is not against the law to be a monopoly. Microsoft controlled more than 90 percent of the computer operating system market in the 1990s. This was fine until Microsoft was accused of abusing its market dominance to drive a small company called Netscape out of business. After that, Microsoft was found guilty of violating antitrust law.

In another famous case in 1980, AT&T was found guilty of breaking the law and was forced to break up into eight regional phone companies that the press dubbed the "Baby Bells." Many economists say this was an extreme measure. However, consumers at the time had one choice of local and long distance provider. Even phones had to be rented from AT&T. Since the breakup, telecommunications have changed with multiple new carriers, the cell phone market, satellite communications, and the Internet. Today, consumers can choose dozens of different ways to communicate electronically, and the cost of some methods is practically free. Do you think free video conferencing over the Internet would exist if AT&T were allowed to continue as it was? Oddly, SBC Communications bought AT&T in 2005 and took its name and logo. At the time, AT&T was a shadow of its former self but has since become a major player in cell phone, Internet, and home entertainment industries.

When monopolies defend themselves in court, they often argue that a large company can actually bring prices down. They have the ability to buy inputs at lower prices than smaller competitors could. The efficiencies that come with size are called **economies of scale**.

Remember, a business violates the Sherman Act only if it "restrains trade." Businesses cannot merge if the merger hurts the market. They cannot conspire together to fix prices, a practice called **collusion**. Last, they are not allowed to write contracts that deliberately harm consumers or producers. Our government tries to keep our markets as free as possible.

Pressing Question

- What is illegal according to the Sherman Antitrust Act?

2J. We Are What We Do

Aristotle wrote, "We are what we repeatedly do." Our jobs define much of who we are. A teacher teaches, a lawyer works with the law, a baker bakes. In the United States, people have thousands of choices when deciding on a job. This was not always the case. Prior to the Industrial Revolution, most people farmed. They rarely traveled more than a few miles from home. They rose at dawn and went to bed around dusk. People worked hard during the growing season in order to grow and preserve enough food to live through the winter. Patterns of life were dictated by the seasons. The work of a farmer who lived in the Roman Empire differed little from that of a farmer in the United States in 1800. Think about it. Thousands of years passed and life did not change all that much.

The Industrial Revolution changed everything. Mass production of goods drove down the price of labor. Mechanization of farming drove down the price of farm goods, causing many families to lose their farms when they did not make enough money to cover their mortgages. Farmers, along with immigrants, moved into cities. City dwellers lived lives governed by clocks, and they resided in cramped and dirty conditions. Urban life was a far cry from the bucolic existence of a farmer. Life would never be the same.

GRAPHIC 2.16

Changing Life in the US

Year	Where do we live?	Predominant jobs in the economy?
1800	Rural	Farming
1900	Urban	Manufacturing
2000	Urban/Suburban	Service

Many industrial jobs required little education. One hundred years ago, few people went to school beyond what we now call high school, much less university. People could manage to live with basic literacy and by learning skills from family. Today, graduation from high school is most common (or a general equivalency diploma, GED). Finding work with a high school education is possible but difficult in the United States; if a worker has a **trade**, he or she has more of an advantage. A trade is an advanced skill level in manual labor. For example, plumbers or electricians must train for years to become adept at their jobs. Generally, a person with a trade will make more money than an unskilled worker. If you do not want to go to college, learning a trade can be a way to make a comfortable living. These **blue-collar** jobs (occupations that require physical labor) are important to a well-functioning society.

More lucrative careers like law, medicine, and accounting require a bachelor's degree and beyond. It stands to reason that the more education a person attains the more valuable he or she becomes to a business. For example, a doctor who has a general practice can see a wide range of people and treat more common medical problems. If there is a problem beyond that doctor's expertise, patients can get referred to a specialist.

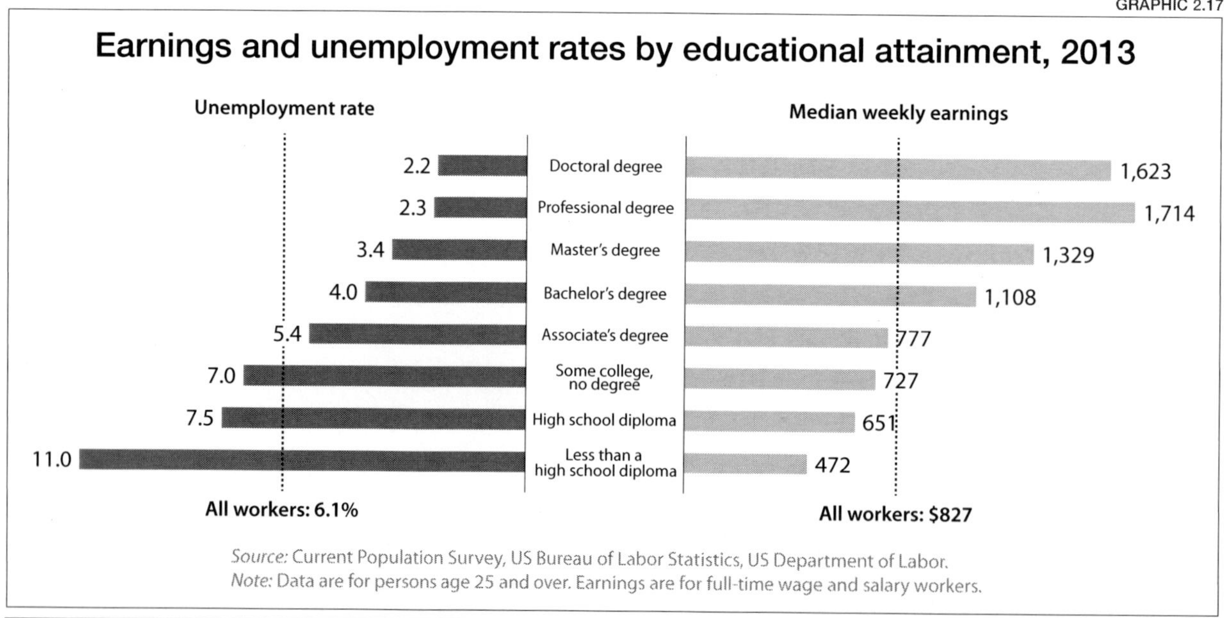

These doctors received additional training and education beyond medical school. For instance, a pediatric neurological radiologist specializes in analyzing the X-rays of children's brains. **Specialization** is the process whereby a worker becomes skilled at a more specific task. Because there are fewer of these workers, the demand for their time becomes more valuable.

Refer to graphic 2.17. While the national unemployment rate was 4.3 percent in 2013, workers without a high school diploma were 11 percent unemployed, and the unemployment rate for those with a bachelor's degree (four years of college) was 4 percent. The earnings difference between education levels is worth noting. A high school graduate will average almost $33,000 per year, while someone with a bachelor's degree makes almost $55,000. In ten years, college can earn you an extra $240,000 in income. It literally pays to stay in school.

2K. Labor Supply and Labor Demand

If you recall the laws of supply and demand from Unit 1, it is easy to apply those same rules to the demand that a business has for workers. Businesses require the factors of production—entrepreneurs, labor, natural resources, and capital. Instead of being a customer and buying things from a business, people are, in a sense, selling their labor to a business.

Labor demand and labor supply can shift like the demand for products. When it snows unexpectedly early in the winter, people will have a need for shovels. The demand for shovels increases. By the same token, the demand for people to remove snow will increase as well. Consider graphic 2.18. The quantity in this graph represents the number of workers in the market. The price represents the wage that a person can get. If this is the market for snow removal workers, then point B represents a new equilibrium in the market if there is a snowy beginning to the winter season.

GRAPHIC 2.18

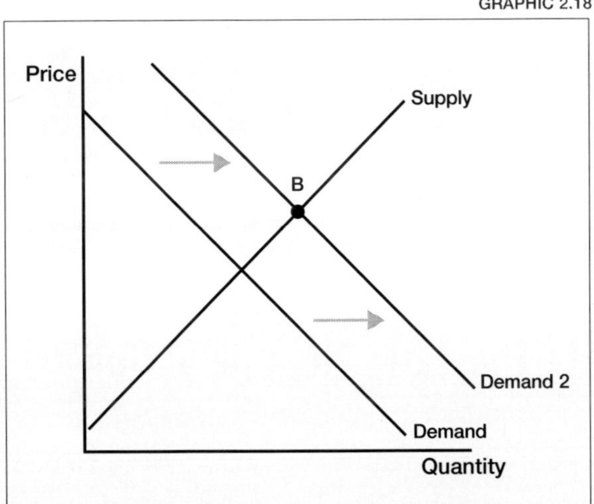

GRAPHIC 2.19

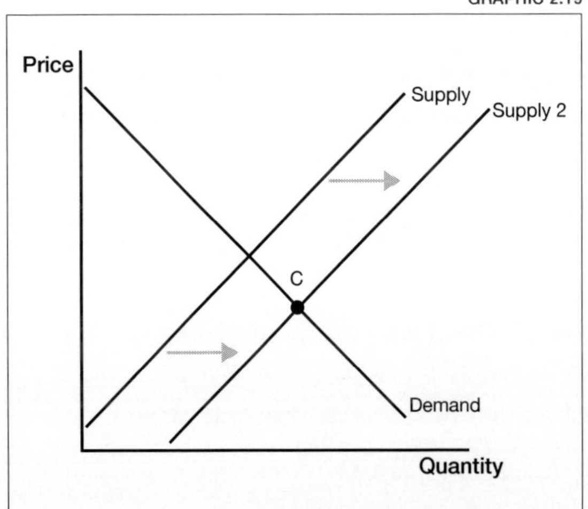

People pay attention to opportunities that will give them higher wages. These price signals entice workers into the market, get existing workers to work longer hours, or convince people who already have jobs to join the market in their free time to make a few extra dollars. This constitutes an increase in the supply of labor. This moves the

Pressing Question

- Compare the salary of someone with a professional degree (doctor or lawyer) to that of someone with less than a high school diploma. Why are they different?

supply curve to the right as seen in graphic 2.19. The new people in the labor market will bring wages back down to point C. The lesson is clear: A higher demand for labor will drive wages up and a higher supply of workers will push pay down.

As mentioned in the previous section, some people attain years of education and training to become more specialized in their work. Because of the expense and difficulty of going to school, receiving additional training, and achieving professional milestones, there are fewer people available to fill these labor markets. For example, a pediatrician is very well paid, because she went to medical school and underwent years of training. Pediatricians who also perform heart surgery, however, will make even more money. In essence, they are more scarce. People will pay a premium for their services.

As our economy changes over the next several decades, many jobs will become obsolete. Have you noticed that in many retail establishments that there are "self-checkout lines"? While it may seem that this is for a customer's convenience, in reality the checkout machinery is less expensive, in the long run, than a worker. A cashier, or person who handles cash, is a rapidly disappearing job. Consider graphic 2.20. As the demand for cashiers decreases, wages will be pushed downward to point D. Those jobs will become harder to find. Workers in that field will compete for scarcer cashier jobs or retrain and switch careers.

GRAPHIC 2.20

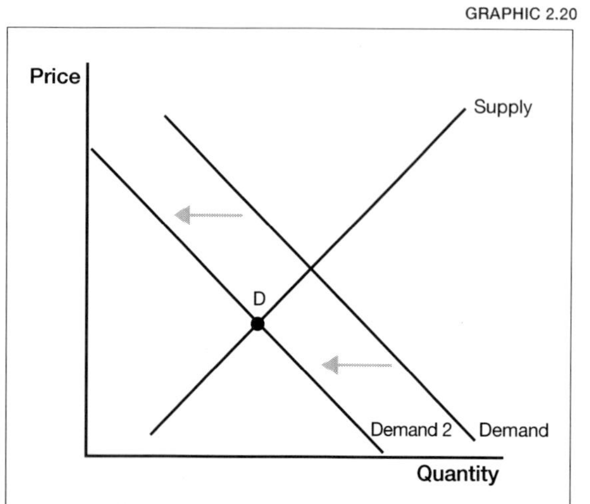

This type of structural unemployment occurs when the actual nature of our economy changes. Many new inventions will quickly become commonplace. Furthermore, those innovations will replace many workers. Driverless cars will replace taxi and truck drivers. Drones will deliver packages. Robots will perform many mundane and repetitive tasks. Humans will need to adapt to these changes by attaining new skills and shifting the focus of their work.

Pressing Question

- If a worker gets laid off, what are some ways he can enhance his skills in order to get a new job?

GRAPHIC 2.21

Noisy and dangerous work for little pay prompted workers to form unions. Children were used to drive down the cost of labor. Here, a young girl (eight to nine years old), works in a textile mill in 1908.

2L. The Early Struggle of Unions

People today have strong opinions about unions in our country. For some, loyalty to unions knows no boundaries. They will never cross a picket line and tend to look for products that were made by union workers. Others tend to distrust unions and believe that the labor market should be left alone. They think that businesses are stifled by the high costs of union labor. Whatever the opinion, there was a time when unions were the only defense that workers had against unfair labor practices.

From the very beginning of our country, labor organizations of some sort have been present.

They took their structure from medieval guilds of Europe. Their function was to set prices, assign product guidelines, and train new workers. A young apprentice would join a guild family and begin learning the trade. After years of service, around the age of sixteen, the apprentice would become a journeyman and was then allowed to offer his services to other employers. Finally, when the young man had created his greatest work, his masterpiece, he was made a master in the guild. Guilds set prices and standards. They guarded the value of their labor.

The earliest guilds and "unions" in the United States were exclusive to those people who had a specific skill. For example, shoemakers, cigar rollers, and printers all had local unions in the United States by the 1790s. Because these crafters had skills that took years to acquire, however, members of **craft unions** set themselves apart from common laborers. Skilled workers did not like to associate with unskilled workers.

As the United States became more industrialized through the late 1800s, more craft unions began to form. They had a lot to defend. The life of a skilled craftsman was more desirable than that of an unskilled laborer. Picture a shoemaker who, with five other workers, made the shoes for an entire town. The complicated tasks of sewing, cutting, and stitching took years to learn. The shoemaker's product was, therefore, of the highest quality. Life in the store was relatively relaxed and the camaraderie of the workers made the work much easier.

When a shoe factory opened up in the area, however, it made shoes that sold at a fraction of the cost at the shoemaker's store. The factory did offer lower prices and higher quantities of shoes, but because of the lack of business, the skilled workers had to close up shop and look for work in the factory. At that point, the jobs they once had of making an entire shoe were broken down into the simplest of tasks—so simple that anyone could be hired to do it.

Because of the lack of skill needed to make shoes in mass production, the workers could not demand high wages. If one complained, then one was simply dismissed and replaced. Workers labored in noisy and dangerous conditions. They had to work long hours and were paid little. Making shoes, once a complex and time-consuming job, was deskilled in the factory. Lower-skilled jobs pay less money. Workers began to see the need to organize **labor unions**, or unions for unskilled workers.

Factory workers had to contend with many problems. First of all, they had to work long days for very low wages, and this was before we had the modern concept of a "weekend." People had to work six to six and a half days per week. The working conditions were often unsafe, noisy, and unsanitary. Factory owners offered few benefits. If workers became sick or injured on the job, other willing workers replaced them. People who complained were fired. Unskilled workers brought nothing to the table but their labor. If they stood up for their rights by themselves, then they had no power over what the company might do. However, if they all stood up together, then they might be heard.

A variety of craft unions and federations of craft unions existed in the 1800s, but the first union in US history to cater to unskilled workers was known as the **Knights of Labor**. Started as a secret organization in the late 1860s, the Knights sought to accept all workers, no matter their skill-level, gender, or race. By 1886, the Knights had close to 700,000 members. It advocated the replacement of capitalism with a system of worker cooperatives, and because of this and other radical ideas, the Knights slowly faded from prominence by the 1890s. It lingered until it dissolved in 1917.

Of the many issues sought to be resolved by unions of the time, none were expressed more vociferously than by the **American Federation of Labor** (**AFL**). Founded in 1886 by Samuel Gompers, the AFL was a federation of smaller craft unions— mainly for skilled workers. Gompers and his followers were most noted for their support of "bread and butter unionism." This meant that they pursued basic goals such as an eight-hour workday, no child labor, safer working conditions, and higher wages. The AFL expanded throughout the first half of the twentieth century. As will be discussed later, it still exists in some form today.

Some unions attracted radicals like communists and anarchists. The **Industrial Workers of the World (IWW)** was founded in the early twentieth century. Led at times by firebrand "Big Bill" Haywood, many members of the IWW believed in the ideas of Karl Marx and saw the working conditions in factories as a reason to organize marches and strikes. A **strike** happens when a firm's employees refuse to work. Many times, IWW protests turned violent as members clashed with police and hired security. Many ordinary Americans began to view unions as havens for radicals and immigrants. Nevertheless, most early unions did not endure, and worker strikes were rarely successful at achieving their goals.

Pressing Question

- Why is it so hard for workers to form a union in a factory?

2M. Labor versus Management

Early unions like the Knights and the AFL had a limited amount of options when it came to getting what they wanted. First, they could strike. At its heart, a work stoppage is a contest to see how long workers can go without pay and owners can go without revenue. During a strike, a **picket line** would form. Workers marched outside their place of employment with signs and tried to draw public attention to their cause. With public support, they could start a **boycott** of the company's products to influence a response from management. Many customers would stop buying the company's products. The lack of sales that came with a successful boycott could force a company to agree to terms with a union. Less formal tactics included work **slowdowns**, during which the pace of production would gradually stall.

In the end, the purpose of this conflict was to sit down with the owners of the company to negotiate a settlement. In a large factory, not every worker would negotiate a contract; rather, the union would select representatives to bargain on their behalf. This is called **collective bargaining**. While this may seem like a logical process, US citizens did not always have a right to form a union. While our constitutional right to assemble is clearly part of the First Amendment, Congress would not clarify a union's rights until the 1930s.

GRAPHIC 2.22

Many labor organizations still have significant presence in skilled trades like plumbing.

Business owners also had ways to counter unions. Many were appalled at the idea of their workers striking or organizing. They believed in an idea called **social Darwinism**. They thought that people who succeeded in life and business were genetically superior to others. In other words, some people were born with the talent to rise to the top, and some were born to be poor. This ideal only strengthened their resolve to fight against unions. To combat them, companies used an assortment of tactics:

- **Scab labor**—Replacement workers. These workers had to cross the union picket lines and sometimes violence would erupt.
- **Yellow-dog contracts**—Companies would only hire people that would sign a contract promising they would not strike.
- **Pinkertons**—These people were hired "muscle" who would infiltrate the unions or simply use violence to break up picket lines. They got

their name from the famous Chicago detective agency that employed them.

- **Blacklists**—The company would compile a list of union members and distribute it to all the other companies. If you were on the list, then you could not get a job.
- **Injunctions**—The company would ask (sometimes bribe) local officials, especially judges, to order the workers back into the factory. If workers refused, they were arrested.

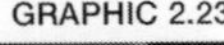
GRAPHIC 2.23

John L. Lewis, the "George Washington of the American labor movement," founded the CIO in 1935. For decades, he championed for the rights of workers.

- **Runaway shops**—If union activity grew too intense in an area, bosses would merely move to another area of the country where the workforce was less organized.
- **Business organizations**—Owners around the country exchanged ideas about keeping workers happy or breaking strikes more effectively through vehicles like the chambers of commerce, which appeared around the beginning of the twentieth century.

Needless to say, unions grew irritated at these tactics and often would lash out against the companies. These violent outbreaks—such as the 1886 Haymarket Riot in Chicago—in which eight policemen died when a bomb was tossed into a crowd—brought publicity to the unions. Between the years 1880 and 1940, multiple violent local and national strikes broke out. On June 30, 1892,

GRAPHIC 2.24

Unions are not as big a part of the labor force as they used to be, but their influence on politics and the economy is undeniable. Here, workers picket a Northern California Kaiser Permanente in 2014.

in Homestead, Pennsylvania, thousands of steelworkers battled with Pinkerton soldiers. The violence (which featured barges, boats, and cannon) lasted for days. At the end, like most other large labor efforts, the union was broken and workers attained none of their goals.

Pressing Question

- In US history, who seems to have had the upper hand in labor disputes, workers or factory owners?

2N. Unions Gain Ground

For decades, the AFL organized for skilled workers, never industrial workers. Hundreds of unions around the United States lost members and disbanded. The 1920s were particularly hard for unions. Numerous national strikes failed. It seemed that workers would never get their basic rights. In the 1930s, however, two men would change all that.

John L. Lewis (graphic 2.23), the president of the United Mine Workers of America, formed the **Congress of Industrial Organizations (CIO)**, the first successful union for unskilled workers. Started in 1935, the CIO saw itself as a direct counterpart to the AFL. Lewis carefully planned strikes in certain industries. In 1937, workers at a General Motors auto plant in Flint, Michigan, all sat down on the job. This "sit-down" strike drew national attention. For more than a month, workers refused to budge from the factory. The government, unlike in the past, merely kept the peace instead of doing the bidding of the owners. Eventually, GM managers met with union leaders and offered a new contract. The United Automobile Workers was born.

Along with Lewis, workers had a friend in the White House. President Franklin D. Roosevelt was born rich but had deep sympathy for workers. He successfully moved legislation through Congress guaranteeing rights most citizens take for granted today. These laws include:

- **National Labor Relations Act** (1935)—Also known as the Wagner Act, for the first time this gave unions the right to collectively bargain. It also formed the National Labor Relations Board to mediate and arbitrate (help resolve) disputes. If both parties consent, the board will use this approach. This means that the suggested solutions must be followed.
- **Fair Labor Standards Act** (1938)—For decades, workers went on strike to gain a shorter workweek and a minimum wage. When FDR signed this bill into law, it guaranteed workers in certain industries a forty-four-hour workweek and a 25-cent-per-hour minimum wage. While these regulations have been updated, it was the first time that many people in the United States rightfully earned a "weekend."

While John Lewis left his union, the CIO continued its success through the 1940s. It opened its ranks to women and minorities, and it stood in direct opposition to the AFL for many years. Ironically, in 1955, the two unions joined to form the AFL-CIO. Today, it is the biggest labor organization in the United States.

Union membership hit a peak during World War II. Since then, there has been a decline in the percentage of the workforce that belongs to a union. Primarily, this is a result of a shift to **white-collar jobs**. These are occupations that tend to be nonmanual and nonroutine jobs like most officework. In addition, bad publicity, corruption, and lack of government support have since then led to a decline in union membership. In the 1980s, the federal government sided with businesses in several high-profile strikes. Air-traffic controllers went on strike in 1981 but were ordered back to work by President Ronald Reagan. When they refused, most of them were fired. In the 1990s, unions found themselves having to shift with the times. According to the Bureau of Labor Statistics, only

GRAPHIC 2.25

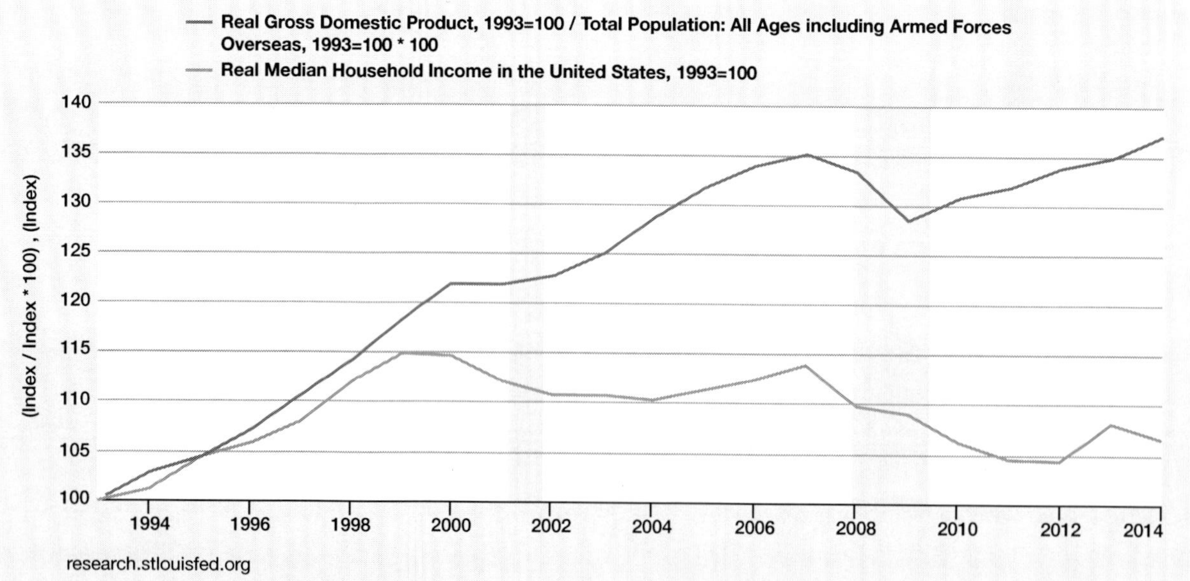

The gap between wage growth and GDP growth (economic growth) is a matter of serious debate. Should workers' wages increase commensurate with what they produce?

about 11 percent of the workforce belongs to a union. Attempts to unionize in retail and fast-food businesses have met with mixed success. Despite this, organized labor remains a formidable political force in the United States.

Pressing Question

- What basic rights did union efforts help secure for American workers?

20. Our Changing Labor Force

While the US population is well over 320 million people, only about one-third of those people are in our labor force. The **labor force** is defined as all of the people in the country who are over the age of sixteen and who are working or looking for work. Not included in this number are people who physically cannot work, retired people, and children. There are also people who have stopped looking for employment, called **discouraged workers**. It is important to remember the exact definition of *labor force*, because it will help clarify exactly what "unemployment rate" means.

In the past 200 years, there has been an almost complete shift in what Americans do for a living. The percentage of farmworkers dropped from 90 percent in 1800 to about 63 percent in 1850. By 1900, only 38 percent of the workers were agricultural. Today, less than 1 percent of the labor force works on farms. In other words, in 1900 it took 90 percent of our people to grow our food. Today it takes less than 1 percent.

Furthermore, in the last forty years there has been a significant drop in the number of manufacturing jobs. Most workers in America are employed in service industries. Instead of building cars and machines, they are providing services like health care, accounting, engineering, and food preparation.

Jobs are also less permanent. Anytime there is a slump in the economy, US businesses lay off workers. People today worry about the security of their jobs. In addition, employees are more transient. It is not uncommon for someone to switch jobs or careers six to ten times in a lifetime. The only way to ensure that you have control over your occupation is to make sure you develop a skill that is in high demand. If a job can be done by a computer or a machine, businesses will invest in that capital instead of continuing to pay labor.

Globalization (to be addressed in Unit 6) has affected our job market. Many people wonder, "what can we do for a living anymore?" Others believe that all of our jobs will leave for places like China. This behavior follows a pattern seen before. The textile industry, once in the northeastern United States, moved to the southern states, then to Mexico, then to China. Still, most people do not know that China is losing those jobs to Cambodia, Vietnam, Bangladesh, and countries in sub-Saharan Africa. This is the nature of international trade. If the cost of production is lower in another country, industries will move their facilities there. Nevertheless, US citizens are still finding work.

New inventions can also change the way we work. When personal computers first appeared in the mid-1970s, businesses were slow to bring them into the workplace. Today, it is expected that employees know how to operate a computer. In accounting for instance, spreadsheets were once tabulated by hand, a painstaking endeavor. Using a PC, one accountant can now do the work it would have taken hundreds to accomplish fifty years ago. This is an increase in productivity, or the marginal revenue that one employee brings into a business.

In the mid-1990s, engineers developed a way to connect all of our computers using the Internet. This technology caught on much faster than any other in the twentieth century. Businesses quickly established websites, and within a few years people used the Internet to shop, trade, and communicate. Today, the Internet is quickly becoming the primary way we do business, entertain ourselves, and access information. New jobs arose from this technology. Cloud database managers, search engine optimizers, social media marketers, webmasters, sustainability experts, and app developers are all jobs that did not exist prior to 2000. Young people, raised on the Internet, are leading the way in developing and managing the new world of constant interconnectedness.

GRAPHIC 2.26

By 2020, the Labor Department estimates that 40 percent of our labor force will be self-employed. This often involves working from home.

Globalization brings competition as well. A college graduate in 1980 had to compete with other young people from the United States for jobs. In 2020, our graduates compete with workers across the globe. Numerous websites allow employers to post job requests online. Interested workers can bid on those jobs. This type of **freelance worker**, somebody who is self-employed and does jobs one at a time on a contract basis, is becoming more common. It is estimated that by 2020, 40 percent of the US workforce will be self-employed. Companies in the United States hire computer programmers from Russia, app developers from China, and website designers from Brazil. The Internet allows us to work with anyone anywhere in the world, and the competition is fierce. Working for yourself can be rewarding, but there is no job security.

Young people today will enter the most competitive job market the United States has ever seen. While the Internet can bring us entertainment and interconnectedness, it also broadens the pool of workers that a business can hire. Your grandparents could graduate from high school, get a job, and work with that same company for decades. This is no longer the case. The United States is not the only player on the world economic stage. You will have to work harder to achieve a standard of living that you find agreeable. Because most workers will switch jobs so many times in their prime wage-earning years, they will need to train and learn new skills on an ongoing basis. Our work must change with the times.

Pressing Question

- Why do most American workers have to retrain so often nowadays?

2P. Your Rights as a Worker

Americans are guaranteed certain rights. Certainly, you have learned about these rights throughout your education. Did you know that you also have many rights as a worker? While some rights, like freedom of speech and assembly, are guaranteed by the Constitution, many others were added by Congress through the legislative process. Unions and other labor activists argued for many of these rights starting in the mid- to late 1800s. It is hard to imagine a day before we enacted laws that gave us basic rights. We have come to see these as normal:

- Minimum wage and a forty-hour workweek
- Overtime pay (time and a half)
- Safe working conditions
- Unemployment benefits
- Unpaid time off to care for a new baby or loved one

On the other hand, there are benefits your employer is not required to provide. These are *not guaranteed:*

- **Retirement contributions**—Aside from Social Security matching funds, your boss is not required to contribute money to your retirement.
- **Paid vacation time**—While many Europeans enjoy up to six weeks of guaranteed paid vacation, workers in America are not granted time

off by law. Hourly workers rarely get paid vacation time. When salaried employees get time off, the standard is ten days.

- **Paid sick days**—Hourly workers who do not work do not get paid. Salaried employees will usually get five to ten paid sick days per year.
- **Medical insurance**—An employer with a small business (fewer than fifty employees) has no legal obligation to provide you with medical insurance. Hourly workers may have to go online to a state health care exchange to find affordable health insurance.

Consider the information in graphic 2.27; notice the years that these laws were enacted. Much of what we take for granted did not exist prior to then. Rights like paid family leave and vacation time may come to the American workplace someday, but that is a political discussion that must take place in Congress. We will see more about that topic in Unit 4.

Pressing Question

- Of all the rights guaranteed by the government, which one is most important? Explain.

GRAPHIC 2.27

YOUR RIGHTS AS A WORKER
(DEPARTMENT OF LABOR)

Laws	Rights
Federal Employers Liability Act (1908) and later state workers' compensation laws	Insurance paid to workers and/or their families for injury or death incurred as a result of their work
National Labor Relations Act (1935)	Right to unionize and collectively bargain
Social Security Act (1935)	Retirement insurance, disability insurance, unemployment insurance
Fair Labor Standards Act (1937)	Minimum wage, overtime, regular hours
Equal Pay Act (1963) Civil Rights Act (1964) Americans with Disabilities Act (1990) Age Discrimination in Employment Act (1967)	Equal opportunity for employment not based on race, gender, age, disability, or creed
Occupational Safety and Health Act (1970)	Safe working conditions
Family and Medical Leave Act (1993)	Unpaid time off to care for a new baby, sick relative, or your sick self

 Name:

Vocabulary Puzzler

Directions: Use your reading to find the answers to the clues on the next page. Fill the spaces in the puzzle below with those words.

Clue Sheet

Across

5. The cost of producing one additional unit
6. The George Washington of the American labor movement
13. A market of only a few producers
16. "__________ of trade"; made illegal in the Sherman Act
18. Officeworker; __________-collar job
20. "No contract, __________, or conspiracy"
23. Your share of the profits for owning stock
24. A person who starts a business
25. Anti__________ law fights monopolies
26. Plumbers and electricians; __________ -collar jobs
27. A refusal to buy a company's products
28. Type of work for self-employed people

Down

1. When a group of workers refuses to work
2. Many producers, many consumers; __________ competition
3. The Federal __________ Commission; (investigates monopolies)
4. Someone who owns their own business; a __________ proprietor
5. Tech giant declared a monopoly in the 1990s
7. The process by which a worker gets better at a more specific task
8. (Protesters outside a business) form a __________ line
9. Gas or cable company; a __________ monopoly
10. Return on __________ (ROI)
11. A business that has filed a charter with its state of origin
12. A market dominated by one business
14. Net income divided by total sales equals profit __________
15. People over the age of sixteen who are working or looking for work
17. A labor organization that represents a group of workers
18. A worker's hourly pay
19. __________ bargaining (allows all members of a union to work under the same contract)
21. Two companies joining together
22. Another word for "new revenue"

Name:

The Business Track

Directions: For each of the following business steps below, fill in the flow chart table with the appropriate terms. Choose from the words in the top table.

corporation	dividends	contracts
franchise	internal financing	business plan
sole proprietorship	initial public offering	salary
bank	stock	wage
chief executive officer	partner	profit margin

If you have trouble, refer to your reading.

Jill did the following:	That is called:
1. Formed a small business in which she is the only owner and assumed full liability.	
2. Found someone to share the risk with and take some of the responsibility.	
3. Wrote down the purpose and focus of her business.	
4. Borrowed money in the form of a business loan from a financial institution.	
5. Incorporated her small business with her state of origin.	
6. Wrote legally binding agreements with her suppliers and customers.	
7. Paid some of her workers an hourly ___________.	
8. Paid other workers set amounts every two weeks.	
9. Sought additional capital from investors by selling stock in her company to the public.	
10. Invested some of her profits back into the company to allow for faster growth.	
11. Sold the licensing rights to sell her products in stores that will look just like hers.	
12. Split the profits among all the stockholders, who get their fair share.	
13. Made sure that her business was profitable when compared to her sales.	
14. Named herself the head of the company.	
15. Divided her company into smaller pieces for sale to the public.	

Name:

Business Facts

Part 1

Directions: Using your reading as a guide, fill in the table below with details about each business formation.

Type of Business	Definition	Examples	Advantages	Disadvantages
sole proprietorship				
partnership				
nonprofit				
cooperative				
corporation				

Part 2

Directions: Answer the following questions with a sentence or two.

1. What are some different ways to make money from investing in a company?

2. What three attributes does a brand-new business need to be successful?

3. What are the components to a business plan?

4. What are some of the ways corporations can combine?

5. What makes a franchise an appealing investment to many people?

6. What role do nonprofits play in our economy? How does the government encourage their survival?

7. What is the difference between a public and a private corporation? Give examples to elaborate.

8. Below list three examples of each of the following that you have encountered: sole proprietorships, corporations, and nonprofits.

Sole Proprietorships	Corporations	Nonprofits
1.	1.	1.
2.	2.	2.
3.	3.	3.

9. What are some of the different ways that businesses can access capital for expansion?

10. What does a venture capitalist do?

11. Describe the structure of a typical public corporation.

Name:

Get to Know Your Costs

Directions: Plot the ATC and MC curves on the graph to the right.

Units	ATC	MC
10	110	60
20	90	50
30	80	40
40	70	50
50	60	60
60	70	80
70	80	90
80	90	100

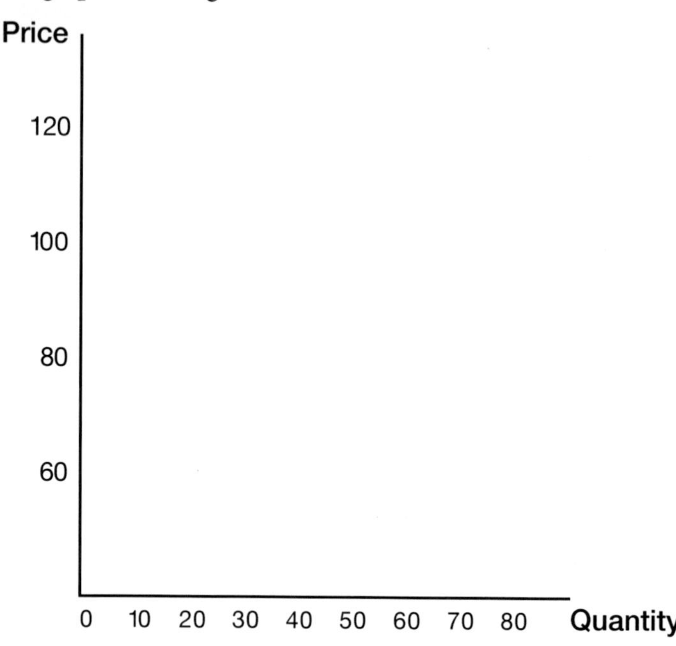

Directions: Answer the following with a sentence or two. Refer to your reading if you need extra guidance.

1. What do ATC and MC stand for?

2. Why does the average cost of making a product go down as you make more?

3. Define the law of diminishing returns.

4. Put a star on the MC curve where diminishing returns set in.
5. Why does the ATC curve start to go up after the MC curve crosses it?

6. Where do businesses in perfectly competitive markets produce? (Hint: It is a formula.)

7. What price does this business need to get from the market to break even?

 Name:

Monopolies and You

Part 1

Directions: Fill in the table below using your reading as a guide. When finished with the table, ask someone you know, preferably an adult, to help you to answer the questions below the table with a few sentences each.

Business Formation	Number of Companies Competing	Entry to Market	Information	Control	Choice for Consumer
Perfect competition					
Monopolistic competition					
Oligopoly					
Monopoly					

Part 2

Directions: Referring to your reading, answer the questions below.

1. How can a monopoly harm consumers? How can it hurt producers?

2. What types of monopolies are allowed to exist in our economy?

3. When does a monopoly break the law?

4. What sorts of market behavior are unique to an oligopoly?

5. Web search: How did De Beers so successfully convince the public that diamonds are rare?

 Name:

The Sherman Antitrust Act

Directions: After the two quotations in italics, answer the questions below them.

Every contract, combination in the form of trust or otherwise, or conspiracy, in restraint of trade or commerce among the several States, or with foreign nations, is declared to be illegal.

Sherman Antitrust Act (1890), Section 1

1. What is truly illegal according to the Sherman Antitrust Act?

2. Define *contract, combination,* and *conspiracy* below.

The purpose of the [Sherman] Act is not to protect businesses from the working of the market; it is to protect the public from the failure of the market. The law directs itself not against conduct which is competitive, even severely so, but against conduct which unfairly tends to destroy competition itself.

Spectrum Sports, Inc. v. McQuillan, 506 US 447, 458 (Supreme Court, 1993).

3. In this case, what does the plaintiff say the true purpose of the Sherman Act is?

4. Is competition bad for the market? Why or why not?

5. Define:
   a. Price fixing:
   b. Bid rigging:
   c. Customer allocation:
   d. Predatory pricing:

6. Bonus research: Using the Internet, briefly describe the following cases:
   a. *Standard Oil Co. of New Jersey v. United States* (1911):
   b. *US v. Microsoft* (2001):
   c. *US v. Apple, Inc. et al* (2013):

 Name:

Labor Supply and Labor Demand

Directions: There is a market for labor, just as there is a market for products and services. In the blanks below, indicate which curve will change and what will happen to wages (see example). Following the example, change the curves in 1–5.

Example: ___*Demand*___ The computer industry is suddenly in need of workers who have high-tech training.

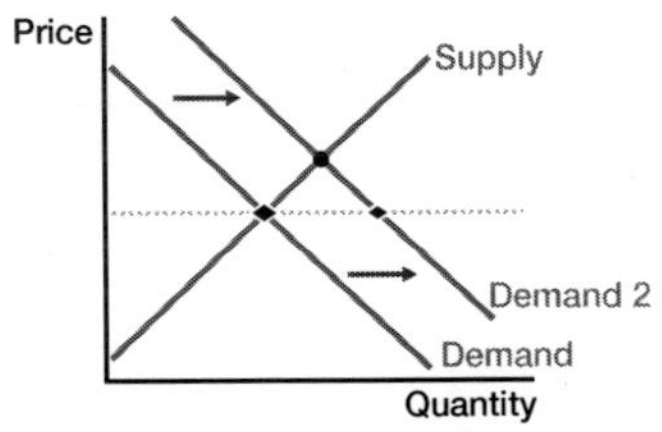

Price
Supply
Demand 2
Demand
Quantity

___*Go up*___ Wages

1. ______________ The economy is very hot. Overall, firms are hiring, but jobs are not getting filled.

   ______________ Wages

2. ______________ You work on an assembly line, and companies across the country are buying robots to do your job.

   ______________ Wages

3. ______________ The number of sheet metal workers has declined on account of the lack of high school grads entering the trade.

   ______________ Wages

4. ______________ Congress just raised minimum wage to $18.00/hour. What would that *price floor* look like?

   ______________ Wages

5. ______________ Colleges are graduating twice as many pharmacists as usual.

   ______________ Wages

Name:

Labor Trends

Part 1

Directions: Go to www.BLS.gov. Using the "Occupational Outlook Handbook," fill in the table below. Try to think as you search and choose five jobs you might be interested in doing.

Occupation	Description	Educational Requirement	Starting Salary
1.			
2.			
3.			
4.			
5.			

Part 2

Directions: Again using the "Occupational Outlook Handbook," fill in the table below.

Top 10 Declining Occupations	Top 10 Growing Occupations
1.	1.
2.	2.
3.	3.
4.	4.
5.	5.
6.	6.
7.	7.
8.	8.
9.	9.
10.	10.

Part 3

Directions: Answer the questions below.

1. Define *labor force.*

2. Define *unemployment rate.*

3. What percentage of our workforce will be "self-employed" by 2020?

4. How do freelancers make a living? What are some challenges they face? Why are these so many now as compared to the past?

Name:

A Worker's Rights

Part 1

Directions: Using your reading, answer the questions and fill in the tables below.

This is my right:	This is the law that guarantees my right:
Being safe and free from dangerous conditions at work	
A government-funded retirement pension	
Several months of unpaid leave to care for a sick relative or new baby	
Minimum wage and a 40-hour workweek	
Meeting with other workers to discuss forming a union	
Compensation if I am injured on the job	

Part 2

Directions: Answer the questions below.

1. In your opinion, what are the most important rights of workers?

2. What rights do Americans currently not have as workers?

3. What are some current trends in our changing labor market?

4. What is job security? What sorts of jobs have more security than others?

5. Using the chart from Section 2J, describe the differences in yearly salaries among three different education levels.

6. How are things better for workers today than they were one hundred years ago?

Unit 3

Financial Institutions

Questions to Consider

1. Why do people not barter as they used to?
2. How does money help us determine value?
3. How is money (currency and coins) made?
4. How does a bank go out of business?
5. What products are most important to our economy?
6. Why do bad economies happen?
7. What sorts of things can make prices go up?
8. Why do most countries have a national bank?
9. Where is our government represented on the dollar bill?

Terms You Need in Order to Read

Bank	Interest	Productivity
Economy	Money	Recession
Inflation		

Financial Institutions

3A. The History of Money

Think back to our earlier readings about economics. In Unit 1, you learned that an economy exists whenever people produce things and consume things (or provide and require services). The constant transfer of goods that goes along with a vibrant economy needs help to continue. Even in smaller countries, an economy would shut down without a viable medium of exchange. In other words, any financial transaction where goods or services are exchanged needs something to come between the producer and the consumer. Like a size medium T-shirt comes between a large and a small, money comes between a producer and consumer.

If we did not have money, we could still **barter**, or exchange goods without the help of money. Bartering can be complicated. Let us say you are a farmer and have some surplus corn. You also need a new pair of tennis shoes. So, off to market you go. You set out across town with a car full of corn only to discover that many people would love to have your corn, but none of these people has any shoes that you would like. At the same time others have the shoes that you want, but they do not want your corn. In essence, you have to find someone who has what you want and wants what you have. This is called the **double coincidence of wants**.

GRAPHIC 3.1

Gold is valuable, because it is rare and we *all* believe it is valuable. Today, governments hold gold reserves as a means to store value. Reserves give a government credibility.

In early economies all over the world, people must have quickly lost patience. Bartering is woefully inefficient. People quickly figured out that there were certain goods that everyone wanted. People accumulated these goods and used them as a medium of exchange. Those items of value that can be stored and transported are called *commodities*. Depending on the area of the world, they could be seashells, animals, precious metals, or an agricultural product. When people use these to more efficiently exchange goods, we call this **commodity money.**

GRAPHIC 3.2

This coin was found in modern Turkey. Made by the Lydians around 560 BCE, these coins are thought to be some of the earliest in the Western world.

All over the world, certain substances seemed to be universally desired. Some substances, like gold (graphic 3.1), were more desired than others. For most people, precious metals have an intrinsic (built-in) value. The problem with trading raw gold or powder was assessing quality and standardizing weights. The next logical step was to take those precious metals and press them, or mint them, into coins.

The first coins began to appear independently around the world between 700 and 600 BCE. The Chinese and people of India were the first to mint coins in Asia. The act of making a coin is "to mint," and the place where coins are made is also called a **mint**. Coins that come from the mint are so pristine that we describe anything in great shape as being "in mint condition." The first people in the Western world to make their own coins were the Lydians (see graphic 3.2), who lived in what is now modern Turkey. From that point forward, civilized people like the Greeks, Romans, and Muslims used precious coins made of gold and silver to make commerce more efficient.

Coins made of gold or silver are called **specie**. In the Renaissance, bankers noticed that people would tamper with coins made of precious metal. Little by little, people would clip or shave a bit of the metal off for themselves. For a few transactions, vendors would accept a damaged coin, not noticing the difference. After this happened repeatedly, however, the once pristine coin became a mangled mess. As a result, it had less metal, and it lost value. People also lost faith in their money, and when they received a perfect piece of **currency** (any type of portable money), they would hoard it. After a while, only the mangled money remained in circulation. Thus, when a society tried to use specie as its currency, bad money with less value drove out the good money. This tendency is called **Gresham law.**

Governments wanted to make sure they could make every little bit of tax that they could from their country's lively trade, so they came up with a solution. They kept the precious metals in a treasury and issued bills that represented the gold or silver. This is called **representative money**. In the 1700s, countries all over the world began to issue their own commodity-backed currencies.

Before the American Revolution, the colonies issued their own local monies (graphic 3.3). After they ratified the Constitution, the Framers debated the need for a national currency. When one was finally issued, local banks still circulated their own money. Bank notes were issued by independent banks, and consumers and travelers were left to figure it out for themselves. Even worse, if a bank failed, its money disappeared and you would be left with worthless paper.

It was not until the Civil War that the United States had its own national currency (the Confederates had their own as well). The bills were black on the front and bright green in the back. We still use the nickname for our money today, "greenbacks." Slowly, states and communities adopted the dollar as their medium of exchange. During the Industrial Revolution, this helped spur interstate commerce.

We continued to use reserves of gold and silver to give value to our money. This representative currency circulated until August 15, 1971. After that, people could no longer convert American money into gold. Today, no country in the world uses precious metals as a means of monetary valuation.

Remember, *our money is no longer backed by gold*. It merely has value because the government says it does. The Latin word for a government decree is *fiat*. Therefore, we call the currency in the United States **fiat money**. This allows our national bank to put money into the economy or take money out of the economy as it deems necessary. You will read later about how important this flexibility is to our economy's well-being.

Pressing Question

- What is the difference between fiat money and representative money?

GRAPHIC 3.3

In the early 1800s, local governments, banks, and even corporations issued their own currencies. If you traveled to do business, you would have to exchange the currency you were carrying for the locally accepted currency.

3B. Guide to Useful Money

Think about the last time you spent some money. Let us say you went and bought clothes and then got some lunch with some friends. Different items that you purchased were given a value according to our currency. Things that people value more require more dollars. Our dollar helps us set the **standard of value** for various goods and services. In many ways, we think in dollars.

To be useful, money must first be a universally accepted medium of exchange. We all value it in common. Next, it must hold its value over time. You may have heard stories of people hiding their money in a mattress or in a vase in a backyard garden. A stable currency will keep its value over the years. This is called a **store of value**. A dollar one year from now will still buy the same amount of goods it does today.

Money must have some other properties in order to be useful to an economy. Because transactions rarely equal an exact dollar, our currency must be easily divided into a fraction. Furthermore, it must be widely recognized by people so there is widespread faith that the money is **legal tender**. This means that it may be used to settle any debts or transactions, public or private. Money in banks or stock is not legal tender or an effective medium of exchange.

Finally, good money has to last. The US Department of the Treasury has long tried to find a dollar bill that can take the punishment that we give it. Despite all of their efforts, the average dollar bill lasts only about a year and a half in circulation. Some even call for phasing out the dollar bill and replacing it with a dollar coin. The main reason for this is the added durability the US Mint could offer in a new coin. That argument has yet to be settled.

No matter what form money takes, it must always have some characteristics that make it easy to use. In earlier reading, you learned about commodity money. In some cultures, the commodity was rice or cattle. Neither of these is easy to transport, much less divide into smaller values. How do you get one-tenth of a cow without killing it? So modern money must be divisible. It needs to be logically and easily split into smaller parts. Second, it must be portable. We have to be able to carry it around with us wherever we go. Last, it must withstand the beating that money must take. It must be durable. Unless it endures multiple transactions over several years, it gets too expensive to maintain.

As society becomes more reliant on the Internet and computers, money is more digital than tangible. That is, more of our money supply lives on computer chips in banks than in our pockets. Consider graphic 3.4. If you add together all the electronic forms of money, they equal 89 percent of our money supply. Currency, what we carry in our pockets, adds up to only 11 percent.

GRAPHIC 3.4

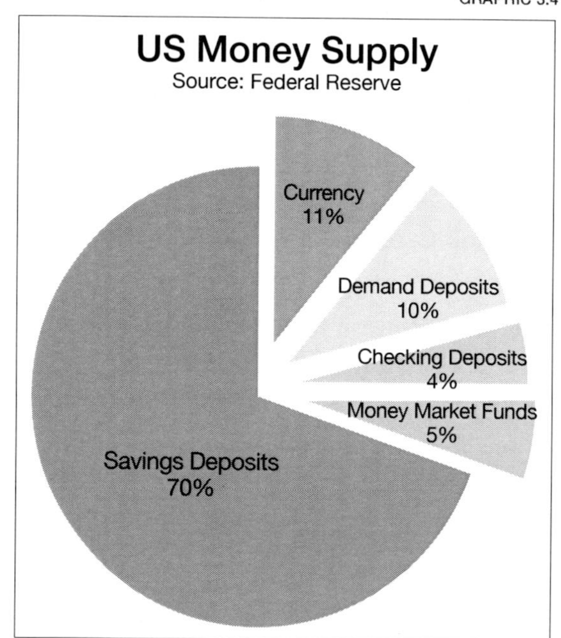

On the Internet, people have even taken to making their own currency. Bitcoin, a completely virtual currency, was developed by a computer programmer in Japan. When people began to use it to exchange goods and services, it became money. Think about it. Bitcoin is finite, durable, portable, and divisible. People who use it believe it has worth. It has everything it needs to be money and so it is. Bitcoin is money.

Money might be an ancient concept, but economies will always have a need for it.

Pressing Question

- What characteristics are necessary to make a useful currency?

3C. The Money Supply

To have value, the supply of anything, even money, has to be finite. As with any commodity, scarcity will give it value. If you want money, then you have to sacrifice something to get it. People work and trade their time and labor for money. People who have excess cash put it in a bank to earn interest. They forgo using that money right now for getting more money in the future. Think of money as just another thing that we trade. There is a supply of it, and there is a demand for it. If there is more money put into circulation, it will lose value. If money is taken out of circulation, then it will gain value. This fact can affect prices of all of the products in our economy. As a result, economists watch the money supply very closely. Even though it can be trillions and trillions of dollars, our money is finite, and we all believe it has value.

Think about the adults in your life. Do you think that most of their money is kept in currency somewhere in the house or in their wallets? Chances are, like most Americans, the bulk of their money is kept in checking accounts and savings accounts. The money held in these accounts is considered **liquid**, as it can be converted to cash very easily. Accountants usually refer to money in the bank as "cash." For many people who make purchases with credit cards and pay bills electronically, their paychecks never even get changed into cash. They are merely deposited into a personal bank account and transferred from one bank to another. Most money in our economy is not even dollars and coins. Most of it is almost cash, in what we call **demand deposits** (commonly in checking and savings accounts). In other words, deposits are "payable on demand." Economists keep track of every penny.

The money supply is such a large number that economists break it down into smaller categories.

- **M1**—This is currency, traveler's checks, and deposits in various types of checking accounts. It comprises about 11 percent of the money supply.
- **M2**—This includes any money that is kept in any short-term investment that allows a person quick access to their money. Mostly, this is in savings accounts. Money market accounts are pools of money invested in different bonds and securities in bulk and pass the interest benefits on to the investor.
- **M3**—This money includes bonds and certificates of deposit. These are places people put their money for extended periods of time. While they are not as liquid as a savings account, they are still counted as money.

Consider graphic 3.4. This pie chart breaks down the various categories of M2. Almost all of our money supply is electronic. This fact is nothing new. Over the past several decades, more and more of our money is "blips on chips." Your short-term cash is not bills and coins, but rather the deposits you have placed in your bank. Most people need to change the way they see money. Cash in the form of currency is rapidly becoming something we will *never* see.

Pressing Question

- What impact does an increasing money supply have on prices? What impact does a decreasing money supply have on prices?

3D. Funny Money

Although the number is difficult to gauge, some economists estimate that almost 75 percent of US currency is held by people overseas. In fact, dollars are the most trusted currency in emerging markets around the world because of the instability of their own governments. Imagine your plane touching down in another country halfway

GRAPHIC 3.5

Security Thread

Hold the note to light to see an embedded thread running vertically to the left of the portrait. The thread is imprinted with the letters *USA* and the numeral *100* in an alternating pattern and is visible from both sides of the note. The thread glows pink when illuminated by ultraviolet light.

3D Security Ribbon

Tilt the note back and forth while focusing on the blue ribbon. You will see the bells change to *100s* as they move. When you tilt the note back and forth, the bells and *100s* move side to side. If you tilt it side to side, they move up and down. The ribbon is woven into the paper, not printedon it.

Bell in the Inkwell

Tilt the note to see the color-shifting bell in the copper inkwell change from copper to green, an effect that makes the bell seem to appear and disappear within the inkwell.

Watermark

Hold the note to light and look for a faint image of Benjamin Franklin in the blank space to the right of the portrait. The image is visible from both sides of the note.

Color-Shifting Ink

Tilt the note to see the numeral *100* in the lower right corner of the front of the note shift from copper to green.

across the globe only to have the cab driver insist that you pay in American dollars. While people like our money because it is stable, it is often in the hands of people who do not know what it should look like.

Counterfeiting, or the creation of fake "funny" money, has become a favorite activity of organized crime and even some governments across the world. Between the 1920s and 1990s, the US Department of the Treasury had not redesigned our currency. This left us vulnerable. One particular hundred dollar bill made by Iran, called the "superbill," was so convincing in the 1990s that many banks were fooled. Merchants refused to accept the note all over the world.

Counterfeiting is a federal crime. It is investigated by the US **Secret Service**, which recommended that the US Department of the Treasury create new security measures to discourage would-be counterfeit operations. This is especially important when you consider that illegal bills sometimes fund terrorism and organized crime. Equally important, citizens need to trust that our money is worth what we think it is. When people lose faith in the money supply, disastrous things can happen to an economy.

Even though currency is only a small fraction of our money supply, the US Bureau of Engraving and Printing (part of the US Department of the Treasury) has added multiple security features to our new bills. Consider graphic 3.5. The paper is secretively made of cotton and wood pulp by one company in the world, Crane & Co. Separate security threads are embedded in the production process. Multiple colors and color-shifting inks allow the holder to check for authenticity more easily. All bills above the one have a watermark, an image of the portrait visible only when backlit. Additionally, if your eyes are very good, you might be able to see the micro printing hidden in Benjamin Franklin's collar. Even the portrait is larger and off center. People have a built-in ability to recognize faces, so if a counterfeit does not reproduce the face perfectly, it is easy to notice.

With electronic scanners, computers, and photo-editing software, criminals have even managed to copy these sophisticated new notes. Other countries are now using plastic and holograms to foil counterfeiters.

If you ever want to copy a bill, think again! It is a very serious federal offense. The bill in graphic 3.5 has the word *specimen* embedded, so your economics book is following the law. If you are going to copy a bill, the law states you must either expand it by 100 percent or shrink it by 50 percent.

Counterfeiting seems like a victimless crime to some. This is far from the case. Whoever ends up holding the bill will be out that money, and it is usually a merchant. The money is in the cash register, and at the end of the day it gets deposited in the merchant's bank. The bank will sort that money and make a deposit in the local Federal Reserve Bank. With sophisticated scanners, the bogus bill will be set aside. It gets turned over to the Secret Service, which will trace it back to the bank and, eventually, the depositor. The money is then subtracted from the depositor's account. In the end, counterfeiting is stealing from the person who finally accepts the money.

Pressing Question

- In a time of war, why do enemies counterfeit and disseminate each other's money as much as possible?

3E. Our Money around the Globe

For the most part, our money is stable and secure. This stability is important to those of us who choose to travel overseas. In addition, thousands of American companies do business in other countries. The United States exports trillions of dollars' worth of goods and services across the globe. If US businesses sell something in another country, then they will eventually have to convert that currency to US dollars. They do this with deposit money or electronic wire transfers. This process is possible only with the help of **foreign exchange rates**.

There are markets all over the world in which people do nothing but buy and sell money all day (that is correct—buy and sell money). For instance, if a trader holds $1 million in US dollars and converts it to 7 million Chinese yuan, he or she will hope that the yuan will **strengthen** (or gain value) against the dollar. Thus, after an hour, week, or month, the trader can change the money back to dollars. More US money will be required to equal the 7 million yuan. In the end, the whole venture could potentially net (or lose) tens of thousands of dollars. The free flow of money around the world is necessary for smooth international commerce.

What happens if you are a business that sells services in China? You hope that the Chinese will buy more of your product. Supposing that the price in China remained constant, higher sales should mean higher profits for your company. If the yuan **weakens** (or loses value), however, it will take fewer dollars to equal the yuan you hold. Your business did everything right. It developed a service, advertised, and delivered. Nevertheless, unfavorable exchange rates can erode your profits.

GRAPHIC 3.6

When traveling, you will need to exchange our dollars into the local currency. You can use credit cards, but cash is still important. Do not exchange your money at airports, hotels, or tourist attractions. For the best exchange rates, always go to a bank.

Businesses and the government watch the value of the dollar closely. Exporters often favor a trend toward a weaker dollar. This means that they can lower their prices overseas. Even with the lower prices, they can still get more dollars back when the profits are moved back into US banks.

If you plan on traveling, root for a stronger dollar. This way, when you get to the other country, you will get more of their money for every dollar you exchange. So, is it better for the dollar to be strong or weak? It depends on who answers the question. Ultimately, we all benefit from a stable and predictable exchange rate.

The currency markets around the world fluctuate in value against one another. These are called **floating exchange rates**. While the dollar might weaken against the euro, it might strengthen against the Japanese yen at the very same time. As with anything else, there is a supply of money and a demand for money. A healthy, growing, and stable economy will make international investors move money into our banks. A rapidly growing economy, like China's, will increase the demand for the yuan. On the other hand, if a country has a financial crisis or civil war, investors and businesses will move their money out of that country quickly. This will make that country's money weaken against other currencies around the world.

One controversy should be noted. Since emerging into the world economy in the early 1990s, China's economy until recently averaged an annual 10 percent rate of growth. This made doing business in China very lucrative. Investors around the world moved money to China, creating a high demand for yuan. This very strong money would make Chinese products more expensive in places like the United States—although Chinese products remain relatively inexpensive. China's government buys US dollars in great amounts to strengthen the dollar and weaken the yuan. This allows Chinese companies to charge lower prices in the United States while still remaining profitable. (See graphic 3.7.)

Pressing Question

- Who wants a stronger dollar? Who benefits from a weaker dollar?

3F. How Banks Work

When you think about banks, the first thing that probably comes to mind is money locked in a safe. The primary function of banks is to be a depository for people's money; so, how do banks make money? As long as we are talking about money, it is about time we addressed the concept of interest.

Interest is the cost of using someone else's money. If you have ever borrowed money from someone, then you may have given that person

GRAPHIC 3.7

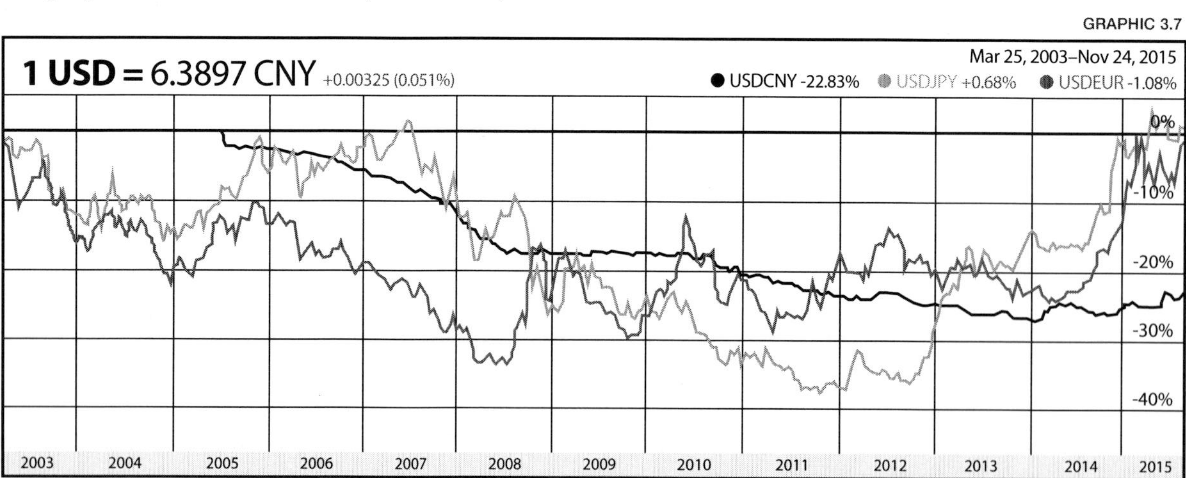

The USDCNY represents the US dollar-to-Chinese yuan exchange rate. The USDJPY line is Japanese yen, and the USDEUR is European euros. Compare the three lines. The USDCNY line fluctuates very little. This is evidence of China's currency market manipulation.

an IOU with a promise to pay on a later date. In the world of banking, it is pretty much the same thing. When you borrow money from a bank, you will sign a contract to repay the bank. The amount you borrow is called the **principal**. The interest is the extra amount added into each payment. This is called the **annual percentage rate (APR)**. For instance, if you borrow $100,000 at 10 percent interest, then you will owe the servicer of the loan $10,000 at the end of the first year. That comes to almost $840 per month to pay the interest alone.

The business model of banking is simple. Consider graphic 3.8. A depositor puts part of her disposable income into a bank. By giving up the utility that the deposited money could give her at that moment, she receives interest (extra money added onto her principal). The bank loans most of the deposit to a borrower. That person then pays interest on his loan. The bank uses that revenue to pay the depositor's interest. It is simple. People will pay banks to use their money, and a bank will pay you to deposit yours.

Banks must follow many government regulations that help discern who should qualify for a loan and who should not. Banking is perhaps the most regulated business in the United States. The government has been setting regulations in the industry since the 1930s, when Congress established the Federal Deposit Insurance Corporation (FDIC). During the Great Depression, thousands of banks closed. Many Americans lost their life savings and refused to trust banks again. To remedy this, the FDIC started guaranteeing all deposits. Today, the amount insured is $250,000. Next time you see a commercial on TV for a bank, listen closely for the "FDIC insured" at the end.

People need money for a variety of reasons—college loans, business loans, auto loans, and purchasing a home to name a few. A person who needs to borrow or save money has several options in today's marketplace. Banks come in a few basic categories depending on who is in charge of supervising and regulating them. Some banks are regulated by the state they are located in while most others are under the jurisdiction of the federal government. Good consumers will choose a bank the same way they choose a car or a lawyer. They shop around.

- **Commercial banks** are the most numerous, profitable, and stable. Bank of America, Chase Bank, and Citibank are counted in this category.

GRAPHIC 3.8

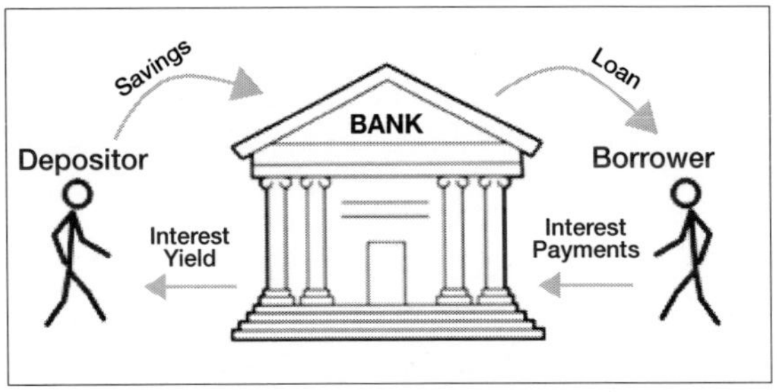

- **Credit unions** are commonly associated with unions, churches, and other social organizations. Members deposit their money in order to buy shares that pay an annual rate of interest. Because they sometimes utilize volunteer labor and capital contributed by a sponsor organization, a credit union is able to loan money to members at lower rates than commercial banks. Also, credit unions are not taxed on their income, while other depository institutions are.
- **Federal savings banks**—These are organized under the federal Home Owners' Loan Act. They primarily serve as **mortgage** lenders (they loan money to buy land or property). They often have the word "savings bank" or "savings and loan" in the name of the company. Often, they are not members of the Federal Reserve System.
- **Internet banks**—Rapidly, the Internet is disrupting many industries. Banking is no exception. Some banks do not have branches. Rather, they are accessible only on the Internet. Depositors can use bank machines, but most business is done on the web. They are often insured by the FDIC, but be sure to check.

Regardless of what you need from a bank, they all function in the same way: They take deposits and give out loans. When choosing a bank, pay attention to what fees they charge and when. Traditionally, most of a bank's profits come from the margin between deposit rates and loan rates. Nowadays, more and more banks rely on fees to pad their profits. If you are careful with your money, you can avoid most charges, but if you make a few mistakes, it could cost you hundreds of dollars.

Banks are finding many new ways to provide people with easier access to their money. It makes their business activity more profitable while making banking more convenient. Most people now carry a debit card, for example. Debit cards may look like credit cards but take money directly from one's checking account. If you are not careful, you can make purchases while still having a check that you wrote waiting to clear. The wise consumer always keeps receipts and keeps close track of spending.

Two last developments in banking today are electronic in nature. ATMs (around for decades) and the Internet give people constant access to their money. These tools make things like demand deposits even more liquid. Banks save millions of dollars when customers use electronic means of doing business rather than going to a teller. With electronic bill paying, debit cards, ATM cards, and direct deposit of paychecks, technology-savvy customers need never visit an actual bank. Some banks will even accept a deposit by simply taking a photograph of the check through a mobile phone app.

Pressing Question

- Explain how a bank makes profits.

3G. Productivity in the United States

One of the most important jobs of our government is to keep a close eye on our economy. An economy exists whenever people get together to make and use goods and services. If we produce a higher dollar amount of goods and services from one year to the next, the economy has grown. The United States produces an extraordinary amount of goods and services every year. It is a monumental task to keep track of all that we consume and produce, but it is the only way to know if the economy is growing or shrinking. The government periodically tries to add up everything we make (called the *gross*). Economists are primarily concerned about what our citizens produce within our borders (domestically). The results of our work are many products, so the final calculation is known as **gross domestic product** (**GDP**).

Think of our economy as a business. The whole point to starting a business is to make money and grow your revenue. Let us say you own a table factory. Your employees are able to manufacture 2,000 tables a month at their maximum efficiency. Your tables are selling well, so you declare to the staff that you wish the factory to hit a goal of 2,200 tables next month. Is it possible? Can you do it without hiring more workers? The answer may be "yes."

You need your employees to become more **productive**, or produce a greater dollar amount of goods in the same time period. This would mean the benefits to your firm by making more goods would exceed the value of the costs. Your company should try to figure out new ways of becoming more efficient. Time has to be used more effectively. Machines could be geared to operate more quickly. If all goes well, your goals might be met. Sales will meet the high demand, and your profits will rise. The best thing is you did not have to spend any more money to produce more.

As a country, we also want to become more productive. In essence, the United States needs to produce more goods and services this year than it did last year. If we do, there will be more jobs for our citizens, more profits for our companies, and more prosperity all around. GDP is the most quoted indicator when describing the health of our economy.

GRAPHIC 3.9

Components of GDP

Category	Symbol	Explanation
Consumer spending	C	All purchases of new and final goods made by consumers. Used goods and raw materials are excluded.
Investments	I	These are not financial investments, only capital investments—roads, factories, and technology, for example.
Government spending	G	Spending by governments at every level. Transfer payments like Social Security are excluded.
Net exports	X_N	Exports are a positive number because they were made into this country. Imports are subtracted, because they were made somewhere else.

Because adding together all of these numbers is difficult, GDP is calculated by using a formula. Consider graphic 3.9. *Consumer spending,* roughly 70 percent of our economy, is the biggest category by far. Keep in mind that only final goods are counted. The wood that the table factory uses is not counted, only the final value of the table itself. Private transactions are not counted either. If somebody sells a used car, it is not counted as productivity this year, because it was produced and counted in a previous year.

Investment spending on capital (not on stocks and bonds) allows our economy to grow in subsequent years. For instance, by building a bridge, a community can become more productive by spending less time in the car and more time working, or when a business buys a new machine, it will be able to produce more goods the next year. Investments usually make up about 5 percent of our economy.

Government spending comprises about 20 percent of the US economy. The federal government alone spends trillions. When the government pays a soldier, buys office equipment, or assists in someone applying for a benefit, it is added into GDP. Transfer payments like Social Security and welfare are not added, because this money goes to citizens and it will be added as consumer spending.

Net exports are calculated by subtracting the dollar amount of imports from exports. While consumers buy imported goods, they are not produced domestically, so they cannot be a part of GDP. If there is a trade deficit, it should be subtracted from GDP.

GRAPHIC 3.10

This container ship is docked in the Seattle, Washington port. If it is loading goods for export, their value will be added to GDP. If those are imports, their dollar value will be subtracted from GDP.

It should be noted that GDP alone cannot help us determine if the economy is growing or not. For example, if the government calculates GDP growth from the previous year at 4 percent, that could be a cause for celebration. However, as you will learn in later sections, the value of the dollar changes from one year to the next. In fact, it usually loses value. This year's GDP was tabulated using this year's dollars, but dollars last year were more valuable. The math must include the change in the dollar's value. If last year's dollars were 2 percent more valuable than they are this year, the GDP must be deflated. Instead of that brisk 4 percent growth mentioned earlier, real GDP (productivity with inflation factored in) actually grew at a sluggish 2 percent.

If the economy does grow, even with inflation factored in, does that mean that we all benefit? It does not. GDP neither factors in for distribution of wealth, how much money certain classes of society control, nor for well-being. To see how a country is doing economically, however, GDP should be divided by the population. This is called **per capita GDP**. A rich country like the United States has a per capita GDP that is more than $50,000, while a poor country might have $3,000. Going further, by factoring in the decreasing value of the dollar, economists calculate **real per capita GDP**. It is the easiest way to compare the relative health of two economies. You will learn more about that in Unit 6.

Pressing Question

- Give three examples of goods or services that fit into each of the following categories: consumer spending, investment spending, and government spending.

3H. Recessions and Business Cycles

If a good economy depends on steadily increasing levels of production and consumption, a bad economy lacks in one of the two. Sometimes, for myriad reasons, people stop buying things. When they do, factories have to slow production. If production slows, then layoffs follow. With people out of work, they will usually not be in the mood to go out and buy any big-ticket items like cars or appliances. This effect, in turn, will cause the factories to slow down even more. As this trend spreads across the country, GDP will decrease. When GDP decreases for six straight months, it is called a **recession**.

GRAPHIC 3.11

Recessions
(triggered by either a supply or demand shock)
People are afraid
They consume less
Businesses lay off workers

Consider graphic 3.11. If people notice that other people in their business or on their street are getting laid off, they will begin to get nervous. Gradually, those people buy fewer large-ticket items. They are afraid. Soon after, as things worsen, people buy less of the necessities they used to buy freely. Conserving cash and saving money becomes more important. As they buy fewer goods, businesses earn less revenue. They cannot afford the workers they have so workers are let go. Alas, this will only make more people afraid. The whole vicious cycle starts again.

It might be helpful to use graphs from Unit 1 to understand our national economy. Instead of the supply and demand for a product in a market, **macroeconomics** is concerned with the supply and demand of everything in the economy. Therefore, the word *aggregate* (everything included) is added to supply and demand. Consider graphic 3.12. This economy is at short-run equilibrium. The supply of goods and services is keeping up with the demand for them.

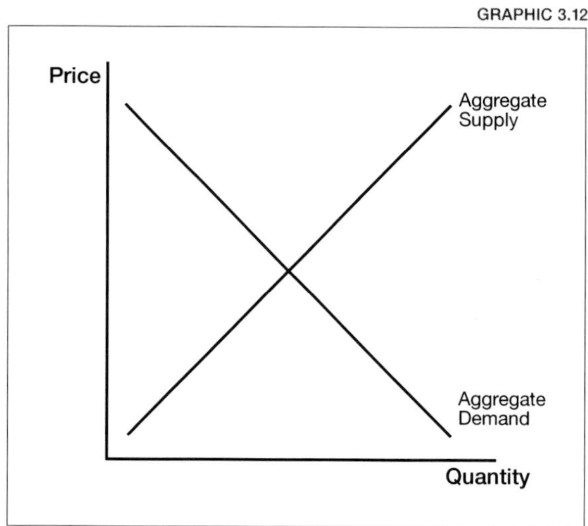

GRAPHIC 3.12

When a recession takes place, one of the symptoms is higher unemployment rates. Our **labor force** is everyone in the country over the age of sixteen who is working or looking for work. So the **unemployment rate** is defined as the percentage of the labor force that is out of work but actively looking for a job. This percentage, released on the first Friday of every month by the US Bureau of Labor Statistics (BLS), is among the most watched and reported economic statistics. It is a figure that every adult seems to know. (See graphic 3.13.)

The unemployment rate is not perfect. During an economic recovery, many people will take jobs that are below their educational or talent level. For instance, someone with experience as a mechanical engineer might take a job working in a ware-

GRAPHIC 3.13

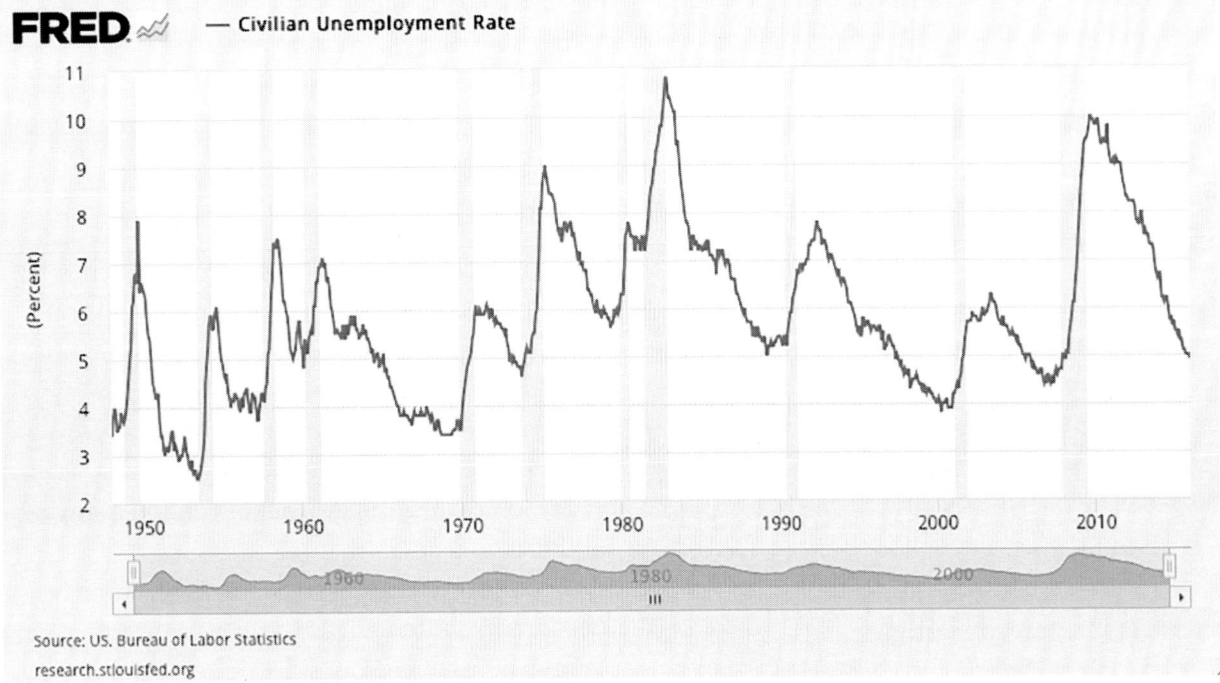

The line on the chart above shows the unemployment rate since 1950. The gray bars are recessions (extended periods of declining GDP). How often do recessions seem to happen? What happens to the unemployment rate when a recession happens?

house. They are underemployed, but still considered employed by the BLS. People who have been looking for job for a long time and stop are called **discouraged workers**—they are not part of the labor force any more. Finally, any person in the labor force who has been unemployed for more than two years is dropped from the labor force. This could make the unemployment rate drop.

In a productive economy, all workers who want to find a job have one. The economy is operating at near full capacity. In the United States, this means that the unemployment rate will drop below 5 percent or so. This is called **full employment**. In the 1990s, unemployment fell below 4 percent for several months. This was the lowest rate since the 1950s. No matter how low the rate goes, it cannot reach 0 percent. People leave jobs for many reasons. They get fired, or they need to move to another city. Whatever the case, even though there are unemployed workers, the economy is operating at full speed.

Economists have identified several different types of unemployment:

- **Structural**—This happens when certain industries become obsolete. Workers with outdated skills get laid off and find new work. Ideally, they retrain and improve their skill set.
- **Seasonal**—Landscapers, farmers, and certain tourism jobs are tossed out of work at certain downtimes during the year.
- **Frictional**—These are people who are just entering the job market or those who have decided to leave their current jobs to find "greener pastures." This is the largest segment of the overall unemployment figure when most of us have jobs. Frictional employment explains why full employment is greater than zero.
- **Cyclical**—Certain industries are hit hard by downturns in the economy. Auto workers are typically laid off during recessions as they wait for consumers to buy more of their companies' products. Companies would rather keep their prices stable than keep their workers.

There is an old joke: If you lose your job, the unemployment rate is 100 percent. While that sounds funny, it is very true. Losing a job can be devastating both personally and financially. In US society, high unemployment rates can mean higher crime rates and more broken families. Structural unemployment has even devastated cities that once depended on the jobs from heavy manufacturing. Cities across the Midwest are a part of what we now call the Rust Belt, because their shuttered factories are left to rust and decay (graphic 3.14).

GRAPHIC 3.14

Cities like Detroit have been devastated by structural unemployment. This massive complex once manufactured cars. Thousands of people worked here to pay their bills and feed their families. Over the last few decades, Detroit has lost more than half of its population.

Recessions happen to every modern economy. Economies move in cycles, having down periods periodically. Consider graphic 3.15. This graph depicts the business cycle. When economies get better, GDP increases. Economists call this an expansion, which eventually peaks. After the peak, the recession begins (highlighted by the gray box). The period of shrinking GDP will continue until the economy bottoms out and business activity picks up. When the expansion begins again, unemployment rates drop and people spend money more freely.

GRAPHIC 3.15

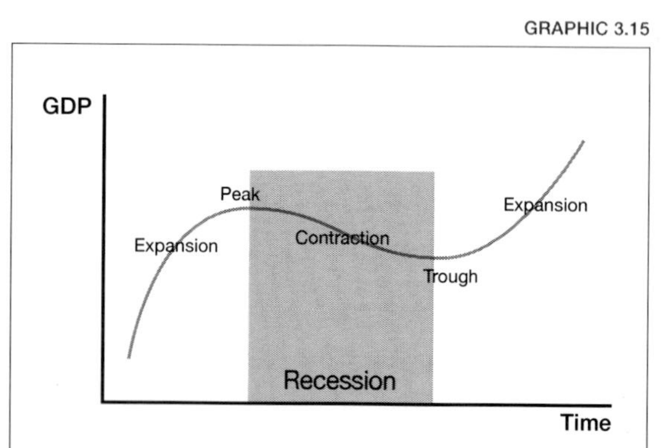

Pressing Question

- When there is a severe recession, which types of unemployment are most common?

31. Runaway Inflation: Economic Enemy #1

Inflation is the steady rise in prices across an entire economy. When it gets out of control, it can destroy an economy. If the economy gets destroyed, governments may fall soon thereafter. Inflation left unchecked is our economy's greatest foe. The government watches prices closely all the time. Once inflation gets out of control, it can be difficult to stop.

Inflation is the rise of *all* prices across an economy, not the price of a single product or group of products. Consider one product in particular, tires. If a rubber shortage causes rubber prices to double, then the price of a set of radial tires will increase; the rise in the cost of one product, however, is not a problem for the United States as a whole.

What if the price of tires, groceries, toys, wood, cars, steel, and everything else were on the rise? It would make it harder for families to live within their budgets. Rapidly increasing prices on consumer goods does not mean that workers will get a wage increase to match. Wages tend to be "sticky" and increases can take years to happen. In the meantime, families will have to make hard choices about what should remain in their budget and what gets dropped.

Across the country, high levels of inflation can lead families into poverty. As prices rise faster than wages, some households will have to make choices between necessities like heat and food. Every person in the country becomes affected negatively in some way. With a recession and unemployment, it is primarily the unemployed people who are affected the most. A spike in the inflation rate, however, reduces the wealth and income of every single person in the country at once. It is as if everyone gets a pay cut at the same time.

While consumers are negatively affected by higher prices, companies have a difficult time planning for the future. They have trouble setting prices. They cannot predict costs. Worst of all, they hesitate to invest in future production. The uncertainty of what their new factory will be worth makes a firm nervous, and uncertainty is bad for the economy.

Inflation tends to breed more inflation. Consumers see the value of their wages begin to drop. They reasonably anticipate higher prices next year. When they get paid, they try to beat the higher prices by spending their wages right away. This tendency may bring about a **wage-price spiral**. The uncertainty about the future makes consumers buy more quickly, so firms raise prices. To compensate for the higher prices, workers demand higher wages. Once they have higher wages, they consume more quickly again. Consider graphic 3.16.

GRAPHIC 3.16

Consuming Increases
Wages Rise
Prices Rise
Consuming Increases

For instance, in the late 1970s and early 1980s, annual prices were increasing at a rate of 13 percent per year. That means that a car that cost $10,000 one year would cost $11,300 the next year and a $100 grocery bill would increase by $13 the next year. Prices would have continued to rise if drastic measures had not been taken by the Federal Reserve.

There is no way to eliminate inflation and have 0 percent price increases every year. The Federal Reserve tries to hit an inflation target of 1 to 2 percent growth from one year to the next. It wants to stay above 1 percent, because falling too low and close to 0 percent could see the economy slip into **deflation**, a period of steadily declining prices.

Inflation has two ways of getting started. It can come from the supply side of our economy or the demand side:

- **Demand-pull (demand-side) inflation**—Rising prices can come from people buying too many goods. In essence, there are too many dollars chasing too few goods. Our producers cannot keep up with consumer demand and they raise the prices. Refer to graphic 3.17.

GRAPHIC 3.17

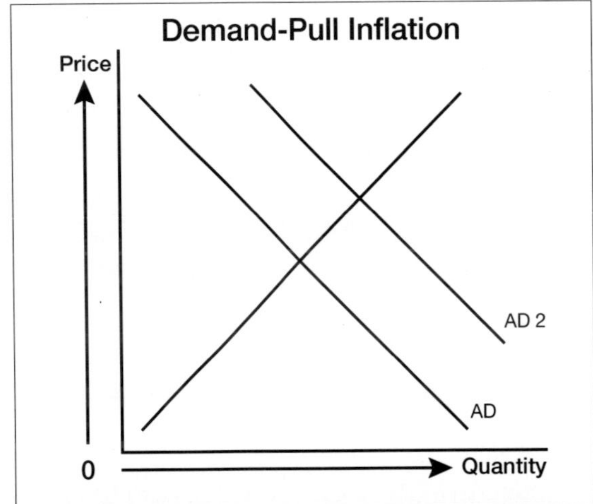

- **Cost-push (supply-side) inflation**—When resource prices like labor and oil go up, this can push the cost of everything else up too. Historically, supply shocks, or unexpected price spikes in important resources prices, can cause a damaging increase in prices. In the 1970s, oil prices shot up and caused a decrease in the aggregate supply.

No matter the cause of inflation, it is important to stop it before it rises too far above 2 percent. Once it gets started, it can be hard to control.

Pressing Question

- What happens to price and quantity in graphic 3.17?

3J. Watching Inflation Closely

Economists track consumer prices with the **consumer price index (CPI)**. There are billions of goods and services in the United States Tracking the prices of all of them is impossible, so statisticians at the BLS choose to follow a **basket** of goods; by narrowing what is tracked to eighty thousand goods and services, the BLS can gather data monthly. Any sign of rising inflation (above a manageable level) will be met with swift intervention by the government. (See graphic 3.18.)

Even a statistic of eighty thousand products is a massive number. It would have little meaning to anyone who heard it. To make the CPI manageable, the sum of the product basket's prices is assigned a base year and given the value of 100. If the next year the basket of goods is 3 percent higher, inflation from one year to the next was 3 percent.

- **Year 1**: Sum of basket is 100.
- **Year 2**: Sum of basket is 3 percent higher than year one. The CPI is 103.
- **Year 20**: Sum of basket is 90 percent higher than in year 1. The CPI is 190.

At times, the CPI overstates swings in prices because food and energy prices are so volatile. **Core CPI** drops those two categories to give a more realistic look at overall price levels.

Remember that the government tries to keep inflation around at around 1 to 2 percent. The Bureau of Labor Statistics (a branch of the Labor Department) releases its CPI finding to the public once per month. It also tracks the prices of producers' goods, like raw materials and other input prices. This statistic is called the **producer price index (PPI)**.

When inflation occurs, a worker has to earn more money to keep the same standard of living that he or she had last year. Because inflation will cause a rise in the price of most goods and services, it will simply cost more to run a household. To keep up with rising costs, wage earners need a **cost of living increase**. This is a pay raise that matches inflation. Many labor contracts and government programs like Social Security are directly tied to the CPI. Most nonunion and private-sector workers must renegotiate their contracts to get a raise.

Pressing Question

- If the CPI was 100 in 1984, and a high-end pair of sneakers cost $80 at that time, how much would those shoes cost today if the CPI is 240?

GRAPHIC 3.18

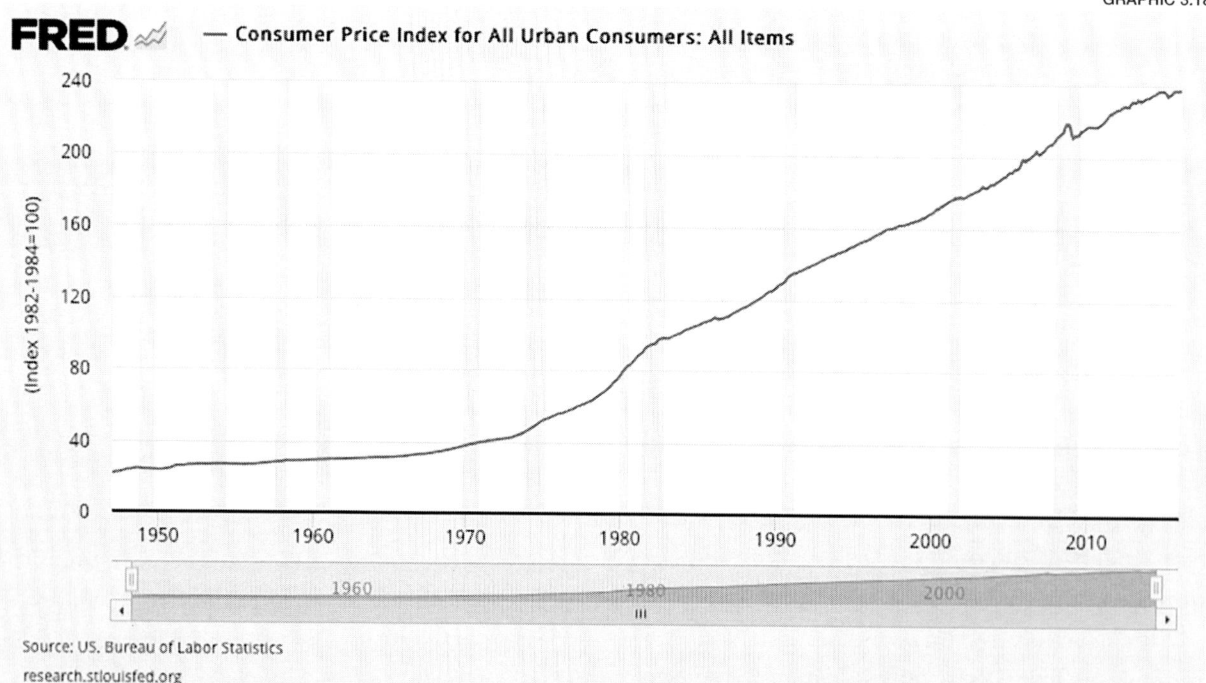

The chart above shows the CPI by percentage change going back to the 1960s. The gray bars indicate periods of recession. Notice what happens to prices during a recession. Also notice what happens to prices directly prior to a recession.

3K. More Details on Inflation

If inflation is left unchecked, people will eventually be unable to afford many products. Banks will raise interest rates higher to maintain their margins. With inflation of 13 percent in 1980, banks raised rates on home mortgages to almost 20 percent, cars to 25 percent. This brought the construction and car industries to a standstill. These sky-high interest rates greatly reduced consumption and eventually lowered prices.

The worst-case scenario comes when the government misses the warning signs like rising CPI or supply shocks. If inflation is left completely unchecked and the money supply continues to grow too quickly, then prices can rise rapidly. For example, Germany in the 1920s printed billions of deutsche marks to pay back other countries for the reparations demanded in the Versailles Treaty. Markets responded to the flood of cheap money by elevating prices to unbelievable heights.

Imagine that this week when you buy a loaf of bread, it costs a dollar. When you go shopping next week, you are amazed to find that the price has risen to five dollars. In the postwar German economy people had to carry baskets full of money just to buy their daily bread. This is **hyperinflation**, with prices rising at a rapid, uncontrolled rate (there is no absolute number, but 10 percent or more annually would be characteristic). It eroded the confidence German people had in their government. Their society had to deal with the chaos. Germany turned to fascism and World War II was the result.

The opposite of inflation, **deflation** is a condition where the average prices for goods and services fall across an economy. In the late 1800s, farmers, who had already been hit hard by the plummeting prices caused by automation, also had to deal with a gold-backed currency that steadily increased in value (because the growth of the money supply did not keep up with the growth of the economy). Crop prices fell even further. When farmers needed to borrow money to save their farms, banks raised interest rates as high as 80 percent. Unable to afford that, many farmers sold their farms and moved to cities.

If inflation does rise above 2 percent, our government will take measures to bring the rate back to our target area of 1 to 2 percent. If inflation falls from 3 percent to 2 percent, this is called **disinflation**; this happens when the rate of inflation falls from a higher rate to a lower rate without becoming deflationary. When inflation rates fell from 13 percent in 1980 to 4 percent in 1985, it was said that the dollar was "disinflating." The United States, and then Federal Reserve chair Paul Volcker, had successfully won the "war on inflation."

GRAPHIC 3.19

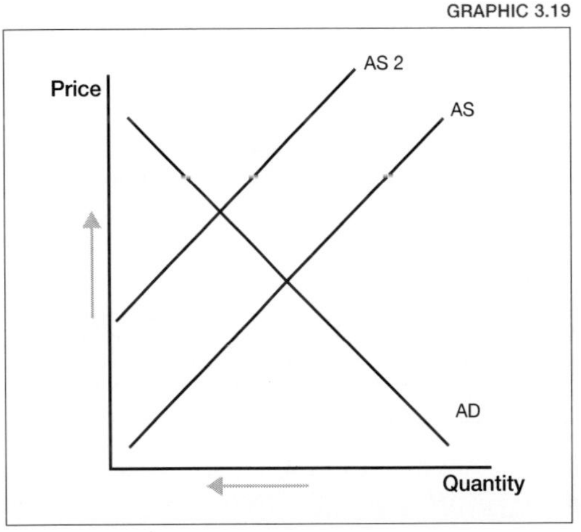

What if the unemployment that usually comes with a severe recession occurs during a period of sharply rising prices? This is a perfect storm of economic bad news. The country must fight high inflation *and* high unemployment. This is called **stagflation**. Refer to graphic 3.19. It is difficult to envision a worse scenario. In the early 1970s, spending on the Vietnam War and social programs was financed with an increase in the money supply. When oil prices shot up from $1 per barrel in 1970 to $35 per barrel in 1982, prices increased in response. Our economy relied heavily on oil and this shortage created a supply shock. Notice on the graph how the aggregate supply (AS) curve of the country moved to the left. This decreased the quantity of goods and services produced, but at the same time prices rose, creating a recession and high inflation at the same time. The result was a period of cost-push inflation. Something had to be done.

For many reasons, inflation is a problem that is best dealt with decisively. The health of our country depends upon the actions of our government. In the United States, much of the job of keeping the specter of inflation at bay belongs to the Federal Reserve Bank.

Pressing Question

- Inflation is bad; that much we know. Why would deflation, however, make it a challenge to pay your mortgage?

3L. Origins of the Federal Reserve

Those farmers mentioned in the previous section raised awareness in the United States of the need for monetary policy. In addition to the Populist movement's cry for currency reform, a financial crisis in 1907 left the nation's banking structure teetering on the brink of disaster. People looked to the government to save the economy, but there were no provisions or agencies to handle the situation. If nothing was done, a depression would have likely occurred.

GRAPHIC 3.20

In the 1800s and early 1900s, the United States faced a series of depressions preceded by waves of bank failures. Above, depositors line up at their bank hoping to withdraw their savings.

All appeared lost until one private citizen, J. P. Morgan, agreed to float the largest banks' massive loans. Someone in the private sector saved us. This alarmed the public and government alike. What if Morgan had not helped? The country would have suffered years of economic contraction. Afterward, Congress engaged in years of debate about how to solve the problem.

In 1913, Congress passed the **Federal Reserve Act** and established the US modern national bank to monitor the money supply and issue more money in times of financial strain. The leaders of the **Federal Reserve** (**Fed**) are the watchdogs who protect the economy from the worst economic problems, inflation and recession. To do this, they track statistics and supervise banks.

The idea of central banking goes back to the very beginning of our nation. Some of the Founders feared putting financial power into the hands of the federal government. Others, including Alexander Hamilton, believed that it was vital to our young nation that a central bank lead our economic growth and competition with foreign countries. A national bank was chartered in the 1790s, but lasted only until 1834, when Andrew Jackson vetoed its renewal.

Congress had other reasons to create a national bank. The traumatic economic events of the 1800s also had a part in our moving toward centralization. Frequent depressions, what historians call "panics," occurred in 1813, 1837, 1857, 1873, 1884, 1893, and 1907. During these events, there would be massive unemployment and stagnant growth in our national product. To make things worse, the banking system would often trigger the panics with widespread bank closures. If one bank failed, it might lose the deposits of other banks. This caused a chain reaction; bank customers reacted by quickly demanding their money all at once, a situation called a *run*. The Fed was created in part to stop these panics and runs by holding a portion of the deposits of most US banks.

Pressing Question

- What prompted Congress to pass the Federal Reserve Act in 1913?

3M. Structure of the Federal Reserve

If you have any paper currency, take a look at it. On the front side at the top is the writing, "Federal Reserve Note." This means that the Fed, as it is called, issues each piece of currency that we handle in the United States. Note that the Fed does not print this money. The US Bureau of Engraving and Printing produces our paper currency and the US Mint stamps our coins. The Fed processes money through its system every time a bank makes a deposit. It removes worn bills and replaces them with newly produced notes.

GRAPHIC 3.21

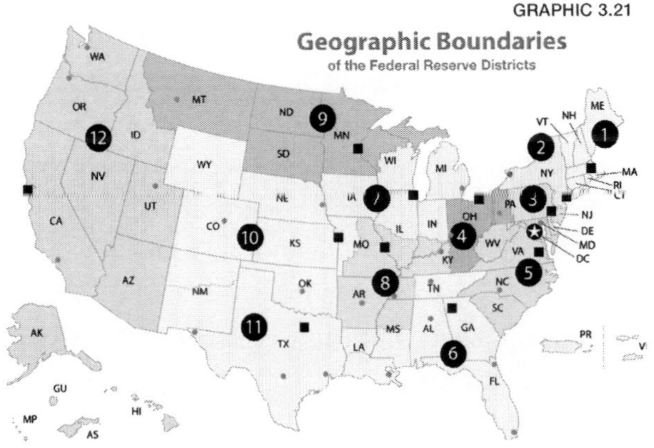

There are twelve branches in the Federal Reserve System. Most of them are located in the eastern half of the country, because when the system started, more of the population lived in the east (graphic 3.21). Primarily, each branch takes deposits from its member banks. It holds a portion of every deposit, around 10 percent usually, for each bank (its **reserve**). In addition, the Fed employs bank examiners who supervise banks to make sure they are well funded and in good financial shape. Each branch also has research departments that gather data about local economies.

The Federal Reserve has a governing structure. The chair of the Board of Governors, nominated by the president and approved by the Senate, is the executive in charge. This board, over which the chair presides, has six additional members. They meet about every six weeks with presidents of different branches. This committee makes all major decisions for the money supply and interest rates. It is called the **Federal Open Market Committee** (**FOMC**). They pour over tens of thousands of pieces of data from around the country, including reports from each of the branches. When their decisions are made, the chair must report to Congress about once per quarter to explain the board's actions. While the Fed must report to Congress to answer questions, it need not do what Congress says.

Member banks are also periodically examined by Fed employees. In order for a bank to be financially sound, it must make good loans. Too many loans that default will cause a bank to lose money, perhaps eating up some of its cash reserve. The Fed watches for this and may force the bank to take measures to fix its situation. The goal is to prevent bank failures.

Pressing Question

- If you were a bank examiner, what factors do you think would be most important to prove the health of a bank?

3N. The Fed Makes Decisions

As we have learned, the Fed is responsible for fighting two main economic problems, inflation and recessions. The worse is inflation, but slips in the economy can devastate families too. The goal of **monetary policy**, actions and rules made by the Federal Reserve, is to control the money supply and interest rates, allowing for steady economic growth. The Fed makes sure the economy does not get "too hot" (inflation) or "too cold" (recession).

Do not confuse the Fed with the **US Department of the Treasury**. The US Department of the Treasury handles the money of the federal government (Congress and the president). The **Internal Revenue Service** (**IRS**) collects several trillion dollars in tax revenue, and then pays the government's bill. The Fed does assist in delivering money from one place to another. It also holds the federal government's cash. In essence, the Department of the Treasury uses the Fed as the bank for its very large checking account.

GRAPHIC 3.22

The Federal Reserve in Washington, DC, is where US monetary policy is made. Decisions about the money supply and interest rates have far-reaching effects on the health of the economy.

In order to more carefully watch the economy, the Fed employs thousands of economists who watch prices, production levels, and local economies. They want to know exactly what prices are and how much companies are producing in their district. These statistics are necessary to make good monetary (money) decisions. Some indicators show us where the economy might be headed while others tend to show us what occurred in the past.

Some of these statistics can show the direction the economy will go in the next six to twelve months. These are called **leading economic indicators**. Some of them include:

- **Average workweek**—If people work more hours, it shows that businesses are trying to produce more.
- **New claims for unemployment benefits**—Fewer claims suggest fewer unemployed people, which in turn might show that people will be spending more money in the future.
- **Capital investments**—These are contracts and orders for new equipment. A business that buys a new machine has faith in its future sales.
- **New building permits**—Large construction projects require lots of material and services. They also show that the builder has confidence.
- **Housing starts**—A consumer who builds a new house will often get a thirty-year loan to pay for it. This shows that she has faith in her financial security.
- **Stock indexes**—Investors want to buy into companies that will make money in the next six to twelve months. If prices are rising, this shows confidence in future sales.
- **Consumer expectations**—These are surveys that ask people how they feel about their future and if they plan on making major purchases.

In addition to all of these, some indicators shed light on how the economy performed in previous months. GDP, for instance, takes months to tabulate. It is such a large number that the "initial" figure is not released until six weeks after the end of the month. The numbers for December do not get released until mid-February and so on. Also, the initial release often gets revised in subsequent months because economists learn of a statistic they did not factor into their calculations or simply because they learn they were wrong. These figures, which take months to calculate, are called **lagging indicators**.

The Fed has a few key tools to keep the economy healthy. Primarily, it monitors the money supply. Putting more money into the economy can increase business activity, because it lowers interest rates. With all of this power comes the awesome responsibility of using that power judiciously. Some of the Fed's functions are:

- **Supervising member banks**—If a bank wants keep money in or borrow money from the central bank, it must follow bank regulations and be audited.
- **Monitoring currency**—Cash is recycled and issued through the twelve member banks.
- **Acting as lender of last resort**—When a bank gets in real trouble and no one else wants to lend it money, the Fed can step in.
- **Regulating the money supply**—The amount of money that is available can affect the rate of inflation and interest rates. The Fed makes

GRAPHIC 3.23

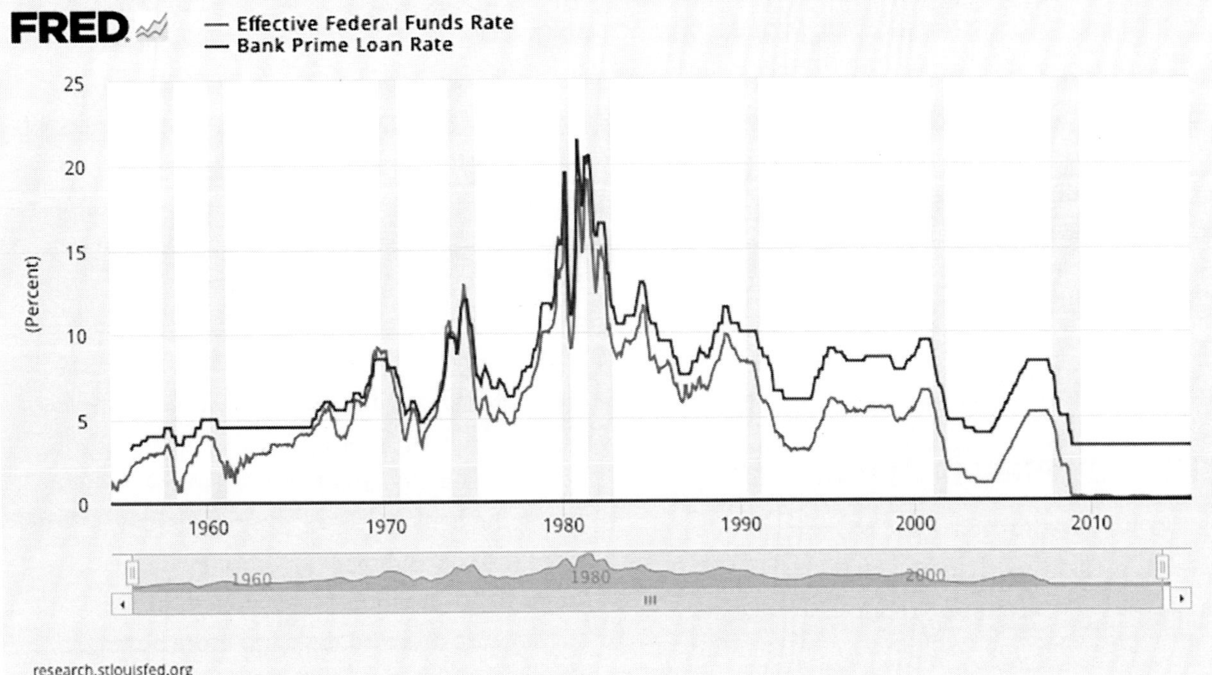

This graph shows the Federal Funds and Prime interest rates since the 1990s. The gray bars indicate times of recession. What do you notice before and during every recession? What is strange about rates since 2008?

monetary policy decisions based on the economic data it gathers.

- **Applying moral suasion**—Officials from the Fed give many public addresses. It is a way to keep the public informed as to what might happen to interest rates in the near future. The chair and branch presidents get attention when they speak in public. Their words can shake markets when people do not like what the Fed might do.

GRAPHIC 3.24

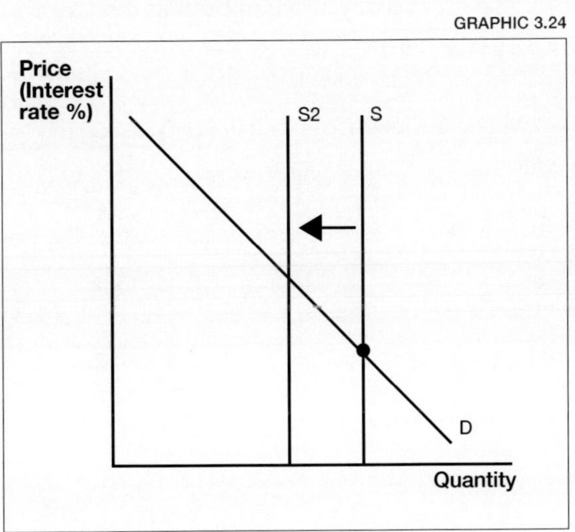

- **Setting interest rates**—This is the most visible of all the Fed's jobs. Consider graphic 3.24. Notice how the increasing supply of money makes the interest rate (y-axis) go down. The **discount rate** (the rate that banks in trouble pay when they borrow from the Fed) affects the **federal funds rate** (the rate that banks pay other banks for overnight loans), which affects **bank prime loan rate** (the rate that banks give to their best customers). Many banks use the prime rate to determine where to set their auto loan and credit card rates. (See graphic 3.23.)
- **Setting the reserve requirement**—Member banks are required to keep a certain amount of a depositor's savings as cash. The rest of it can be lent back out. For example, if you deposit $1,000 and the reserve requirement is 15 percent, the bank must keep $150 in the vault. The other $850 does not stay in the bank; it is lent out. Lowering the reserve requirement will increase the money supply.
- **Check clearing**—Every check written in the United States must go from one bank to another. These are physically scanned and cleared by the district Fed bank. This task is also shared with some outside companies.

Monetary policy can affect how much we earn in bank accounts and how much we pay for a student loan. It helps the economy avoid inflation and keeps prices steady. A steady and growing economy can ensure that you find a job after high school or college. Some people argue that the Fed chair is the most powerful person in the world.

Pressing Question

- What are the two lowest interest rates set by the Federal Reserve?

30. Fed Policy in Action

As we have learned, if the economy is in recession, many workers will be laid off. Less money is being spent on products, so factories will slow production, leading to more layoffs. It is difficult to get worried consumers to make more purchases, but if the cost of borrowing money makes a desired product more affordable, some consumers may be lured back to the marketplace. When sales pick up, businesses will hire more workers again.

For instance, if someone wants to build a house for $200,000 at 12 percent, then it will cost about $2,500 per month on a thirty-year mortgage to repay the principle and interest (P&I) on that loan. That is out of the price range of many people. If the rates fell to 7 percent, the P&I payment for the same house would be about $1,500 per month. Even lower, a 4 percent loan will have a payment of $955. The same impact that interest rates have on the housing market can be applied to the purchase of cars, appliances, factories, or heavy equipment. Interest rates affect both consumers and producers.

Recall the economic indicators from the previous section. Use graphic 3.25 as a reminder. These indicators help the Fed figure out whether the economy is getting too hot or too cold. After careful consideration and multiple meetings, the FOMC chooses a **bias**, or the inclination the Fed has to fight either inflation or recession. During a period when a recession is feared, rates are lowered. In a period of inflationary bias, however, they are raised.

Refer to graphic 3.24. Notice that the supply curves for the money supply are perfectly vertical. The Fed tracks every dollar in our money supply, so the quantity is set. The availability of money around the economy can alert banks as to what to do about commercial interest rates. Banks are just like any other business. If a shoe store has too many shoes piling up in the store room, they will have to have a sale. It is the same thing with a bank. If there is too much cash piling up in the vaults, the banks will be prompted to have a "sale." Since the cost of borrowing money is interest, they will lower interest rates. Lower interest rates might cause more buying, and more buying means more hiring, which could lift the economy out of a recession.

If the Fed bias is toward inflation, it will take money out of the economy. By doing this, the money supply curve moves to the left. Look to graphic 3.24 again. If the supply curve moves left, then the price of money (interest) will increase. Higher interest rates discourage bigger purchases. Businesses cannot raise prices when people are not buying. Inflation can come under control.

The contraction and expansion of the money supply is done through an activity called **open market operations.** Because money cannot simply be given away, the Fed buys and sells bonds. Here is how it works:

GRAPHIC 3.25

Ideal Statistical Numbers

Indicator	Annual Growth Rate
GDP	3%–4%
CPI	1%–2%
Unemployment	4%–5%

- **Increase the money supply**—The FOMC will buy bonds from investors with cash from its own vaults. The money will end up in banks, which will then lend the money to producers and consumers. This is commonly called **loose-money policy.**
- **Decrease the money supply**—The FOMC will sell bonds from their vast holdings to the bond markets. This will draw money from banks' reserves, and thus there will be less money to lend to producers and consumers. This is also called **tight-money policy**.

Businesses need easy access to capital to grow and prosper, but too much cash in the hands of banks and consumers can cause a rise in inflation. To get a better understanding of what the Fed's two choices entail, refer to graphic 3.26.

GRAPHIC 3.26

Monetary Policy

	Loose-Money Policy	Tight-Money Policy
Open market operation	Buy bonds	Sell bonds
Money supply	Increases	Decreases
Interest rates	Lowers	Raises

There are limitations to monetary policy. First of all, markets are slow to react to stimuli and these **time lags** can be as long as six to twelve months. The Fed might pump money into the economy to lower rates, but the impact of the action could take a while to be noticed. Second, the Federal Reserve is run by human beings and mistakes can be made. Some data can be incorrectly gathered, and that could lead to a bad decision. In the past, the Fed has sometimes failed to see signs of economic problems coming. The board is not perfect, but the people of the Fed do an adequate job of managing the money supply.

Third, many people feel that the Fed makes mistakes when it tries to steer the economy. People called **monetarists** believe that all the Fed should do is let the money supply grow slowly and not respond to the temporary fluctuations in the economy with the discount rate. Fourth, the Fed has no control over the actions of Congress, and many times the big spending and low taxes of a generous government can counteract the stringent measures of a more disciplined Fed.

GRAPHIC 3.27

Current and former chairs of the Federal Reserve Bank (left to right): Janet Yellen (2014–), Alan Greenspan (1987–2006), Ben Bernanke (2006–2014), and Paul Volcker (1979–1987).

Part of the monetarists' reservations center on the chairs of the Federal Reserve—public figures who have significant influence on the economy. Their words can move markets and shift trillions of dollars across the globe. As mentioned earlier, Paul Volcker, as the Fed Chair, famously declared a "war on inflation." Under his leadership, the Fed raised interest rates to historic levels, thereby bringing inflation under control. In the 1990s, Alan Greenspan, who dealt with an economy that was growing too quickly, caused a panic in the financial world when he said that the rising value of the stock market was caused by "irrational exuberance." The stock market lost much of its asset value, because the harsh words could have indicated an impending interest rate hike. Two words from the Fed chair cost investors around the world billions of dollars.

Nobody in the world, however, can effectively predict the direction of the economy. In essence, it is predicting the future. The Federal Reserve uses carefully collected data to make a bias. It monitors our fiat money and by doing so can make our interest rates go up and down. People react to these rates by either buying more or buying less. By ensuring the soundness of our banks and money supply, the Fed helps the United States achieve slow and steady growth over the long term.

Pressing Question

- Why is Fed policy action sometimes very unpopular?

Name:

Vocabulary Word Find

Directions: Write the appropriate word in the blank provided. Then in the word find on the next page, circle the words that correspond with the clues.

1. ________________ He led the Federal Reserve during the "war on inflation" in the early 1980s.
2. ________________ He led the Federal Reserve in the boom years of the 1990s.
3. ________________ This type of suasion is the use of words to encourage more appropriate behavior.
4. ________________ To exchange goods without the use of money is _______.
5. ________________ Gold or silver currency is an example of this.
6. ________________ Our money today is known as _______ money.
7. ________________ The first people in the Middle East to coin money were the _______.
8. ________________ His law stated that "bad money drives out good money."
9. ________________ The amount of money borrowed in a loan is the _______.
10. ________________ The cost of using someone else's money is the _______.
11. ________________ is the abbreviation for the agency that insures your bank deposits to $250,000.
12. ________________ The lowest interest rate set by the Fed is the _______.
13. ________________ How many districts are in the Federal Reserve system?
14. ________________ Overall prices are rising steadily.
15. ________________ Money that consisted of shells or other trinkets is known as ______ money.
16. ________________ The rate that is given by banks to its best customers is known as the ______ rate.
17. ________________ Inflation fell from 5 percent to 1 percent. This is an example of _______.
18. ________________ Inflation rose to 500 percent in less than a year. This is an example of _______.
19. ________________ The Fed is the "_______________ of last resort."
20. ________________ is the abbreviation for the main decision making body of the Federal Reserve.
21. ________________ is the abbreviation for the main gauge for measuring consumer prices.
22. ________________ A slump in the economy is known as a _______.
23. ________________ is the abbreviation for the answer to this formula: C + I + G + Xn = ?
24. ________________ Agency in charge of investigating counterfeiters is the _______.
25. ________________ Money used during the gold standard was known as _____________ money.
26. ________________ Policy formulated by the Federal Reserve is known as _____________ policy.

Puzzle Sheet

(Hint: Search both across and down.)

R P C D I S I N F L A T I O N M F O M C X Z A P O P Y U T U
E L K J E S O H D Y B V B X Q O E A O X B M L P I R N K L E
C G D P E T O U M N H G Y R I P L E D C X X M I H I U I O J
E C F R S E F V B N R E P R E S E N T A T I V E U N N F R K
S K G M D T Y O P F D R E B N K P F G H J D G J K C H U F D
S G J O J J O P E W D V N J U G E G H J J K D E S I D H J C
I H I N T E R E S T D N C T G R E E N S P A N C B P B X V P
O V C E N J F S F T G H S F G O P D S G J Y J E O A K L E I
N C D T G H T L H S F C V B M H Y U K D G H J F D L S V V N
C B O A I H L E J L U G R E S H A M P O G F Y D N J K F D Y
H U K R V D J N F O U I L L G L R J I F T F D I S C O U N T
F J I Y K Y F D J D M M K D V J D E X D G J C C X H U S X B
T O R J V K S E C R E T S E R V I C E V I H G B C K Y D C J
H C T Y O P G R K I K B F H D G N J I F C F R G V N K S G U
I D P L L C D S A X D F E X Z S F F S W Z V X V V Z C P I I
B A R T E R K J Y H G F D S C S L A S D F G H O H J K E I Z
S O I I N B Y T D G H J H F D G A D E E S X V L V C D C P O
T L M J C O M M O D I T Y H G V T F D D D D X C X V S I P T
I H E H J N B V C D E W Q A S F I A T X C V B K B H F E F W
N X Z S P X V G V T B N K O H V O I U G J D H E C N M K D E
K H K G G L Y D I A N S J L D X N B N M C M O R A L X E R L
S V N B G B J F G Y H U H U I O E A S F S F D H J D Y I N V
G H D N D V H M L O H F H Y P E R I N F L A T I O N M J L E
V J O K P K I B H E S S K J B K O J R V R N M R E X H J H I

 Name:

My Family, My Economy

Directions: You will be conducting an interview, so it is imperative that your conduct is at its best. Remember that you represent our class.

Ask a parent and/or guardian to respond to the following survey questions using the numbering system described below. Please be thorough, as the class will use the information gathered at a later time in Unit 3.

1. Completely disagree 2. Disagree 3. Neutral 4. Agree 5. Completely agree

My family and I are better off than we were at this time last year.	1	2	3	4	5
I feel secure about my family's financial future.	1	2	3	4	5
I feel secure in my employment.	1	2	3	4	5
I see no need to alter my family's budget at this time.	1	2	3	4	5
The business I (or my spouse) work(s) for continues to grow.	1	2	3	4	5
We plan to take a vacation this year.	1	2	3	4	5
I am anticipating some major purchases in the near future.	1	2	3	4	5
I feel comfortable with the level of debt my household carries.	1	2	3	4	5
I feel optimistic about the direction of our nation's economy.	1	2	3	4	5
The business I (or my spouse) work(s) for continues to hire people.	1	2	3	4	5

Sum your score: ______

Class total: ______

______________________ Parent or guardian signature

Parents/Guardians: Please feel free to be as candid or discreet as you want to be with the following questions:

1. What are your greatest financial concerns for your family right now?

2. In what ways do interest rates affect your family? When have rates influenced your behavior (if ever)?

3. How do you feel about the current state of our local and national economies? Why?

4. What are the worst economic times you can remember?

5. What is the best advice you can offer a young person regarding financial management?

6. What financial mistakes have you made in the past that you wish you could redo?

7. How do you see the economy changing in the last few years? Is it a good thing or a bad thing?

8. What is the best financial decision you have ever made?

9. What do you find challenging and rewarding about your work?

Name:

History of Money

Part 1

Directions: Using the table below, place the types of money or exchange from the list and place them in chronological order in the first column. Then use your reading to fill in the rest of the information.

Word List: representative money, commodity money, bartering, fiat money, specie.

Type of Exchange/Barter	When It Was Used	Problems with This Exchange

Part 2

Directions: Answer the questions below with the help of your reading or to your best knowledge:

1. How has our money supply been changing over the last fifty years?

2. What are the new security features on our currency?

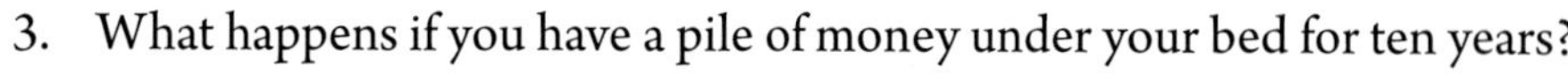

3. What happens if you have a pile of money under your bed for ten years?

4. If something cost $5 in 1984, what should it cost today?

5. List as many ways as you can that people can exchange money today.

 Name:

Guide to Useful Money

Part 1

Directions: Look up the definition of *bitcoin* in Wikipedia. Then look at up the history of the dollar. Using your reading, fill in the remainder of the table by explaining how these two monies are portable, divisible, and durable.

Attribute	Dollars	Bitcoin
Define	*What is the origin of the word "dollar"?*	*What is a bitcoin?*
Portable		
Divisible		
Durable		

Part 2

Directions: Answer the questions below using your reading:

1. Money has to have a store of value to be useful. Explain.

2. Money has to have a standard of value to be useful. Explain.

3. What does the sentence, "This note is legal tender to settle all debts public and private" mean?

4. What two government seals appear on our currency?

5. What is the difference between money and currency?

6. How much of our money supply is currency and how much is on computers?

Name:

Foreign Exchange

Part 1

Directions: Using the Internet, list the names of these countries' currencies in the appropriate column. Then convert their money into one hundred US dollars.

Country	Symbol	Money	Converted into $100
Canada			
China			
Mexico			
Germany			
Singapore			
Australia			
Egypt			
Brazil			
Indonesia			
India			
Russia			
South Korea			
Japan			

Part 2

Directions: Answer the questions below using your reading.

1. What does it mean when the dollar gets stronger? When the dollar is weaker?

2. List four countries whose currency is also called a *dollar*.

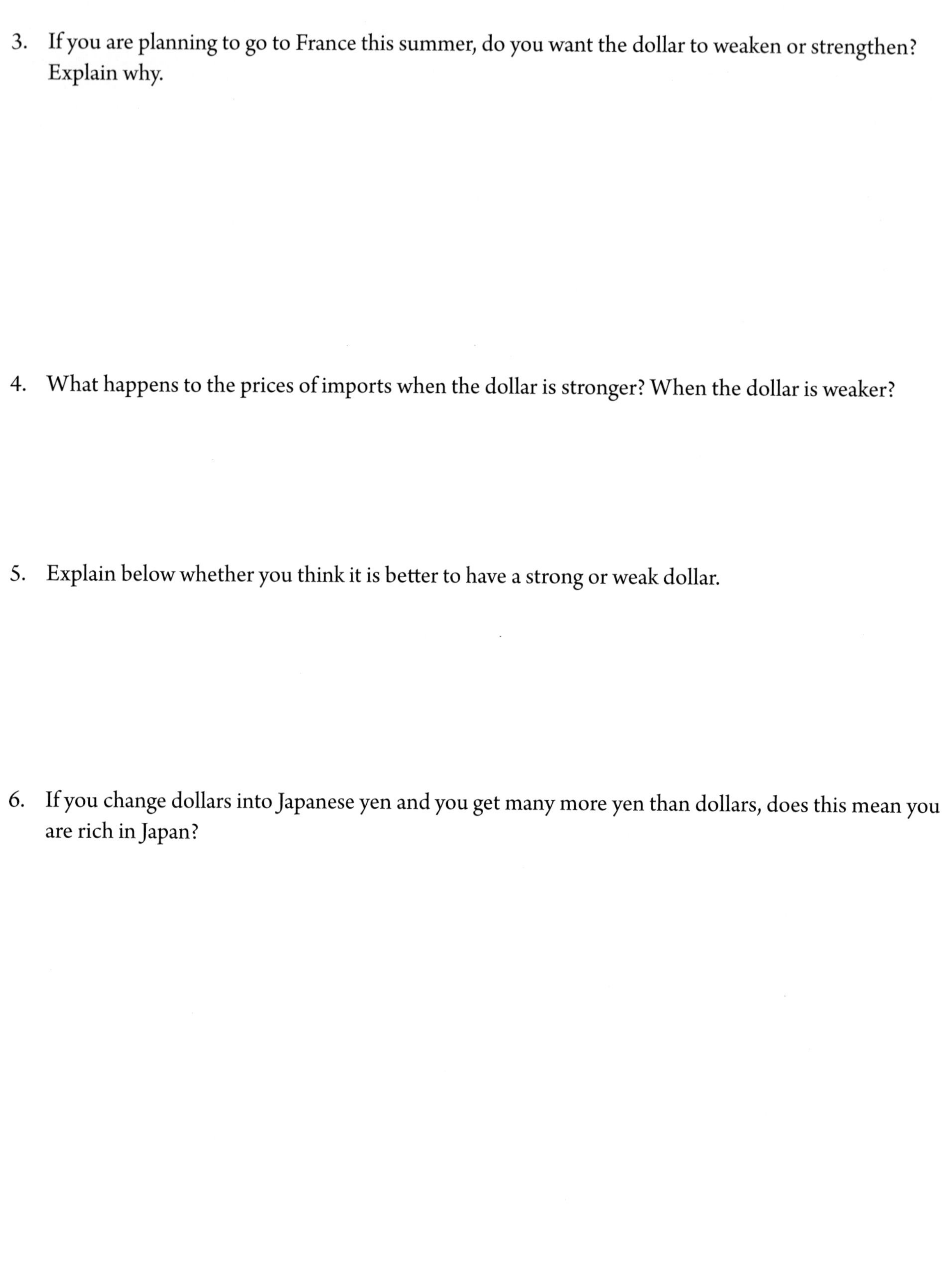

3. If you are planning to go to France this summer, do you want the dollar to weaken or strengthen? Explain why.

4. What happens to the prices of imports when the dollar is stronger? When the dollar is weaker?

5. Explain below whether you think it is better to have a strong or weak dollar.

6. If you change dollars into Japanese yen and you get many more yen than dollars, does this mean you are rich in Japan?

Name:

Where Do These Fit?

Directions: Review this list: What type of spending does each scenario represent? Fill in the table below by placing the scenario's number in the appropriate row of column 3. *Warning*: some items are **not** part of GDP.

1. A business buys a new computer system.
2. A college graduate buys a new car.
3. A local community builds a new bridge.
4. A company buys plastic pellets to make new toys.
5. You buy a phone made in South Korea.
6. A man visits his doctor for a physical.
7. The government buys food to feed the army.
8. A grandmother sells her old car to her granddaughter.
9. A US car company sells a car in Europe.
10. A family stays in a hotel.
11. An athlete makes money in an exhibition game overseas.
12. A stay-at-home father provides home care for his children.

GDP Component	What does the letter stand for?	Which items from the list above are part of this GDP component?
C		
I		
G		
X_N		

Name:

Inflation, GDP, Unemployment

Part 1

Directions: Finish the following paragraph with the correct vocabulary from your reading.

The CPI, or ________________ (1), is an ________________ (2) indicator collected by the Bureau of Economic Analysis. It is the primary indicator of ________________ (3) in our economy. The CPI does not track every good in our economy. It watches a ________________ (4) of 80,000 goods. Another indictor, called the ________________ (5) Price Index, watches a variety of raw materials. Rising prices during a recession is called ________________ (6). It is also called ________________ (7)-push inflation. Demand-________________ (8) inflation occurs when consumers' aggregate demand moves to the right on a supply/demand graph. Prices falling across the economy are called ________________ (9), while a decreasing rate of inflation is called ________________ (10). ________________ (11) inflation is the rate of rising prices with food and energy omitted. The graph below is called the ________________ (12) cycle.

Part 2

Directions: Label the graph according to the steps below.

1. Label the x and y axes.
2. Place the following words on the curve:
   a. trough
   b. expansion
   c. peak
   d. contraction
3. Shade in the area of the graph that indicates a recession.
4. Highlight the curve where you think inflation is most likely to occur.

Part 3

Directions: Write the type of unemployment being described in the blanks below.

________________ Unemployment that occurs when an economy contracts and is in a trough

________________ Workers lose a job when an industry gets a machine to do it more cheaply.

________________ People are between jobs or have been fired.

Part 4

Directions: For the individuals described below, check either the Yes or No column to indicate whether they are employed.

Are They Part of the Labor Force?	Yes	No
A fifteen-year-old gets fired from a bike shop for showing up late too often.		
An unemployed worker has stopped looking for a job after twelve months.		
A nuclear physicist takes a job working in a warehouse.		
A father leaves his job to stay at home full time to raise his children.		
An auto worker is laid off during a recession.		
A teacher retires and will not seek a new job.		
A nineteen-year-old leaves her summer job as a lifeguard and goes back to college.		
A college student graduates and seeks his first job.		

Name:

Prices Are Relative

Concept: *People think that consumer goods in the past were all less expensive. While that is sometimes true, marveling at a low price in the past ignores the effects of inflation.*

Directions: First, find the "current US CPI." Using the formula provided, figure out what the following products and services *should* cost in today's dollars. Simply use a ratio and basic algebra to find the cost in today's dollars. Then, in the next column, jot down what it *actually costs*. You may consult other people or sources if you are unsure of today's price.

1. The current CPI is ______________.

The formula is: $\frac{\text{old CPI}}{\text{old price}} = \frac{\text{today's CPI}}{\text{X (what it should cost now)}}$

Product	Year	Old Price	Old Year CPI	It Should Cost	It Actually Costs
Three-Bedroom house	1948	$10,000	19		
Loaf of bread, pound of butter, gallon of milk, and a pound of ground beef	1940	$4.15	14.1		
Cheap seats at a Major League baseball game	1960	$1.00	29.5		
Movie ticket	1975	$2.00	53		
One semester at state college	1985	$400	31.6		
VCR	1978	$875	74		
CD player	1985	$250	108		
Apple LLE computer	1980	$1600	82		
Average income of a high school graduate	1940	$2200	14.1		
Model T Ford (use a modern equivalent)	1925	$525	18		

2. What products and services seem to be more expensive today in real prices?

3. What products and services are less expensive in real dollars?

Name:

Keeping on Track—Web Research

Directions: Dividing up the work in your groups, do an Internet search for "economic calendar." Fill in the chart with the appropriate information for each of of your three assigned indicators. (Use the blanks in the column heads to fill in your indicators.) Do a good job and be prepared to present your findings in class.

Group One	Group Two	Group Three	Group Four
• CPI • PPI • Leading Economic Indicators Index	• New home prices • Consumer confidence • Unemployment rate	• Factory orders • Dow Jones Industrial Average • S&P 500	• GDP (initial) • Capacity utilization • Jobless claims

Question	Indicator: ___________	Indicator: ___________	Indicator: ___________
Who gathers it?			
How is it calculated?			
When is it released?			
Historic highs and lows?			
What is an ideal level?			
What is it now?			
What is the trend for the last twelve months?			

Name:

Monetary Policy for Beginners

Directions: For each of the following circumstances listed below, check a box to indicate whether you think it suggests inflation or recession.

What's Happening?	Inflation Bias	Recession Bias
Thousands of workers are being laid off across the country.		
People feel great about the economy and prices are rising.		
The economy is getting too hot.		
The stock market is falling and car sales are dropping.		
New home sales are rising fast and consumer confidence is high.		
The economy is in a slump and prices are falling.		
The CPI is at 4 percent.		
There was a terrorist attack and people are losing their homes.		
GDP has shrunk for eight straight months.		
Unemployment has gone from 6 percent to 9 percent in the last year.		

Part 2

Directions: Write the word that is being described in the blank provided.

1. The abbreviation for the decision-making body of the Federal Reserve is ______________.
2. The Fed adjusts the money supply by selling and buying ______________.
3. Consumers will buy more durable goods if the Fed ______________ interest rates.
4. The number-one enemy of our economy is ______________.
5. A slump in the economy is called a ______________.
6. Inflation that goes higher than 10 percent is called ______________.
7. Inflation with a recession at the same time is called ______________.
8. Lowering rates is part of a ______________-money policy.
9. ______________ rates is part of a tight-money policy.
10. If the Fed increases the money supply, interest rates will ______________.
11. The Fed is in charge of ______________ banks.

 Name:

Advanced Monetary Policy

Directions: Label the graphs below. They represent the money supply. Then, follow the directions.

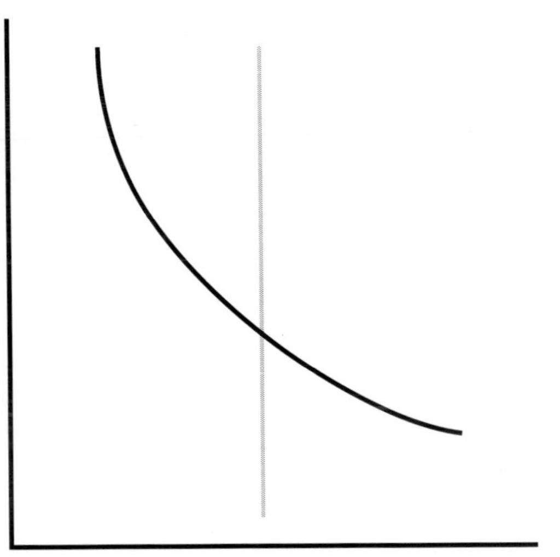

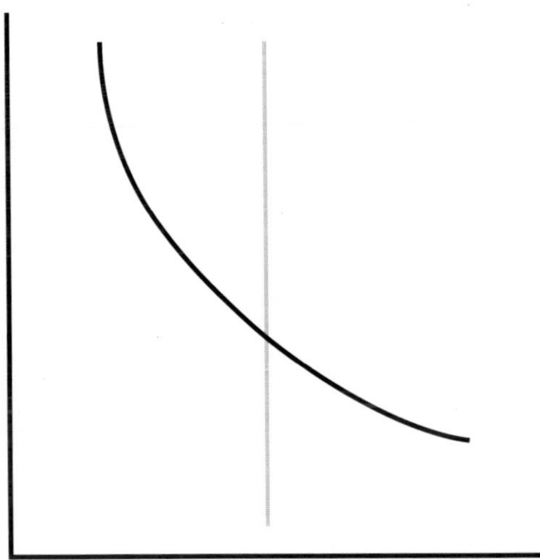

1. Label the x and y axes on these graphs.
2. Label the curves.
3. In the graph on the left, draw in an increase in supply.
4. In the graph on the right, draw in a decrease in supply.

	Left Graph	Right Graph
What happened to money supply?		
Will interest rates go up or down?		
Does the Fed buy or sell bonds to do this?		
Is this in response to a recession or inflation? (bias)		
Would this be a loose or tight money policy?		

Name:

Monetary Policy Decisions

Directions: For each of the following scenarios, a certain course of action is called for. In the column marked "Bias," write in *inflation, recession,* or *neutral.* In the column marked "Monetary Policy Decision," choose *loose money policy, tight money policy,* or *nothing.* If you need to review what those choices actually mean, refer back to your reading.

Economic Problem	Bias	Monetary Policy Decision
1. Stock prices decline for the last two weeks.		
2. GDP dipped from 3 percent to 1 percent in the last year.		
3. The CPI and PPI have risen 3 percent in the last twelve months.		
4. The prices of microchips have tripled in the last year.		
5. GDP is growing steadily at 3 percent and the CPI has climbed 2.5 percent in six months.		
6. The US is experiencing both high inflation and high unemployment.		
7. The CPI and PPI are rising at 5.5 percent and housing starts are at a fifteen-year high while inventories are at a ten-year low.		
8. We are in a recession, factory orders are down, and the economy appears to be slumping.		
9. Consumers feel worried, inflation is low, and spending is sluggish.		
10. Unemployment is low and prices are rising at a rate of 1.7 percent per year.		
11. The index of leading economic indicators shows a strong move towards inflation		
12. The Fed senses that people are not saving enough money		
13. Jobless rates are pushing 11 percent while the CPI has fallen from 8 percent to 2 percent growth		
14. The money supply appears to be tight and prices are on the rise at a 5 percent rate.		
15. Prices are stable and the GDP is growing at a 3 percent pace.		

Financial Armageddon

Directions: Match the words from the word bank to the description. As a class, discuss how all these items and events fit together.

Word Bank			
9/11/2001	GM and Chrysler	AIG	pensions
sub-prime	consumer credit	Trouble Asset Relief Program	adjustable rate mortgage
credit agencies	mortgage	Glass-Steagall Act	Iceland
foreclose	investment banks	Federal Reserve	treasure
credit history	bond		

Description	Answer
In the 1990s, the amount that households borrowed skyrocketed.	
Congress repealed the 1930s law that kept banks from being investment houses.	
A recession was triggered by a shocking terrorist attack.	
This institution lowered interest rates to help avert a recession.	
Getting a loan to buy a house became much more affordable.	
Borrowers who were not qualified began to get loans. They were not likely to pay those loans back.	
These borrowers had bad track records at paying back loans.	
Banks convinced these borrowers to take a lower-interest loan that adjusts ever year to market rates.	
Banks sold these loans to big financial institutions that structure huge financial deals.	
All these risky mortgages were bundled into this type of investment (the type of investment that pays holders interest on their money).	
Companies that are supposed to put a "grade" on the risk of an investment gave these investments a AAA rating, the highest possible.	
Big funds that give money to retired people invested in these bonds filled with rotten mortgages.	
American Insurance Group sold insurance on many of these bogus, rotten bonds.	

This country in Europe invested heavily in these terrible, no good, rotten investments.	
By 2006, many of these adjustable mortgages reset permanently at high interest rates. People could not pay their mortgages, so banks had to . . .	
September, 2008. Panic set in. The Secretary of the ______________, Congress, and our national bank had emergency meetings.	
The government established a massive fund of $700 billion to bail out thousands of banks and AIG.	
The government even loaned these two auto companies billions of dollars in exchange for partial ownership in them.	

 Name:

Noticing Trends

Directions: Using the four graphs on the following pages, answer the questions below.

1. What is the subject of the first graph?

2. What is the subject of the second?

3. What is the subject of the third?

4. What is subject of the fourth?

5. List the recessions after World War II:

6. What happens to GDP during a recession? Which recession stands out?

7. How often do recessions happen prior to 1980?

8. How often do recessions happen after 1980?

9. What happens to unemployment prior to a recession?

10. What happens to unemployment during a recession?

11. What happens to prices before a recession?

12. What happens to prices during a recession?

13. What are interest rates doing before and during a recession?

14. How is the Federal Reserve trying to help the economy during a recession?

15. What seems to be the worst economy since 1950? What data back up your answer?

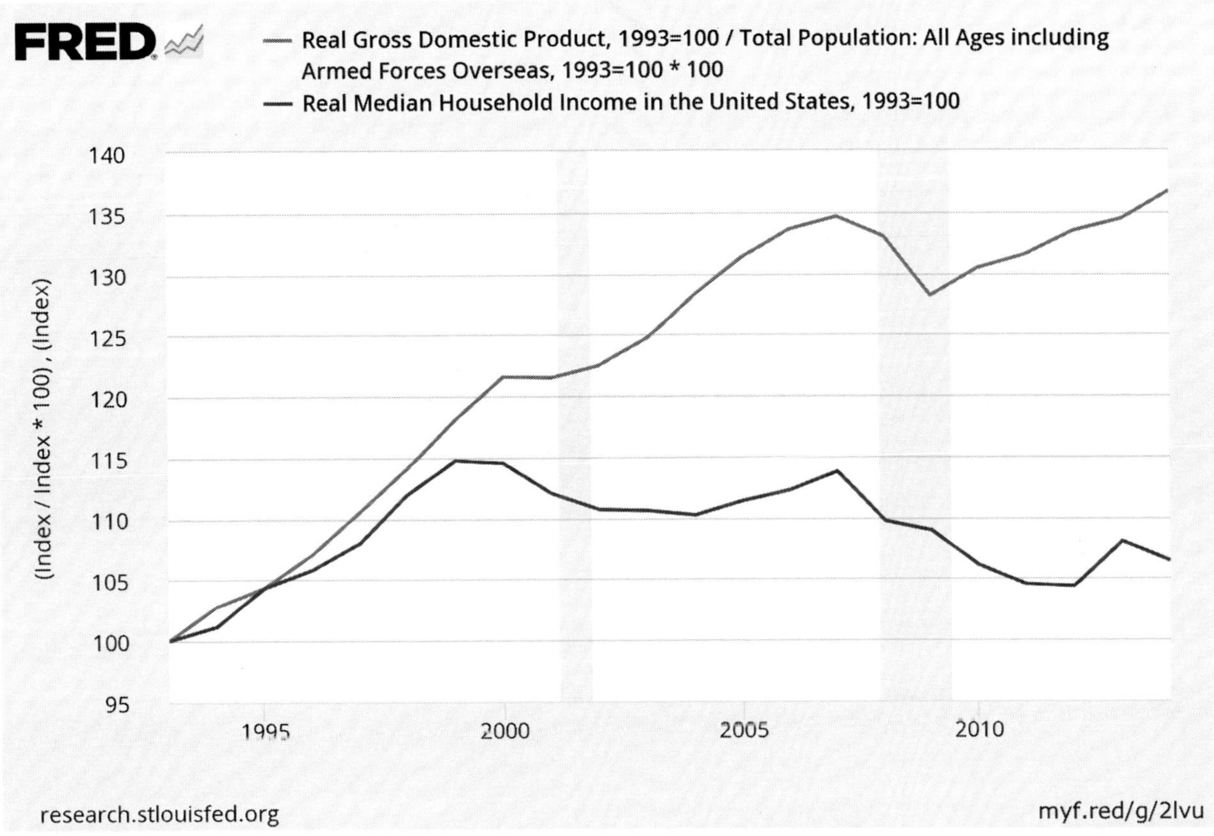
FRED
— Real Gross Domestic Product, 1993=100 / Total Population: All Ages including Armed Forces Overseas, 1993=100 * 100
— Real Median Household Income in the United States, 1993=100
(Index / Index * 100), (Index)
140
135
130
125
120
115
110
105
100
95
1995
2000
2005
2010
research.stlouisfed.org
myf.red/g/2lvu

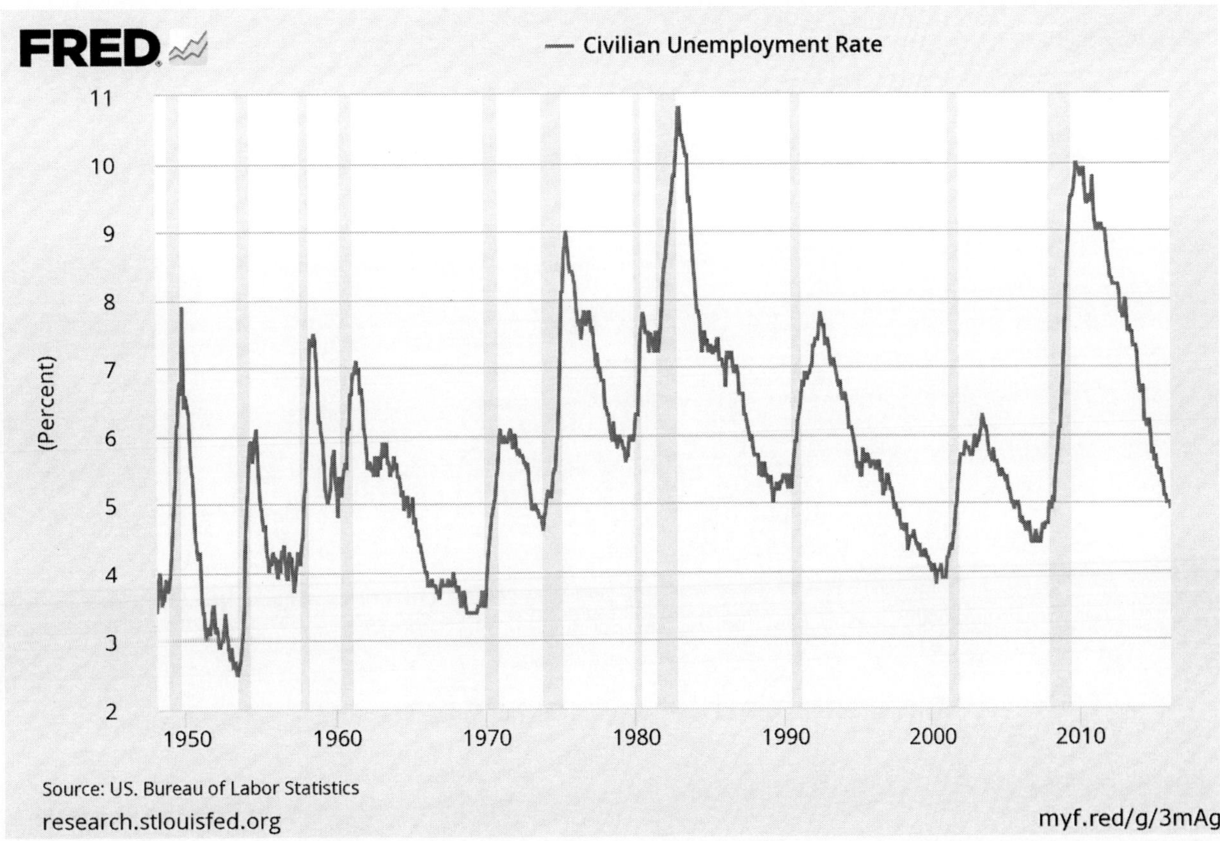
FRED
— Civilian Unemployment Rate
(Percent)
11
10
9
8
7
6
5
4
3
2
1950
1960
1970
1980
1990
2000
2010
Source: US. Bureau of Labor Statistics
research.stlouisfed.org
myf.red/g/3mAg

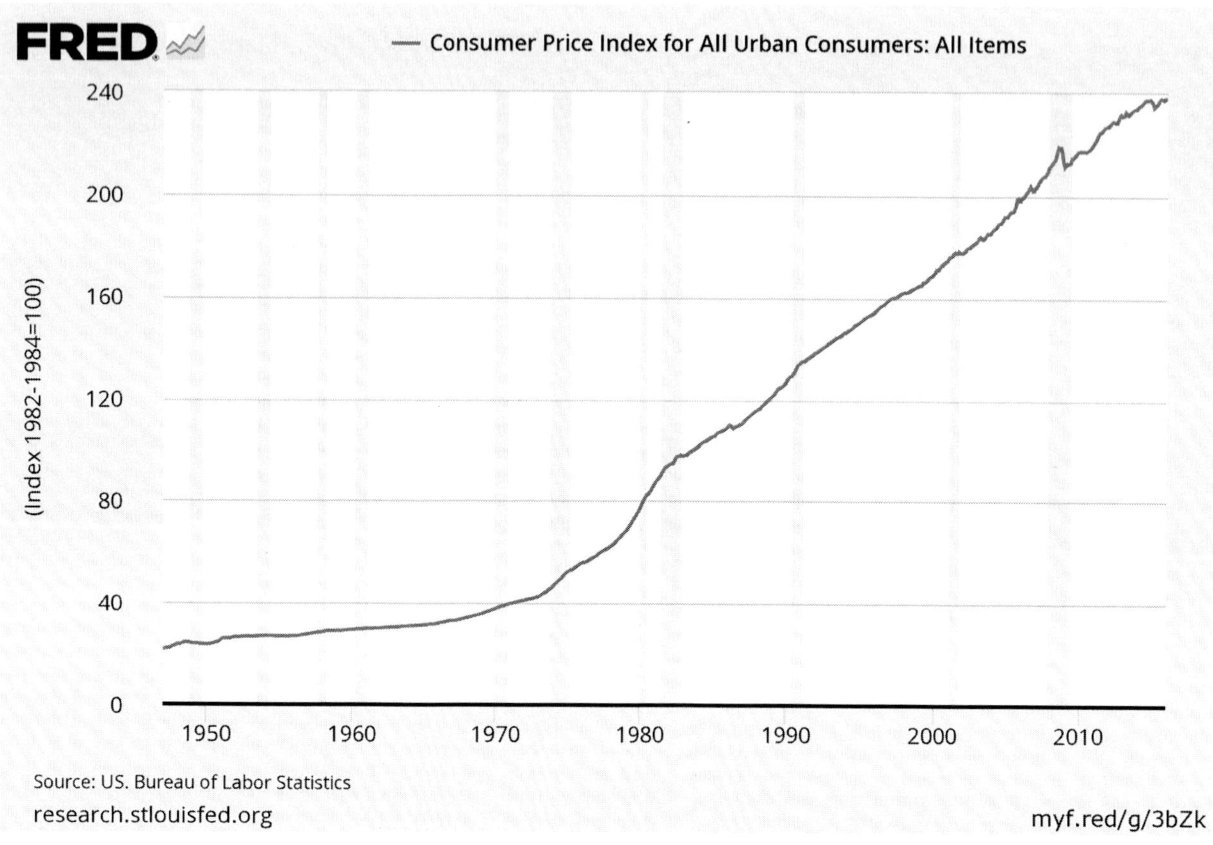
FRED
Consumer Price Index for All Urban Consumers: All Items
(Index 1982-1984=100)
240
200
160
120
80
40
0
1950
1960
1970
1980
1990
2000
2010
Source: US. Bureau of Labor Statistics
research.stlouisfed.org
myf.red/g/3bZk

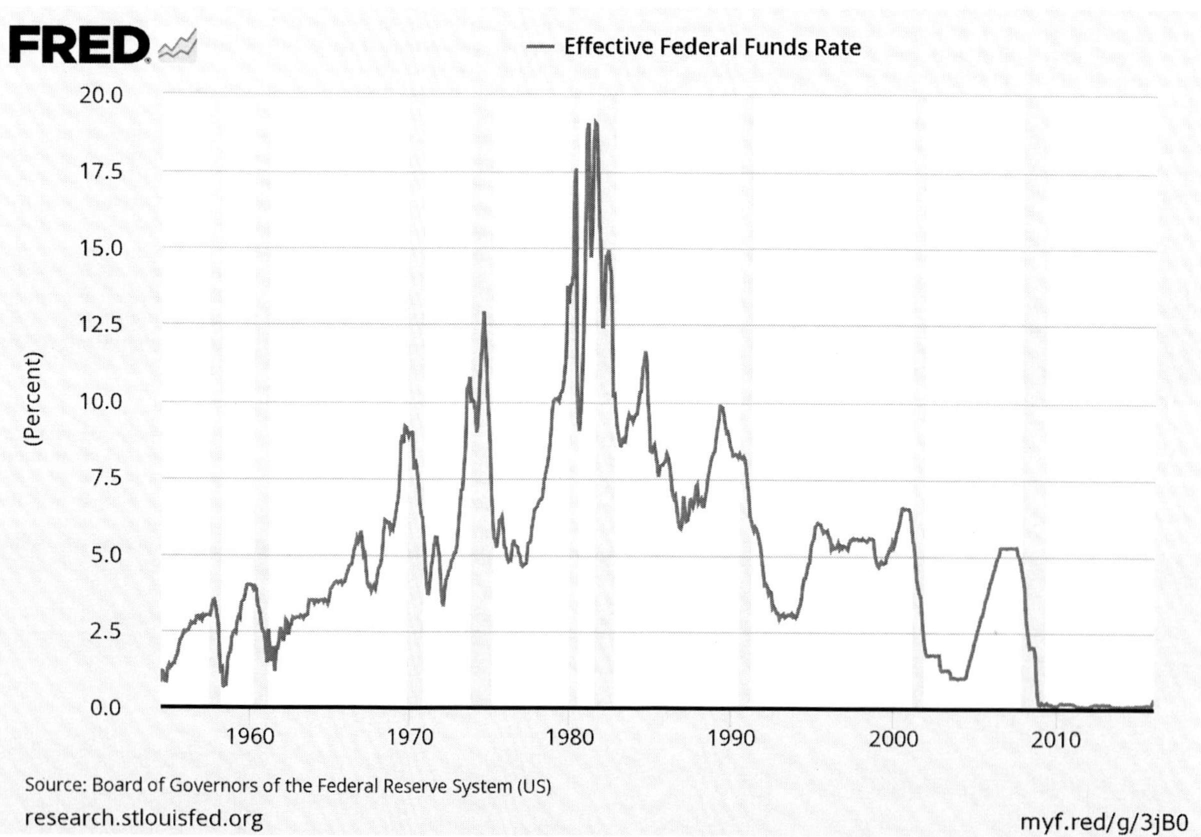
FRED
Effective Federal Funds Rate
(Percent)
20.0
17.5
15.0
12.5
10.0
7.5
5.0
2.5
0.0
1960
1970
1980
1990
2000
2010
Source: Board of Governors of the Federal Reserve System (US)
research.stlouisfed.org
myf.red/g/3jB0

Unit 4

Government and the Economy

Questions to Consider

1. Do you consider yourself to be a conservative or a liberal? Why?
2. Are people in your family Democrats or Republicans? Why?
3. What basic economic rights do you have?
4. How involved is our government with the economy?
5. How much does our government spend?
6. What levels of government influence your life?
7. How many types of taxes do we pay?

Terms You Need in Order to Read

Conservative
Liberal
Republican
Democrat
Regulation
Tax
Entitlement

Government and the Economy

4A. Basic Functions of Governments

For much of human history, people lived under socioeconomic systems like feudalism. People who controlled the land allowed other people to work on it. The farmers kept some of the product, but the lords received most of it. In exchange for their work, the farmers received protection from various outside invaders. This was how society was organized for thousands of years. Not until the French and American Revolutions did the old way of doing things begin to subside.

Two hundred years ago, there were fewer than five democracies in the world. Today, that number is more than 150. What accounts for such a global shift? While there are many reasons for a country to adopt democracy, the primary reason is economic. When the world industrialized, people no longer had to farm. In the process, people made more money, and a middle class slowly developed. Middle-class people owned property and had a higher standard of living. Literacy rates increased to meet the demand for more skilled workers. Simply put, richer and smarter people wanted a government that would protect their property. They wanted a say on how their society functioned.

Today, people in the Western world enjoy a great deal of freedom. Their rights fit into three basic categories: life, liberty, and property. Consider this story. A man is walking down the street, and he is struck in the head and knocked to the ground by a mugger who takes his wallet. Which of the pedestrian's rights were violated? All three of them. Being hit in the head could kill somebody. His life was threatened. His right to walk down the street without being accosted—his liberty—was violated. Finally, that wallet is his private property, not the mugger's. We expect our government to protect these three rights.

A **government** is a system for determining and enforcing public policy. Laws are made and executed by the government. We also grant it the power to use force to enforce the law. For example, ordinary citizens do not have the right to arrest and incarcerate someone, but the government does. Early sociologists wrote that governments have a "monopoly on violence." In essence, government alone is allowed to use force against citizens.

GRAPHIC 4.1

Peasants exchanged labor for protection. Here, a French illustration from 1310 shows a noble overseeing fieldwork. This was a primary form of social order up until the nineteenth century.

Keep in mind, this does not mean brutality but rather the ability to confiscate property, arrest and detain someone, and enforce contracts. For our work, we are primarily concerned with how the government involves itself in our economic lives. We pay taxes, follow regulations, and receive services or benefits from the government. This unit takes a deeper look at all three of those powers.

Pressing Question

- Are there any rules that the government compels you to follow?

4B. The Foundation of US Politics

From the very beginning of our country's history, Americans debated the government's involvement in the economy. These debates were as heated in the 1790s as they are today. You may recall from

GRAPHIC 4.2

Thomas Jefferson strongly opposed giving too much power to the federal government. He wanted more rights to be given to states.

your American history class two groups called the Federalists and the Anti-Federalists. Some people believed that the federal (national) government should remain small and rarely interfere with the economy. Others believed that it was in our national interest that the government be directly involved with our economic affairs. The argument between the two factions is at the heart of our political system.

The **Anti-Federalists**, led by Thomas Jefferson, had a fundamental distrust of government. Having ousted an obtrusive monarchy from England, they were not anxious to let another government start taxing them and telling them how to live. Their conservative beliefs are still around today in the Republican Party. Economically, the modern **conservative** wants lower taxes, less spending by the federal government, more power to the state governments, and fewer regulations placed upon business.

The **Federalists**, led by Alexander Hamilton, believed that the federal government, not the states, should monitor and engineer the growth of the economy. They wanted to see the United States develop as an industrial power and compete with Europe. Because they advocated a stronger central power, and a change from things in the past, the Federalists were liberal for their day. Today, **liberals** advocate a stronger federal government, regulating businesses more stringently, and programs that alleviate social problems. In order to do this, the government becomes more involved in our economic affairs.

If you already have some political opinions, try to clarify them as you read this section. Some ideas are controversial, and some may even anger you. Try to be open to new ideas, but also be firm in what you hold most dear. We live together in the one of the oldest democracies in the world. The ability of our government to function is vital to the health of our society. Because you are a citizen, you must take part in determining the direction of our country.

A society is only as strong as its economy. You have to ask yourself the question, "Does the government help the economy or hurt it?" The answer is at the very heart of your political beliefs.

Pressing Question

- Construct two separate definitions for the following words: *conservative* and *liberal.*

4C. What Governments Provide

Americans expect to have the freedom to choose how to live their lives, spend their money, and spend their time. We have a very high standard of living. If you have ever received a paycheck, however, then you remember the shock you felt when you saw your pay stub. About 20 percent or so was gone. It is a reminder of how the government is part of our lives. At all levels, governments provide services, protect our rights, and ensure efficient commerce with that 20 percent.

A necessity to the health of any modern economy is a **rule of law**. This means that we have a system of laws that is written down, consistently applied, and predictably enforced. If you build a factory, you expect that nobody else can take it from you. Your competitors are not allowed to burn it down, nor are they allowed to conspire to put you out of business. These assumptions are essential to our **free enterprise** system. Our system has five characteristics:

- Private property
- Freedom to choose
- Voluntary exchange of goods and services
- Competition
- Consistent rule of law

Remember from Unit 1, the US economy is mixed. While our government taxes us and provides services, citizens make most of the decisions on what gets produced, how it gets produced, and who gets the goods and services. The government's involvement can be understood in the circular flow diagram shown in graphic 4.3. Businesses get labor and resources from households and, in turn, sell the household's (people's) products. In the middle of all that, the government regulates and taxes.

Every time Americans get in a car and go out for food, they do not realize the extent to which government is involved with their lives. The car that they drive is registered with the state, manufactured according to federal standards, and driven on roads maintained mostly by local and state governments. The food that is bought must be supplied and prepared according to local, state, and federal cleanliness regulations. Taxes will be assessed at the time of purchase. Just on this little trip, there are more rules and regulations than we can count.

GRAPHIC 4.3

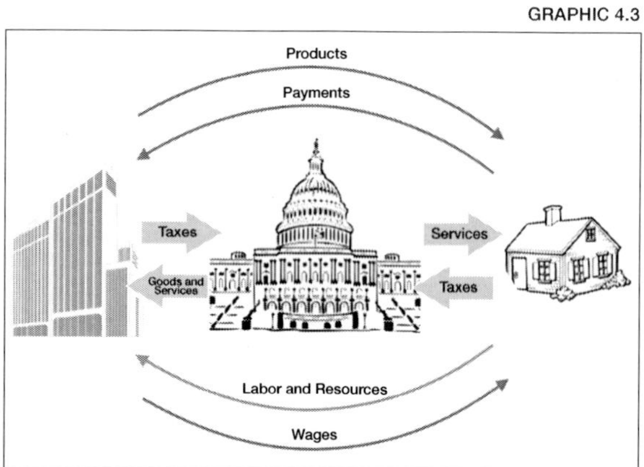

Just driving down the road involves multiple levels of government. The shared responsibility among city, county, state, and federal governments is a system called *federalism*. For example, cities maintain local parks, states maintain your highways, and the federal government provides Social Security assistance to older people in your area. Our governments promote fairness in competition by enforcing antitrust laws, protect consumers from harmful products by inspecting food, and try to maintain economic well-being by managing social assistance programs. Many large infrastructure projects like airports, roads, and bridges involve funding from multiple governments at the same time.

Americans have come to expect quite a bit from their governments. If we are thrown out of work, then we expect the state to provide unemployment benefits. If there is a national emergency, the federal government is expected to maintain order. We expect the government to handle virulent disease outbreaks. If there is injustice, then Americans expect all levels of government to adjudicate. The public expects these goods and services, more than they usually know.

In our mixed economy, products are divided into two groups. **Public goods** are goods that cannot be denied to anyone, whether or not they pay taxes. For instance, nobody in the United States is excluded from the protection of national defense. It is a benefit best supplied by our government. On the other hand, a **private good** is a good that people can be denied. If you buy a new computer, it is yours and you have the right to deny others the use of it. While our government protects your right to private goods (property) through the law, it is also committed to providing numerous public goods.

GRAPHIC 4.4

LEASE

This lease is a legal and enforceable contract; Please read it carefully.

This lease agreement was entered on _______________, between Joseph Febeetz ("Landlord") and _____________ ("Tenant"). With this written document, which is the entire agreement between them, the landlord and tenant agree to the following:

The Landlord shall lease to the tenant the __________ premises located at 3098 Carroll Avenue in Cleveland, Ohio for a period of ________ ( ) months beginning on _____, ____ and ending on _______, ___

The number of persons that shall occupy thus unit is _____.

One of the most important ways government protects your private property is through the enforcement of contract law. A **contract** is an agreement between two or more people to perform a service or to provide a good. Consider graphic 4.4. A lease is a common contract between a landlord and tenant. Both parties agree to terms, date the document, and then sign it. This process where two parties agree to do something and cooperate is fundamental to our free-enterprise system.

To elaborate, Mrs. Garcia signed a contract with Jones Construction to build a new bathroom. She was very specific about what she wanted and when it was to be finished. When the crew left, however, they did not finish the job according to Mrs. Garcia's satisfaction. The contract specified how the job was to be completed. With contract in hand, Mrs. Garcia can use the local court system to arbitrate a settlement. The court can enforce the contract and make the contractor finish the job or pay Mrs. Garcia damages.

Across the United States, almost 22 million people work for a government (2.8 million are federal and the rest are state and local employees). Despite its size and complexity, the government's primary role in our economy is to ensure that commerce is promoted and protected. Whether the case is small, like a homeowner versus a contractor, or is large, like the breakup of a massive corporation (AT&T in 1982), people need to rely on a predictable rule of law. Our freedoms to start a business and engage in commerce are clear, but not always honored.

Pressing Question

- Is the government effective in the jobs we expect it to do?

4D. Basic Tax Theory

A **tax** is a required payment to government revenue, levied by the government on workers' incomes and businesses' profits. They are sometimes added to the cost of some goods, services, and transactions. Taxes provide a cash flow so the government can operate. This money provides for services, government regulatory agencies, and the redistribution of income. The amount of money that the government brings in every year in fees, charges, and taxes is known as **tax revenue**. Our elected representatives decide how the money is spent. How much we pay and how much we spend can have a tremendous amount of influence on the health of our economy.

Mark Twain once remarked that there were only two sure things in life, "death and taxes." Ever since, people have lived with governments, forfeiting some of their earnings to the government has been a dreaded necessity. There are many differing opinions and theories when it comes to how our government should take money from us. At the core of each opinion are issues of fairness and justice.

Our current federal income tax is known as a **progressive tax**. Refer to graphic 4.5. As people make more money, they will have to pay a larger percentage of their income to the government. In the current system, the lowest income tax bracket is 10 percent and the highest is around 40 percent. Keep in mind that these rates are not applied to the entire income. They are marginal rates, meaning that the percentage is applied to the amount of money made in that bracket. In 2016, a single filer who made $35,000 per year paid 10 percent of $9,275 ($927.50) plus 15 percent of the rest ($25,725 × 0.15 = $3,858.75); this person's final federal income tax bill was $4,786.25.

Some believe that just because an individual makes more money, he or she should not have to pay a higher percentage. They believe that taking more of a person's income will act as a **disincentive**, or a reason to work less and not more. In other words, if individuals feel that they are paying too much in taxes, there might not be a point to making more money. They might not decide to work harder or start a business.

GRAPHIC 4.5

Tax Bracket 2016 Example		
Tax rate	Single	Married filing jointly or qualifying widow/widower
10%	Up to $9,275	Up to $18,550
15%	$9,276 to $37,650	$18,551 to $75,300
25%	$37,651 to $91,150	$75,301 to $151,900
28%	$91,151 to $190,150	$151,901 to $231,450
33%	$190,151 to $413,350	$231,451 to $413,350
35%	$413,351 to $415,050	$413,351 to $466,950
39.6%	$415,051 or more	$466,951 or more

Opponents to progressive taxation argue for a **flat tax**. In this system, every taxpayer applies the same percentage to their income. No matter how much a person makes, each would send the same percentage of income to the government. If the flat rate were 15 percent, then a person who makes $1 million per year would pay $150,000. A person making $10,000 per year would pay $1,500. Currently, with the deductions and assistance, the latter taxpayer would pay no income tax. The government hopes to improve the standard of living of the poor and create more financial equity in our society. Proponents of the flat tax argue that the government is treating people who are more successful unfairly.

The federal income tax is progressive on purpose. Our society has decided that it is in our best interest to have tax brackets in order to make higher-income people pay higher percentages. Other taxes, when levied, end up costing a poorer person a higher percentage of her income. A **regressive tax** is a type of tax that takes a higher percentage of people's income as they make less money. State and local sales taxes are the best examples of this. For example, two women go into a car dealership to buy the same $20,000 car. The sales tax on the car will amount to $1,400. The first woman makes $35,000 per year. The tax amounts to 4 percent of her yearly income. The second woman makes $135,000 per year. The sales tax on the car will amount to about 1 percent of her income.

GRAPHIC 4.6

"Taxes are what we pay for civilized society."—Oliver Wendell Holmes, Jr., US Supreme Court Justice

"The power of taxing people and their property is essential to the very existence of government."—James Madison, US President

"The hardest thing in the world to understand is the income tax."—Albert Einstein, physicist

"Taxation with representation ain't so hot either." —Gerald Barzan, humorist

"Where there is an income tax, the just man will pay more and the unjust less on the same amount of income." —Plato

"Income tax has made more liars out of the American people than golf."—Will Rogers, humorist

Opinions about fairness in taxation vary with people's social concerns, value systems, and economic positions. The two basic stances are:

- **Ability-to-pay principle**—Those who make more money should pay a larger portion of their income or wealth to the government. People who believe in this idea believe that the government should take an active role in achieving more income equality.
- **Benefits-received principle**—This idea states that those who get more of the government services should pay for them. For example, only those who use gasoline pay the excise tax on gasoline. If one uses more, then one pays more in taxes. While it is difficult to figure out how much a citizen benefits from other services, proponents of this theory say it is fairer, because it more accurately mirrors how a free market works. In other words, if you get a good or service from the government, then you should pay for it just as you would pay any other business.

Pressing Question

- Considering the differing ideas about taxation, explain what idea you consider to be most fair.

4E. The Litany of Taxes

Today, taxes at all levels of government add up to about 25 percent of GDP. Depending on one's income and financial situation, the percentage of income given up to government varies. The rates charged on sales, property, and income differ from state to state.

The largest amount of money US citizens pay is to the federal government. Most people are familiar with income tax, but there are so many more that get collected:

- **Income tax**—This tax is progressive according to an individual's income. The IRS withholds money from each paycheck. States and local governments may collect income tax as well.
- **Social Security tax**—Also known as FICA tax (after the 1935 Federal Insurance Contributions Act), this money helps to support the Social Security programs that pay retirement pensions, aid for the indigent, and survivor benefits for orphans. It is a flat 6.2 percent of income that is matched by employers. Income exceeding $115,000 is not taxed.
- **Medicare tax**—Along with Social Security, Medicare tax is referred to as a **payroll tax**. Regardless of income, all citizens who make money pay these taxes. This is a flat 1.45 percent of one's income that funds the health care of retired or disabled Americans. There is no income cap on Medicare contributions.

Look at the pay stub in graphic 4.7. Notice the different taxes that are assessed. First, the largest amount will be federal withholding tax. Below that are Social Security and Medicare taxes. The state and local income taxes are also listed. The gross pay is totaled in the lower left-hand box. After subtracting the taxes and other deductions, the remainder is what you take home. It is known as *net pay* or disposable income.

In addition to these payroll taxes, there are many more taxes to be paid.

- **Capital gains tax**—If you make money in an investment that has increased in value, the extra money is a *capital gain*. For instance, if you buy stock at $20 per share and sell it for $30 per share, then you will have to pay tax on the *gain*, or the amount your money grew, $10. While the same applies to real estate, much or most of the money you made on the sale of the house you live in is exempt from capital gains tax.

GRAPHIC 4.7

A Typical Pay Stub

Employee Name	Social Security Number	Pay Period	Date
Josephine Febeetz	000-00-0000	04/10/16—04/24/16	04/30/16
Company Name	**Exemptions**	**Status**	**Adjustments**
Initech, LLC	2	Single	None

Earnings			Taxes			Deductions		
	This Pay	Year To Date		This Pay	Year To Date		This Pay	Year To Date
Salary	1,119.00	9,878.00	Federal	122.40	966.72	401(k)	100.00	800.00
Overtime	158.00	442.00	State	33.12	259.87	Medical	52.00	416.00
Bonus	57.00	695.00	City	44.33	178.17	Flex Pay	50.00	400.00
			Social Sec	69.77	555.33	Charity	10.00	
			Medicare	19.98	124.54			
Total	**1,334.00**	**11,015.00**	**Total**	**288.60**	**2,084.63**	**Total**	212.00	1,616.00

-Taxes	288.60	
-Deductions	212.00	
Net Pay	893.40	

It is important to know how to read a pay stub and know where your money is going. Did you know that some retirement savings, medical insurance premiums, and charitable contributions can be subtracted from your gross income PRIOR to paying tax? These are called "pre-tax" benefits. Be sure to talk to your human resources advisor.

- **Corporate income tax**—Corporations are taxed different rates according to their net income. Many expenses like capital improvements and charitable contributions, however, are deducted from their taxable revenue. All levels of government can collect tax from businesses.
- **Excise taxes**—These are taxes on particular products or services. Gasoline, tobacco, alcohol, gambling, and telephone service are just a few of the excise taxes that Americans pay. These are collected at all levels of government.

GRAPHIC 4.8

The excise tax on gasoline is a good example of the benefits received principle. This revenue pays for the upkeep of roads. On average, Americans pay 48.5 cents per gallon.

- **Estate tax**—Sometimes called inheritance tax or the "death tax," this is imposed when a person dies and leaves money or property to someone else. These too are levied at all levels of government.

The federal government is not the only one to collect taxes from us. The following are some of the payments we must make to our state and local governments:

- **Sales tax**—Most states collect sales taxes. Some counties also collect them. In a particular state, one might pay 3 percent to the county and 5 percent to the state for a total of 8 percent. A $100 purchase will therefore cost you $108. The merchant sends the payment to the governments.
- **Property tax**—Homeowners and businesses pay tax on houses, buildings, and land. These taxes vary from locale to locale. Tax is levied upon the estimated value of the property. For example, a city has a rate of 2.53 percent. On a $100,000 house, the yearly tax bill is $2,530. Homeowners usually pay this money when they make their monthly mortgage payment. Most communities depend on property tax to supply most of their operating revenue. Typically, public schools require the most tax dollars. Next time your community wants to raise taxes for schools, listen for the word *mills*, or 1/1000th of a dollar.
- **More local income tax**—The money deducted on the "city" line in the pay stub goes to the city in which the person works. In some states, the community that you live in may also charge an income tax. The only way to avoid this would be to live and work in the same city.

There are even more taxes than are listed here. It might seem that people and businesses are overburdened by taxation. In reality, the US economy manages to grow consistently. Overtaxation would hinder that growth.

Pressing Question

- How could too much taxation hurt the economy? How could it hurt you?

4F. How We Pay Taxes

Anyone who has received a paycheck has paid taxes. Most times, when something is purchased, a sales tax is collected. When it comes to income tax, it is more complicated. There is a process that must be followed. Every year, in order to settle accounts with the IRS and other collection agencies, taxpayers need to send in a **tax return**, the official form that documents a year's income and tax activity.

As a year goes along, employers withhold taxes from their employees' paychecks to pay the government on the employees' behalf. This way, the government gets monthly operating revenue and people do not get an unexpected tax bill. People at every income level will owe the government a specified amount of tax. At the end of the year, if the government took too much in taxes, you will get a refund. If too little was taken, you will owe the difference. These calculations are made using the government's tax return forms. Every taxpayer must file the previous year's tax return by April 15th.

GRAPHIC 4.9

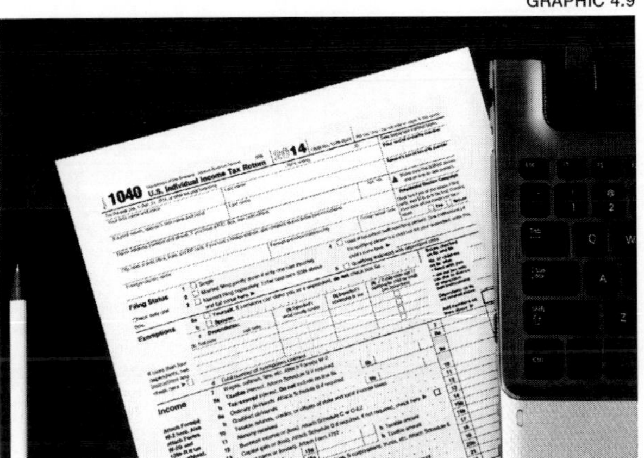

Doing taxes is like homework for adults. Forms have math, complex instructions, and take a lot of time. Unlike homework though, you might get money for turning them in on time.

On every tax return, taxpayers list all the money they made from each employer. Wages, salaries, and tips are the most common income sources. Dividends from stock and interest earned from banks are also taxed as income. Royalties from a published work get added in. The total of all these amounts is called **adjusted gross income**. The good news is you do not have to pay tax on the entire income you brought home.

Following the instructions on your tax return, you are allowed to subtract some money from your gross income. Every subtraction is called a **deduction**. If you gave money to a charity, you can subtract that amount. In essence, the government encourages donations by not charging tax on them. Home mortgage interest, business expenses, and taxes you pay to other governments are all sizable subtractions. The remainder after all the deductions is your **taxable income**.

Although there are thousands of tax forms in the United States, there are a few that are the most common. Some of them are:

- **1040**—This is the standard federal return form (graphic 4.9). It allows the person to account for deductions. Whether filled in online or by hand, it goes to the IRS. Young people who do not have major deductions or income can use a short form called the **1040 EZ**.
- **W-2**—This is the form that each of your employers will send you sometime in January. It is a declaration of all the money you made and taxes you paid in the previous year.
- **1099**—This is proof of income for freelance workers. No payroll or withholding tax was deducted from that income, so a self-employment tax will need to be paid.
- **W-4**—This form must be filled in when you get a job. You get some control over your withholding tax on this form. Taking an **exemption** will mean that the government will take less money from each paycheck. Remember though, if enough money is not withheld, you will pay what you owe at the time you file your return. Follow the instructions or ask for help when you start a new job.

When it comes time to file your taxes, you should take time to get organized. Gather all the forms you need and get a couple of folders. A 1040 form can be printed out from IRS.gov. Many Web services like TurboTax take their customers through the process step by step. No matter what method you choose, remember that the IRS must receive all returns by April 15th. If you own your own company or have very complex tax returns, accountants offer professional advice and electronic filing services. Be warned though, accountants can be expensive.

Pressing Question

- What percentage of taxpayers do you think still send in their tax forms by mail?

4G. Basic Fiscal Policy

Governments collect revenue from the public in the form of taxes and fees. Executives like presidents and governors then deliberate with legislatures on how to spend that money. This spending is called **government expenditure**. If the revenue matches the spending, then the budget is balanced. The means by which a government adjusts its spending levels and tax rates to

GRAPHIC 4.10

Major Categories of Federal Income and Outlays

Income and Outlays. These pie charts show the relative sizes of the major categories of federal income and outlays for Fiscal year 2013.

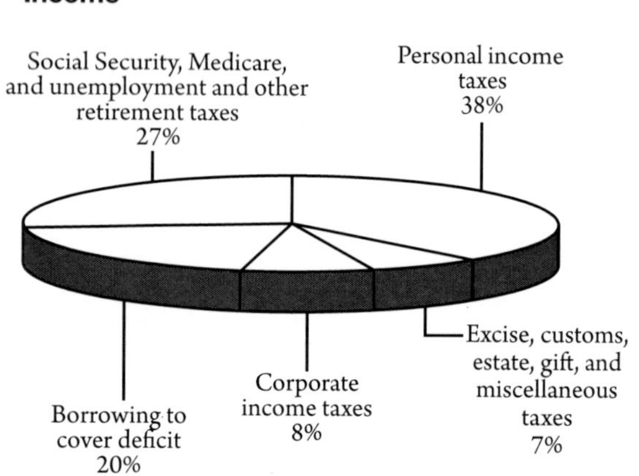

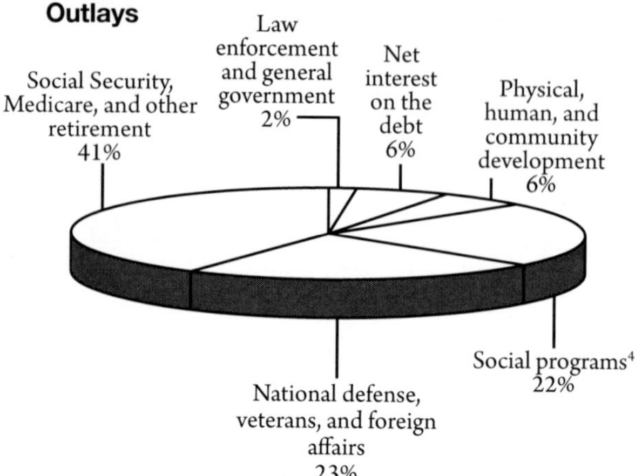

influence a nation's economy and social norms is called **fiscal policy**.

If someone you know is described as *fiscally responsible*, it means that he rarely spends more than he makes. Because of this, he avoids getting in debt. Our national government has been less than fiscally responsible over the past few decades. Since the late 1960s, the federal government has run a yearly deficit, except for a few years in the late 1990s. A **deficit** is the amount of spending that exceeds revenue. In other words, the federal government spent more money each year than it brought in from taxes. In times of crisis, such as the years of the Great Recession, the federal government will typically run higher deficits.

Consider graphic 4.10. The two largest areas of revenue for the government come from personal income and Social Security tax (about 38 percent and 27 percent respectively). Corporate tax only accounts for about 8 percent of our tax revenue. The rest of the revenue comes from many smaller taxes and borrowing. As mentioned before, the federal government typically spends more than it collects. This borrowing (20 percent) pays for the rest of the budget.

On the other end of the process, our national budget funds many programs. Caring for seniors with Social Security and Medicare (health care for retired persons) takes up the largest portion of the budget. National defense and international relations cost 23 percent. Other social programs like Medicaid (health care for the poor), public housing, and health research take up 22 percent. Paying the interest on past debt costs us 6 percent of our budget every year. Where in the budget can you find support for education and college students? It is in the human development component, which is only 6 percent of the budget.

GRAPHIC 4.11

Budget Processes

	Federal	State	Local
Budget Starts with	President	Governor	Mayor
Budget gets Deliberated by	Congress	State Legislature	City Council
Biggest Expenditures	Social Programs	Education	Education

Some programs started by Congress, like Medicare and Social Security, can only be changed by Congress. They must be funded every year, because it was determined that citizens are entitled to them. These mandatory expenditures are called **entitlements**. Spending on Medicaid and food stamps comes to about 15 percent of the budget. When added, these entitlements occupy almost 60 percent of the budget. With the implementation of the Affordable Care Act in 2010, this number has risen and will increase in the future.

When discussing any government budget, it is important to think like an economist. Pay attention to how money is spent and moved from one part of our society to the next. Social Security transfers money from current workers to program beneficiaries. Sums moved from one place to another are called **transfer payments**. Remember though, people who pay the tax are deprived of the utility that tax money could bring them. Money spent in one place cannot be spent in another. Why not spend more on high school and college education for instance? Or perhaps the government should give more grants for medical research.

The budget process starts with the executive. Consider graphic 4.12. Mayors, governors, and presidents propose their plan on how to tax and spend the public's money. In this proposal, they need to estimate how much money they think the government will collect in taxes. The legislatures always have their own ideas on how money should be collected and spent. After a series of committee meetings, backroom discussions, and calculated compromises, a final budget is voted on. Once the executive signs it, it becomes law. After that, taxes are collected and programs are funded.

GRAPHIC 4.12

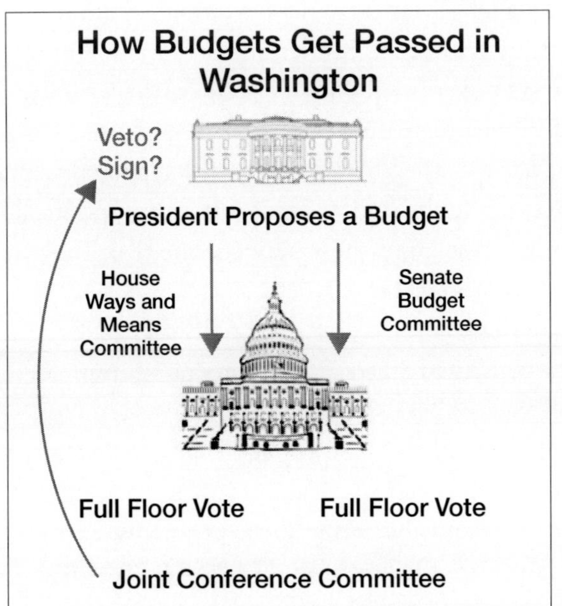

Refer to graphic 4.12. In Washington, members of the House and Senate try to reach a consensus after they both pass their own versions of the budget. If they hammer out their differences in the Joint Conference Committee, the budget will be held up to a vote in both chambers. If it passes, the president then has the option of signing it into law or refusing to sign it with a **veto**.

GRAPHIC 4.13

When the executive and legislative branches of the federal government cannot agree on a budget, a shutdown can occur. The effects can be immediate.

Because the government's fiscal year runs from October 1 to September 30, the budget debates must start early in the year. If a budget is not agreed upon by the end of September, then the government will usually operate on the previous year's budget. Even then, Congress must allow the government to borrow money to cover any deficit in tax revenue. In the last twenty years, Congress and the president have had profound disagreements about policy matters. In 1995 and 2013, Congress let the government shut down in order to get the president to compromise. In the end, little gets accomplished when the budget process diverges from the model in graphic 4.12.

Pressing Question

- If we have a budget deficit, what are some ways to eliminate it?

4H. Advanced Fiscal Theories

Arguments about taxes go back to the very beginning of the United States. Colonists objected to being forced to pay taxes and wanted to have their say through representation in the English Parliament. Economists also have strong opinions about taxes. If the government taxes the sale of a product, how will the quantity supplied and the quantity demanded be affected?

Consider graphic 4.14. In this market for batteries, a certain quantity is supplied and demanded. This quantity is shown with the equilibrium at point A. If the government decides that the disposal of batteries is harming the environment and levies a per-unit sales tax on each one, then the supply of batteries will decrease from S_1 to S_{tax}. The price goes from point A to point B. Now, follow the supply curve down from point A to point C. That section represents the producers who dropped out of the market, because they can no longer afford to compete. The price is higher and the quantity supplied is lower.

The government will collect revenue from the battery tax, but not the amount that it thought it would. The quantity supplied is lower because of the higher price, so there are fewer batteries to be taxed. Above point B and below point C, the reduced size of these areas represents lost utility for consumers and lost profits for producers.

What about the triangle formed by points A, B, and C? These batteries will be neither produced nor consumed. As a result of the higher price and lower quantity, some consumers are pushed out of the market, and some producers go out of business. In essence, that part of the market is lost to everyone in the battery market. Economists call this a **deadweight loss**. This is the loss of efficiency that occurs when the equilibrium for a product or service cannot be achieved.

Graphic 4.14 provides a strong argument against taxation. On the other hand, what if the production of a product is actually harmful to the public? For example, if manufacturers of batteries habitually pollute rivers, does that cost our society anything? A canoe rental business and a restaurant both go out of business as a result of the new pollution. The battery business may be efficient and profitable, but there was an external social cost, or **externality**, when batteries were produced. As seen in the same graph (4.14), the original supply curve is what producers bring to market. The second supply curve is what should get produced because of all the damage done to other businesses. Supporters of the tax might argue that the tax revenue should be used to clean up the pollution and compensate the other businesses.

GRAPHIC 4.14

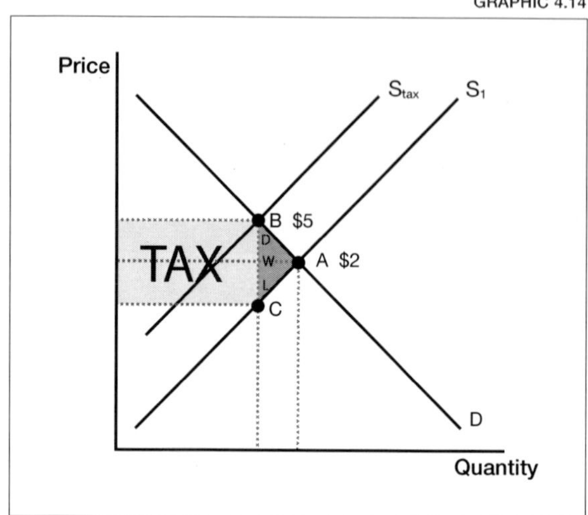

Recall the definitions of *conservative* and *liberal* from Section 4B. While conservatives want a smaller government, less taxation, and more business freedom, modern liberals want a more active government, higher taxes on the wealthy, and strict regulation of business. In graphic 4.15, notice that the liberals are to the left and conservatives are to the right—most Americans' political beliefs rest somewhere between the two. They are called **moderates**.

There are two dominant political parties in the United States. The Democrats comprise primarily liberals, while conservatives tend to vote Republican. The average Democrat wants the government to play an active role in creating more equality and alleviating social problems. Republicans want the government to lower taxes and lighten the regulatory requirements on businesses. In a labor dispute, Democrats normally side with the union, and Republicans side with the business. On taxes, Democrats want higher marginal tax rates on the rich and think that money should be used in social programs and education. Republicans prefer a flat tax and believe that too many social programs can harm people and society. Simply put, one party has favorable view of the government and the other does not.

Economists can be liberal and conservative as well. Some say that the government should step in and help prevent recessions and business malfeasance. Others maintain that governments hurt efficiency and create deadweight loss. Both liberals and conservatives have valid points. It is up to you to decide where you stand.

GRAPHIC 4.15

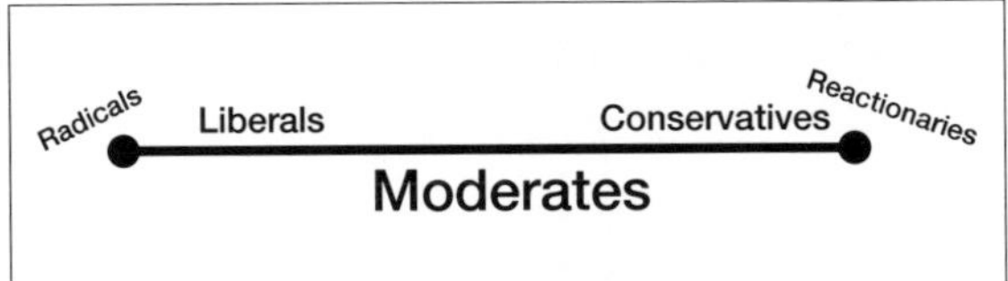

Conservative economic thought views government attempts to control the economy as problematic. Many ideas about free markets and individual freedom originated in the eighteenth and nineteenth centuries with economists like Jean-Baptiste Say and John Stuart Mill. Their theories hold that most government intervention is harmful to a nation's economy. Excessive rules and regulations in combination with high taxation stifle the growth of business. Ultimately slow business activity will cost jobs. The theory is aimed at promoting growth by providing full freedom to producers to produce more. Say is best known for Say's law, which states that "supply creates its own demand." This idea suggests that if firms produce more goods and services, then inflation will be reduced as more goods are created to fill the demand.

Conservative ideals have lived on through the twentieth century to today. Economists like

GRAPHIC 4.16

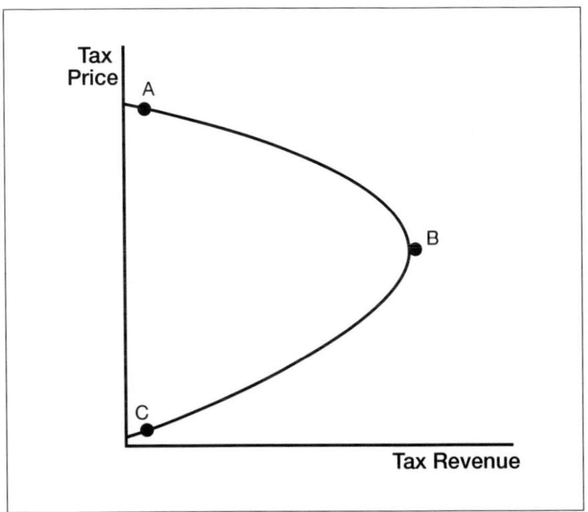

Austrian Friedrich Hayek wrote about how money can affect the fluctuations of the overall economy. Hayek's views influenced other economists at the University of Chicago. Men like Milton Friedman and Arthur Laffer urged governments to lower taxes, promote free markets, and deregulate industries. President Ronald Reagan used Laffer's ideas to convince Congress to lower taxes. The Laffer curve (see graphic 4.16) shows that too much taxation will be a disincentive to work. At point A, the tax rate is very high but the tax revenue is low. The same amount of tax revenue exists at point C. Reagan lowered all the tax brackets to 28 and 15 percent.

GRAPHIC 4.17

John Maynard Keynes (left) believed that governments should intervene and direct the economy. Friedrich Hayek (right) thought that governments disrupted the long-run equilibrium of economic growth.

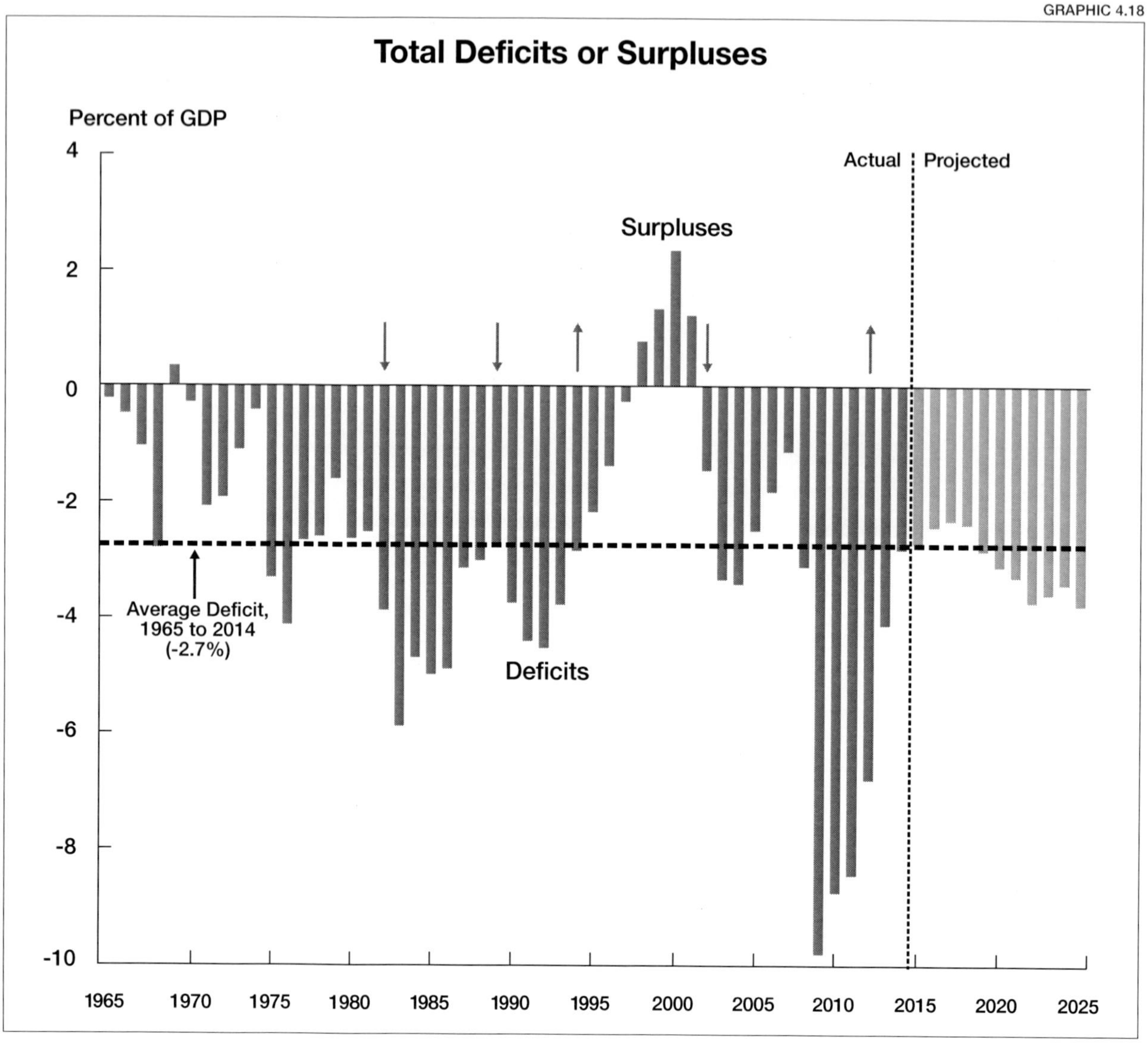

Liberal economists opposed "Reaganomics," as it came to be known. They argued that the tax breaks to businesses and the rich were unnecessary. Because of this opposition, liberals dubbed these policies "trickle-down economics." This fiscal policy approach coincided with the economic growth that followed the stagflation of late 1970s. However, as deficits grew later in his administration, Reagan did agree to some tax hikes.

Liberal economists see the government as a positive tool in controlling the ups and downs of the business cycle. Furthermore, they believe that the government should take measures to relieve poverty and keep corporations from abusing their power over workers. Demand-sided theory originated in the 1930s with the writings of John Maynard Keynes (rhymes with rains). In his book *The General Theory of Employment, Interest, and Money*, Keynes states that the government can stabilize the economy by stimulating aggregate demand with fiscal and monetary policy. This idea contrasted with those of the conservative theorists, who believed that long-run economic growth always stabilized. Keynes quipped that in the long run, "we are all dead." Keynes urged governments to get involved in the present.

Keynes writes that a government can lower taxes and start social programs when the economy is bad. This would boost GDP and make up for the lack of consumer spending and investments. If inflation is threatening, then taxes can be raised and programs shrunk. The new idea was shocking. Keynes wrote that during bad economies, government spending might require incurring a deficit. Keynes hoped that government intervention would eliminate the boom and bust trends of the 1800s and prevent damaging depressions in the future. Today, Keynes's ideas are adopted and proliferated by economists like Paul Krugman. In writing about Japan's long recession of the 1990s, Krugman theorized that fiscal policy should be used to combat severe recessions and unemployment with fiscal spending and targeted tax cuts. Krugman also argues that sometimes economies cannot be helped with monetary policy alone in severe recessions. People will tend to hoard their money (resulting in a "liquidity trap") and aggregate demand will fall. Krugman believes that government spending is the best way to turn an economy around.

Most people hold a combination of all these ideas, and most Americans are moderate. It is important to remember that the two basic points of view have an impact on the people who control fiscal policy. After all, you will pay taxes. Consider graphic 4.18. The arrows point up for major tax increases and down for major tax cuts. While we want lower taxes, we need to lower spending when we cut taxes. Historically, deficits have increased when taxes were lowered.

These ideas seem complex. You should know, however, what your representatives are thinking when they change the law. No matter where you stand, over the last one hundred years the United States has found a good balance of economic freedom, taxation, and government.

Pressing Question

- How does a tax cause a deadweight loss? When does a tax on an externality make sense to some economists?

4I. Fiscal Policy in Action

In 2002, the US economy contracted and entered a recession. In response to this, President George W. Bush and Congress passed a series of tax cuts to stimulate the economy. They followed up with an adjustment to the marginal tax rates. This followed a pattern in which Democrats and Republicans readjusted the tax brackets about every ten years.

The first income tax was collected by the federal government in 1913. Since then, tax rates have gone up and down with different presidential administrations. The first tax brackets started at 1 percent for lower-wage earners and 7 percent for top incomes. During World War II, the highest bracket topped out at 94 percent. It stayed that high until the 1960s, when it was reduced to 70 percent. In the 1980s, top earners had the rate lowered to 50 and then 28 percent. Bill Clinton's tax policy raised the top bracket to 39.6 percent. It was lowered by George W. Bush to 35 percent and raised by Barack Obama ten years later back to the Clinton administration's level of 39.6 percent.

Presidents must get their budgets though Congress (graphic 4.12). By the time the process is over, the finished budget might be vastly different from the one the president proposed. Such is the nature of politics. Between budgets, the executive branch can adjust the spending in certain departments. Other programs cannot be touched.

GRAPHIC 4.19

Nondiscretionary	Discretionary
Social Security	Science
Medicare	Space
Medicaid	Energy
Interest on debt	Natural resources
Income security	National parks
Defense	Agriculture
	Commerce
	Transportation
	Community development
	Education
	Veterans' benefits
	Justice
	Affairs of state

- **Discretionary spending**—These are programs with budgets that the president can adjust according to the politics of the day and needs of the economy. (Refer to graphic 4.19.)
- **Nondiscretionary spending**—Some programs (see graphic 4.19) cannot be changed without an act of Congress. They even expand if the economy goes into recession. These are also known as **automatic stabilizers**. For instance, unemployed people can get insurance from their state. The long-term unemployed can collect food stamps or welfare. The impact of injected money into the economy can stimulate growth and soften the impact of a trough.

Mentioned in the previous section, Keynesian economists like Paul Krugman favor the use of fiscal policy to ameliorate the worst impacts of a recession. To this end, they would favor the use of an **expansionary fiscal policy**. The government can lower taxes and boost spending on programs. In the process, aggregate demand should increase. However, the increased spending with less revenue will prompt borrowing, which will incur a **deficit**. Repeated deficits over time add up to the current federal debt (now measured in tens of trillions of dollars).

It is important that the government not borrow too much of the country's money. If it uses too much of our money supply, then interest rates could be driven higher. Consumers might not buy more durable goods and businesses might not invest. This is called **crowding out**. Running deficits would not contribute to an ever-growing debt if the government raised taxes and lowered spending in good economies. Raising taxes and lowering spending is called **contractionary policy**. When revenue exceeds spending, it is called a **budget surplus**. At that point, the debt can be reduced.

What has more impact on an economy? It depends. Spending programs and transfer payments increase aggregate demand in the short run. Tax cuts can help too, but only if people spend that money. If the United States is heading into a recession, people tend to be scared and pessimistic. If you give them money, they will tend to save it or pay down debt. The percentage of money they save is called **marginal propensity to save** (**MPS**) and the amount that they will spend is called the **marginal propensity to consume** (**MPC**). Government accountants in the Congressional Budget Office estimate these percentages and advise Congress on how impactful a tax cut would be.

Cutting taxes when people will spend that money will have a greater impact when the MPS is low and the MPC is high. For example, if the MPS is 0.10 (10 percent), then the MPC is 0.90 (90 percent). Therefore, if a person gets a $1,000 tax cut, she would spend $900 and save $100. The people who get that $900 of spending will also spend and save, and so on. At the end of the cycle, a $1,000 tax cut ripples across the economy to become $10,000 of spending. This is known as the **multiplier effect**. On a national scale, a $10 billion tax cut will grow the economy by $100 billion—that is, if the MPS is 0.10. But what happens if people save more and the MPS is 0.5? The overall impact of that $10 billion tax cut will fall to $20 billion.

Changing your tax structure can have more impact over the long term. It is hard to predict what will happen five or ten years after a tax cut or hike, but economic growth will be affected for good or for bad. Striking a good balance among taxes, government services, and financial freedom can affect long-term growth.

Pressing Question

- What is the difference between expansionary and contractionary fiscal policy?

4J. Our Government Regulates

The safety devices in your car, the purity of the medicine you take, the speech you get from a flight attendant on a plane, and the accuracy of the labels on food are all examples of the government making rules for business. A **regulation** is a rule or restriction passed by local, state, or federal government that businesses must follow.

Regulations exist at every level of government. Cities tell you where you can park and where you can open a business. Your county issues liquor licenses to bars and your state tells you when alcohol can be sold. The federal government has millions of employees. In order to enforce these laws and to guard against violations, our governments have numerous agencies to watch businesses. Here are just a few of the more prominent regulatory agencies:

- **Food and Drug Administration (FDA)**—Founded in 1906, the FDA, along with the Department of Agriculture, inspects the nation's food supply. This agency is also in charge of approving new drugs and cosmetics for consumers.
- **Federal Trade Commission (FTC)**—Founded in 1914, the FTC works for the promotion of consumer protection and the elimination and prevention of anticompetitive business practices. It watches for violations of US antitrust law.
- **Securities and Exchange Commission (SEC)**—Founded in 1934 in response to the crash of the stock market, the SEC watches for insider trading and fraudulent activity in the bond, stock, and futures markets.
- **Federal Deposit Insurance Corporation (FDIC)**—The FDIC, formed in 1933, insures bank deposits up to $250,000 and supervises banks to make sure they are financially secure.
- **Federal Communications Commission (FCC)**—Founded in 1934, the FCC issues licenses for the use of public airwaves and sets standards for all electronic communications.
- **Environmental Protection Agency (EPA)**—Formed in 1970, the EPA sets environmental standards for industry and oversees inspections of the fitness of the outdoors.
- **Occupational Safety and Health Administration (OSHA)**—Part of the Labor Department and founded in 1970, OSHA inspects workplaces and sets standards for job safety.
- **Consumer Product Safety Commission (CPSC)**—Founded in 1972, the CPSC regulates the safety of consumer products. For instance, when a car has a safety issue, the CPSC will inform the public and might suggest a recall.
- **Consumer Financial Protection Bureau (CFPB)**—Founded in 2011 in response to the 2008 economic meltdown, the CFPB alerts consumers about scams and questionable financial practices.

GRAPHIC 4.20

The CFPB is the newest of the federal regulatory agencies. Founded in 2010 in response to the 2008 financial collapse, it warns consumers about predatory lending practices and scams.

Opponents of regulation say that too many rules and laws cost businesses and hurt productivity. These higher costs might be passed on to consumers. Supporters argue that businesses would abuse consumers, workers, and the environment if it were not for the government acting as the watchdog. Like all issues in economics, regulations have two sides to consider. While a rule or law is intended to do one thing, there will always be an opportunity cost to consider. In the end if the cost of regulation is lower than the potential problems that not regulating would allow, then the regulation makes economic sense.

Pressing Question

- When does it make sense to regulate a business?

GRAPHIC 4.21

K Street in Washington, DC, is home to dozens of lobbies, interest groups, and think tanks. Lobbyists visit Capitol Hill on a regular basis in hopes of influencing votes of members of Congress.

4K. Campaign Finance

A common complaint among most members of Congress is about the time spent fund-raising. It is not uncommon for a member of the House to spend millions, a senator to spend tens of millions, and two final presidential candidates to both spend billions together.

This money comes from individual donors, parties, unions, or lobbies. Historically, rules limited the amount of money that individuals can donate. Supreme Court decisions changed the landscape considerably in 2010.

Currently, there are still limits on what individuals can give candidates and parties. The Federal Election Commission (FEC) is in charge of tracking compliance with existing campaign laws. In *Citizens United v. Federal Election Commission,* the Supreme Court declared that the First Amendment to the constitution prohibits the government from setting limits on how much a nonprofit organization can give to a candidate. Another case in 2014 lifted the limits on contributions to national parties. As it stands, some nonprofits give money to candidates, create television commercials, and stage events while spending hundreds of millions of dollars. Furthermore, they are not required to declare who their donors are.

Many businesses and special interest groups gather their money together into what is known as a political action committee (PAC). In these organizations, resources are pooled, and because there is no limit to the donation size of a PAC, a considerable amount of cash can be channeled to a candidate.

The question remains, How much do one person's contributions influence an election? To keep pressure on our elected representatives, many special interest groups hire lobbyists, or professional advocates, to visit Congress daily and put direct pressure on the members to make decisions and votes that favor their interest. For instance, if there is a pending vote in Congress to decide on requiring American car makers to lower the emissions of their vehicles, several environmental lobbies will dispatch lobbyists to Congress to remind certain representatives of their responsibility to the environment and to their organization. On the other hand, the automakers will also have lobbyists of their own trying to remind them that these stricter regulations will raise the cost of cars and potentially cause job losses in home districts. Usually, there are ten to fifteen thousand registered lobbyists in Washington. Including the unofficial lobbyists, the number might be closer to one hundred thousand.

GRAPHIC 4.22

Former Speaker of the House Tip O'Neill once said, "All politics is local." What he meant was that elected officials always have to answer to the people they represent, their constituents. No matter what is happening in Washington, DC, they always have to go home and get people to vote for them again.

For example, earning local votes can be done through the use of **earmarks**, money appropriated by a legislature for a specific project. These can be part of an original bill or attached at the end as a rider. Allocating money from an act of Congress to the people in a home district is referred to as **pork-barrel spending**. In the past, members of Congress would secure the votes of their colleagues with the promise of sending money back to a home state to fund a pet project. These funds were not specifically authorized or awarded by competitive bid. Rather, the appropriation was made at the very end of the bill.

By circumventing the normal committee process, representatives could secure funds that helped serve their local and special interests. While the practice is often criticized as wasteful, the money for these projects can sway votes and make the legislative process more efficient. A primary concern for the public when it comes to all the new money flooding into elections is whether our representatives answer to the voters back home or to their big-money donors.

Conventional wisdom in the United States says that "you cannot fight city hall." Actually, that is false and unwise. People take on the government all the time and sometimes win. Citizens have an obligation to vote, question their government, and demand accountability. If you feel like the government is wasteful or unfair, then go online and find out who represents you at the local, state, and federal levels. Your representatives will get back to you and many times can offer real help.

Pressing Question

- Should citizens be allowed to give as much money as they want to a political candidate? Why or why not?

Name:

Government Puzzle

Directions: Use your reading to find the answers to the clues on the next page. Then, fit the words into the puzzle below.

Clue Sheet

Across

3. A person who favors faster change and government intervention in the economy
6. A member of the more liberal of our two main political parties
9. Shared governance between local, state, and federal governments
12. The primary federal tax form that we send to the IRS (Hint: spell it out.)
14. The third president and conservative Founder of the United States
15. Income tax that charges a higher percentage of your income as you make more money
16. The _________ effect; amplifies the impact of a tax cut
19. The money left over when you've paid all the bills in a budget
20. A person whom an elected official represents
23. A tax can sometimes push consumers and producers out of a market; creates a _________
25. He said, "The hardest thing in the world to understand is the income tax."
26. Program providing medical care for the elderly
28. The amount of money you are lacking to meet your budget
29. The more conservative of our two main political parties

Down

1. A rule or guideline that businesses must follow
2. An Austrian economist who advocated less government economic control
4. Tax money collected by the government; _________
5. A person who roams the halls of Congress trying to influence votes
7. Political action _________
8. A British economist who advocated government intervention during recessions
10. The FICA payroll tax pays for this program
11. An old form of social control in which lords let peasants work the land
13. A tax on alcohol or gasoline
15. __________ goods; cannot be denied to anyone
17. Governments form _________ policy; budgets revenue and spending
18. A person who favors the status quo and slower change
21. A person in the political middle
22. ___________ tax; levied on your house
24. A required payment to the state
27. Crowding_________

Name:

Getting the Facts Straight

Directions: Using the website www.usdebtclock.org or another Internet source, fill in the tables below.

Statistic	1800	1900	2000	Today
US population				
US GDP				
US GDP per capita				
Federal budget				
Number of states				

Statistic	1980	1990	2000	Today
Number of state/local employees				
Social Security spending				
Medicare spending				
Defense spending				

1. List five conclusions or concerns you have about the data in these two tables.
   a.
   b.
   c.
   d.
   e.
2. Why have some of these programs become more expensive in the past few past decades?

3. What national fiscal challenges might face young people as they get older?

Name:

Government Basics

Part 1

Directions: Using your reading, fill in the blanks in the paragraph below.

Thomas ______________ (1) was opposed to a strong federal government. He is considered the ______________ (2) forefather of American politics. Alexander ______________ (3) wanted a strong central government, and he led an early political party called the ______________ (4). Early on, the US government had trouble collecting money, or tax ______________ (5). A government that wants to promote free markets needs to have a consistent rule of ______________ (6). It should protect our freedom to ______________ (7), promote ______________ (8), and defend our right to own private ______________ (9). Key among a government's powers is the right to levy ______________ (10) and to enforce legal agreements called ______________ (11). The process of taxing citizens and spending that money is called ______________ (12) policy.

Part 2

Directions: Place the words in Box 1 on the political spectrum below:

Box 1
Conservative
Liberal
Reactionary
Moderate
Radical

Box 2
House Ways and Means
Senate Budget
Full floor vote
White House
Joint Conference
Veto
Budget bill

Part 3

Directions: Using the words in Box 2, describe how a budget is approved in complete sentences.

Name:

Tax Basics

Part 1

Directions: In class or on your own, answer the following two questions on tables below by placing a check mark in the correct boxes.

Who collects these taxes?

	Federal	State	Local
Income			
Excise			
Property			
Sales			
Estate			
Import (customs duties)			
Social Security			
Medicare			

Who provides these services?

	Federal	State	Local
National defense			
Recreational football league			
Highways			
Traffic lights			
Education funding			
Local high school			
Food stamps			
Airports			
Car safety standards			
Colleges			
Law enforcement			
Garbage collection			

Part 2

Bonus research: In Article I, Section 7 of the US Constitution, what economic powers does Congress have?

Interpreting Your Pay Stub

Directions: Study the pay stub below; then answer the questions. If you have trouble finding a definition in the reading, use the Internet.

A Typical Pay Stub			
Employee Name Josephine Febeetz	***Social Security Number*** 000-00-0000	***Pay Period*** 04/10/16—04/24/16	***Date*** 04/30/16
Company Name Initech, LLC	***Exemptions*** 2	***Status*** Single	***Adjustments*** None

Earnings			***Taxes***			***Deductions***		
	This Pay	Year To Date		This Pay	Year To Date		This Pay	Year To Date
Salary	1,119.00	9,878.00	Federal	122.40	966.72	401(k)	100.00	800.00
Overtime	158.00	442.00	State	33.12	259.87	Medical	52.00	416.00
Bonus	57.00	695.00	City	44.33	178.17	Flex Pay	50.00	400.00
			Social Sec	69.77	555.33	Charity	10.00	
			Medicare	19.98	124.54			
Total	**1,334.00**	**11,015.00**	**Total**	**288.60**	**2,084.63**	**Total**	212.00	1,616.00
-Taxes	288.60							
-Deductions	212.00							
Net Pay	893.40							

1. Define:
   a. Salary:

   b. Deductions:

   c. Social Security:

   d. Medicare:

   e. 401(k):

   f. Flexible spending account:

   g. Pre-tax deduction:

2. What behaviors is the government encouraging by allowing pre-tax deductions?

3. Who collects taxes on behalf of the federal government? What department is that agency in?

4. What three governments collect income tax in Josephine's location?

Name:

Filing Taxes

Directions: Go online to www.irs.gov, and look up a 1040 form for last year. There are two pages to this form. Complete each of the exercises below. If you are confused by any of the terms, search the Internet or ask an adult.

1. Define the terms below:
   a. Filing status:
   b. Exemptions:
   c. Income:
   d. Adjusted gross income:
   e. Taxes and credits:
   f. Other taxes:
   g. Payments:
   h. Refund:

2. From graphic 4.10, list from largest to smallest:
   a. Federal government revenue sources:
   b. Federal expenditures:

3. What forms will you need in order to fill in your 1040?

4. Complete the table below.

Ways to File Your Taxes		
	How Does It Work?	**How Much Does It Cost?**
Print and mail		
IRS.gov Free File		
H&R Block		
TurboTax		
Professional accountant		

Name:

Fiscal Policy Closer to Home

Directions: Using the Internet, go the website for your city, county, and state. Try to find the information to fill in the tables below.

Your City	
Executive's name:	Five biggest expenses the city had to pay:
City council is called:	
Primary sources of revenue:	

Your Country	
Executive:	Five biggest expenses the county had to pay:
Your county legislature is called:	
Primary sources of revenue:	

Your State	
Governor's name:	Five biggest expenses the state had to pay:
State legislature:	
Primary sources of revenue:	

 Name:

Graph a Tax

Part 1

Directions: The government wants to keep people from smoking cigarettes. To make this happen, it imposes a tax of $5-per-pack tax on packs that now cost $2. Follow the numbered instructions below and see what the graph shows you.

Supply Curve 1 (S_1)	Supply Curve 2 (S_{tax})
Quantity—30 million	Quantity—22 million
Price—$2	Price—$5

- Label the initial equilibrium point A and the equilibrium price (on the price axis) as $2.

1. If there is a tax, which curve will move?

2. Which way will that curve move?

- Draw in a new curve parallel to the old one. Label it S_{tax}.

3. What happened to price and quantity at the new equilibrium point?

- Draw a vertical line down from the new equilibrium point to the x-axis.
- Draw a horizontal line across from the new equilibrium point to the y-axis.
- Notice where that vertical line down from the new equilibrium point crosses the S_t curve. Mark it with a dot labeled C.
- Shade in the area that you think represents the tax and label it "tax."
- Shade in the area you think is the deadweight loss and label it "DWL."

Part 2

1. Why is there less quantity supplied in this market?

2. What is the tax revenue?

3. Why is there less quantity demanded?

4. Who gets the deadweight loss area?

5. Why are cigarettes a logical thing to tax?

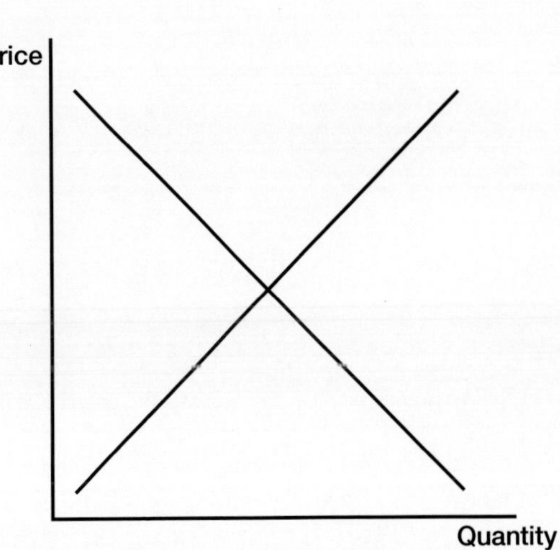

Name:

Keynes versus Hayek

Directions: Place the terms and phrases below under the appropriate economist in the table below. Use the Internet to search for unfamiliar concepts. Place a checkmark next to those statements that most closely match your opinions. Then answer the question at the bottom.

- long-term focus
- liberal
- respect for entrepreneurship
- Government acts in best interests of the public.
- Value of saving is disorted by monetary policy.
- Government causes mal-investment.
- Economy will settle at a long-run equilibrium without help.
- some bailouts
- no bailouts
- Markets can be steered.
- Markets are unpredictable.
- Savings get hoarded in recessions.
- conservative
- People are rational.
- short-term focus
- respect for human suffering and job protection
- People act in their "animal spirits."
- Bad businesses should be liquidated.
- Some bad businesses can be saved.
- Regulations are good.
- Regulations are bad.
- Democrats
- Republicans

Keynes	Hayek

Would you be a liberal economist or a conservative economist? Explain.

Name:

Political Party Platforms

Directions: With the help of an adult, or by looking up the websites of the Democrats and the Republicans, briefly describe the stances of the two main parties of the United States in the boxes provided. Place a checkmark next to those statements that most closely match your opinions. Then answer the question at the bottom.

Democrats	Issue	Republicans
	Taxes	
	Business Regulations	
	Environmental Issues	
	Unions	
	Minimum Wage	
	Social Security	
	Medicare	
	Immigration	
	Gun Conrol	
	Free Trade	
	State or Federal Government	
	Hayek or Keynes	
	Hamilton or Jefferson	

Do you think you are a Republican or a Democrat? Why?

Unit 5
Personal Finance

Questions to Consider

1. How much money does it take to retire comfortably?
2. What is the difference between an asset and an expense?
3. Where are some places to save money?
4. How does a loan work?
5. What is insurance for?
6. How much does the average house cost?
7. How much do cars cost?
8. What is credit?
9. Why are some investments riskier than others?
10. Why is stock in some companies more valuable than others?

Terms You Need in Order to Read

Asset
Bond
Expense
Interest
Investment
Market
Stock
Yield

Name:

Personal Finance

5A. Respect Your Money

Are you good with your money? If you have a job, does it seem your bank account grows month after month? If you answered yes to either of those questions, then you have some personal inclinations that can really help you out in life. For many young people, savings disappear quickly or never exist at all. Some adults live their lives in a constant financial crisis. They spend money faster than they make it, make impulsive decisions with their money, and save nothing for their future. There is no magic bullet to help you build wealth, retire comfortably, and avoid financial problems. Anyone with the ability to do fourth-grade math, however, can master their money. You have choices. You can learn to take control of your finances.

The title of this section is "Respect Your Money." There is no mystery here. Money is hard to make, and too often we spend our money without enough thought. One recurring statement that should never leave your mind is, "take time to think." Grocery stores put candy right next to the checkout, because people will **impulse buy**, or purchase something without much thought.

Buying a car can be a dizzying experience, especially when it comes to negotiating a price. Dealers know that two out of three people will buy a car once they go into a showroom. They know you want that car, and you know you want that car. If you *take time to think* and go home before buying anything, then chances are that the dealer will call you up to offer a better deal. Wanting something like a new car can lead us to making rash decisions.

In Unit 1, you learned the difference between a want and a need. Impulsive purchases are usually made to buy a want. Nobody needs a candy bar, but there it is. You tell yourself you deserve it so you make a snap decision. You told yourself on the way to the dealership that you were looking for a monthly payment around a certain amount, but the dealer up-sells you on the navigation and Internet system for only an extra $50 per month. If you take time to think, then you could go home and sleep on it. Simple math dictates that $50 per month equals $600 per year. The trouble is many people do not think and take time to distinguish a want from a need. If you want to control your finances, then you will need to control your impulses and be honest about your motivations.

Buying something new can be fun. Shopping is the number-one leisure activity in America. Overspending, however, can get people into financial trouble very quickly. Like a drug, the act of purchasing and consuming goods can be intoxicating. In fact, shopping can activate the same part of the brain as substance abuse. We feel the need for something, and we feel satisfied immediately afterward. Try to remember the last time you made a big purchase. Recall how you felt when you got home. What happened to that feeling? Why did the purchase not make you feel great forever? Buying new things will make you feel good for a little while, but that feeling will always go away. In the end, you are left with only yourself. If you are not happy, no purchase will ever help fix that.

If you are about to purchase a want, step back and consider what you are doing. If you have to borrow money to buy it, then perhaps you should consider **delaying gratification**, or putting off the rush of ownership until a later date. If you take time to think, you can weigh the cost and benefit of that purchase. Consider the utility (satisfaction) that the spending will bring you. Compare that feeling to the price. Ask yourself, "How long did it take me to earn that much money?" This process can bring you back to your senses. Realizing that the thrill of the purchase will quickly fade and that you need to work many hours to afford that item, you might change your mind. This thought process is called a cost-benefit analysis (recall the term from Unit 1).

GRAPHIC 5.1

Recall Jill from Unit 2. She trained as a chef at a local community college while working in a restaurant. After years of reliable service, showing up on time, and learning from her bosses, she opened her own restaurant.

By spending a lot of time on the Internet and watching TV, Americans have the misconception that getting rich is easy. The reality is that only 25 percent of workers make more than $85,000 per year. Only 2 percent make more than $200,000. The rest of the country earns an income around $55,000. It sounds like a good amount of money. You will have to work hard to earn that money when you have a job. Until then, you're going to have to work hard to qualify for a job like that. People who work, shop smart, and save have learned to respect their money.

Pressing Question

- List and describe the worst consumer product you ever bought.

5B. Career Goals

The work that we do, as much as anything else, defines and molds who we are. A **career** is a job that requires specialized training and education, and it typically becomes one's life's work. Too many young people take early job decisions lightly and think that they have plenty of time to find the right path. Before they know it, they have been doing a job for five or ten years and come to the conclusion that they do not like what they do.

Ask yourself some questions (really pause and think for a minute):

- What are my passions?
- What do I value the most? Possessions and comfort? Happiness and fulfillment?
- Where did I experience the greatest success in school?
- Where do I see myself in five years? Ten years? Twenty years?

Careful consideration of these questions can help you establish some goals. Try to imagine yourself working in a job that you find fulfilling and rewarding. Choose to study what you love if you go to college. If you only have a high school diploma going into adulthood, then consider learning a trade. Either way, you may not earn a large salary, but there is a better chance you will be happy if you enjoy your job. As you will learn in a later section, there are ways to build wealth with a modest income.

GRAPHIC 5.2

A worker with a trade needs specialized training and sometimes does dangerous work; because of those factors, he may earn a high salary.

Here are some options for young people ready to hit the "real world":

- Get a job right out of high school. Live at home or move out of the family house.
- Start a business.
- Get a two-year associate degree.
- Get a four-year bachelor degree.
- Undertake postgraduate study.

People with more education make more money per year and over a career. Consider graphic 5.3. Notice that these decisions will have consequences. The yearly salaries are different. Think about how much difference a worker's lifetime earnings will be. Over a forty- or fifty-year work life, a person might pay an opportunity cost of millions of dollars for not finishing school. Also, note the vast difference in unemployment rates. It is simple. People with more education get paid more and have easier times finding work.

You need to consider the benefit of each decision versus the cost. For instance, heading out into the world and getting a job right after high school is one option. You will have to weigh the pros and cons of that decision. In the past, it was possible for someone with only a high school education to advance to the upper levels of a corporation. However, in today's job market, businesses are usually unwilling to promote beyond a certain level if an employee has no college degree. While many high school graduates can secure work for a while, they will often have to go back to school to attain a degree or advanced skill.

It is never too soon to start thinking seriously about a career. Ask yourself what class you enjoy the most. It may be the class that you find the easiest, or it could be a subject that you enjoy. If you do not enjoy any of your classes, perhaps there is an extracurricular activity or hobby about which you are passionate. If you are interested in anything, there is probably a career that will suit your interests. Again, choose work that you enjoy. There are few things more depressing than being stuck in a job you find unfulfilling.

If you have trouble choosing a job or career, talk to a counselor or family member. They can be a source of reliable advice. If you are determined, then you can accomplish your goals. First, set some short-term goals. These are things you have to accomplish in the next few months. Write those goals down and put them somewhere you can see them every day. Also write out your long-term goals—for instance, owning your own business or working as an accountant. These goals can take years to accomplish. Focusing on them alone can

GRAPHIC 5.3

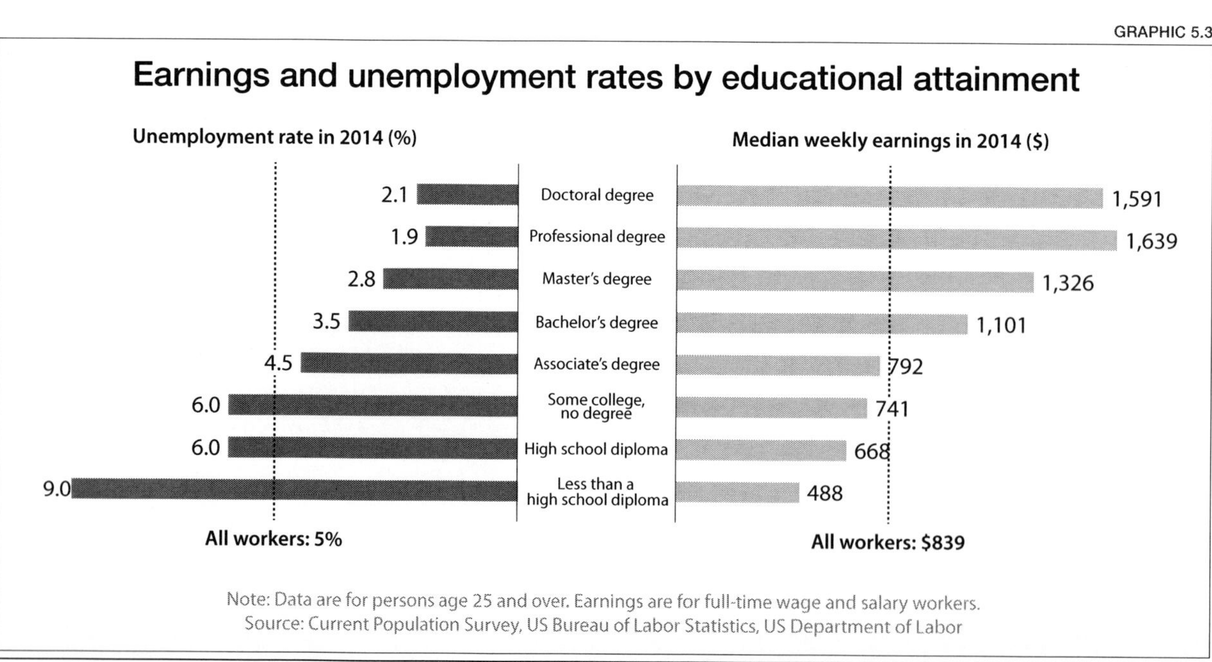

GRAPHIC 5.4

FASTEST-GROWING JOBS, 2012–2022		FASTEST-DISAPPEARING JOBS, 2012–2022	
JOB	GAIN	JOB	GAIN
Industrial-organizational psychologist	53	Fallers	-43.3
Personal care aids	49	Locomotive firers	-42
Home health aides	48	Shoe machine operator and tenders	-35.3
Insulation workers, mechanical	47	Postal service mail sorters and processors	-31.8
Interpreters and translators	46	Log graders and scalers	-31.6
Diagnostic medical sonographers	46	Postal service clerks	-29.8
Occupational therapy assistants	43	Semiconductor processors	-27.1
Genetic counselors	41	Textile cutting machine setters	-27.1
Skincare specialists	40	Postal service mail carriers	-26.8
Physician assistants	38	Motion picture projectionists	-26.5
Helpers-electricians	37	Sewing machine operator	-25.8
Information security analysts	36	Word processors and typists	-25.1
Occupational therapy aides	36	Fabric and apparel patternmakers	-25
Physical therapist	35	Data entry keyers	-24.6
Brick masons	35	Textile knitting and weaving	-24.5
Orthotists	35	Postmasters and mail	-24.2
Nursing instructors	35	Superintendents	-24
Nurse practitioners	33	Textile bleachers	-23.4
Audiologists	33	Animal breeders	-22.5
Dental hygienists	33	Drilling and boring machine operators	-20.5
Convention planner	33	Farmers, ranchers	-19.3
Market research analyst	31	Meter readers, utilities	-19.2
Ambulance driver	31	Pourers and casters, metal	-18.7
Family therapist	31	Computer operators	-17

be daunting, so start with the smaller goals first. Last, you will need a **work ethic**. This is your ability to work when you really do not want to. If you want to reach goals, then you need to make a plan and get to work. Successful people work hard to achieve that success. Talk is cheap, but accomplishments are priceless.

Pressing Question

- What is your dream job?

5C. Labor Force Issues

Another factor that makes education beyond high school vital to your work is the changing nature of careers today. **Job security**, or the length of time that a worker can expect to have a specific job, does not exist as it did in past decades. If you listen to the news, **downsizing**, or the elimination of jobs, sounds like a common occurrence (even for companies that are doing well). Often, the largest expense businesses have is their labor. When they have to trim their budgets, they lay off workers. Where a high school graduate in the 1950s could find a lifetime job, buy a house, and raise a family, workers today rarely plan to work their entire lives for one company. In fact, the average worker today will spend less than 4.5 years at the same job. Younger people spend even less time at each job.

For your generation, the Internet and global competition are changing the labor force in the United States. If you have a job that can be done by a computer program, it will disappear. Furthermore, if it can be done more cheaply by someone in another country, then it will probably move outside the United States. The twenty-first-century worker needs to be flexible and pick up new skills quickly. You need to be willing to change paths for the rest of your life; your job may depend on it.

There are several factors that can affect a worker's **wage** (paid by the hour) or **salary** (paid as an annual sum divided into equal monthly or bimonthly payments). First, skill level and labor specialization often determine the demand for one's labor. If someone goes to college and attains a specialized skill, that person will be in high demand and can thus expect a high salary. For example, a specialist in medicine (neurology or cardiology) will tend to make more than a general practitioner (the doctor you go see on a regular basis). Second, if the economy is doing poorly, many firms may lay off workers. Across the entire economy, this can slow the increase of average wages and would mean that the demand for labor will decrease. Third, a worker who is seen by a firm to be a valuable member of the organization more likely will stay employed as opposed to someone who is seen as of marginal value. Good employees should show up on time, work hard, solve their own problems, and get along well with their team.

Other factors can determine salaries, wages, and job security:

- Labor market demand
- Education level
- Skill level
- Work ethic
- Dependability
- Intelligence
- Reputation
- Track record

GRAPHIC 5.5

If you have trouble choosing a career path, go to BLS.gov. There, you can find the Occupational Outlook Handbook, which gives accurate research about thousands of different jobs.

For the foreseeable future, it appears that there are some jobs and careers that will be in higher demand than others. Labor demand is not an ideal way to choose a career, but if your passions lie somewhere in health care or geriatric (elderly) services, there will be plenty of jobs out there for you.

Workers in your generation need to be adaptable, willing to learn new skills, and creative. Creative people are difficult to replace, and employers want employees who can solve their own problems. Let us examine a job like photography. In years past, photographers could work for a large newspaper or magazine and earn a steady paycheck. They would get daily assignments, go to a photo shoot, and then deliver the undeveloped film to their boss. Today, a photographer uses a digital camera, edits the pictures with a computer on site, then delivers the finished product over the Internet. When a new technology appears, photographers learn how to do use new software and hardware. If they do not, they might lose their jobs.

As mentioned in Unit 2, more than one-third of the labor force does freelance work. Gone are the days of the steady job, steady paycheck, and retirement parties. Today, workers depend on relationships and per-job income. Websites like LinkedIn assist people today with finding jobs and communicating. **Networking** is interacting with other people to exchange information, develop contacts, and further one's career. The Internet also centralizes the search for a new job. Sites like Monster, Indeed, and CareerBuilder allow people to post their resumes and apply for jobs online.

Losing a job can be terrifying. Having a college degree, specialized training, and strong references will give you options and an easier time finding a new job. Your connections and networks can give you an edge during the interview process. If you do get an interview, then remember to be on time, dress appropriately, and make sure you know about the company. After the interview, be sure to send a thank you note to your potential new boss.

Pressing Question

- What skills do you have now that could be useful to an employer?

5D. Getting a Paycheck

You can learn a lot by looking at an earnings statement (graphic 5.6). The pay stub is an inactive check that signifies that a direct deposit was made to your bank account. Rarely does an employer give you a live check that needs to be hand delivered to the bank or ATM (automatic teller machine). Instead, most workers have their pay moved to a checking account via **direct deposit.** This is a safe and secure electronic delivery system by which money is moved from bank to bank. However, your boss may still give you a pay stub to verify that the funds transfer took place.

If you have ever received a paycheck, you will undoubtedly recall the disappointment of seeing the actual amount of money that went home with you. You spent the first few weeks of your job doing the multiplication of your expected hours and wage. Like it or not, as an American citizen, you have responsibilities that go beyond your own personal finance. The first is taxes. Taxes removed from everybody's pay are Medicare, Social Security, and withholding tax. Many young people expect to get most of their taxes back when they file their return, but this is not the case. Only if the government withheld too much money from your pay in the previous year will you get a refund.

Along with tax obligations, most workers decide to withdraw money from their paychecks to make contributions for other needs. Because the government wants to make it easier for us to pay for these things, the expense is subtracted from our gross pay *prior* to paying any withholding tax or payroll tax. We call them **pre-tax deductions**. Some of these are retirement savings, medical insurance premiums, and flexible savings accounts. Remember that the government uses these deductions as a way to encourage people to save for themselves and become less dependent on government benefits.

GRAPHIC 5.6

DEFENSE FINANCE AND ACCOUNTING SERVICE MILITARY LEAVE AND EARNINGS STATEMENT

ID	NAME (Last. First, MI)	SOC.SEC.NO.	GRADE	PAY DATE	YRS SVC	ETS	BRANCH	ADSN/DSSN	PERIOD COVERED

	ENTITLEMENTS		ENTITLEMENTS		ALLOTMENTS		SUMMARY	
	Type	Amount	Type	Amount	Type	Amount	+Amt Fwd	.00
A	BASE PAY	2247.30	FEDERAL TAXES	88.46	DISCRETIONARY ALT	1521.00	+Toc Ent	4266.73
B	BASE PAY	2247.30	FICA-SOC SECURITY	139.33	TRICARE DENTAL	11.58	-Tot Ded	1570.22
C	BASE PAY	2247.30	FICA-MEDICARE	32.59			-TCT Allt	1532.58
D				27.00			=Net Amt	1163.93
E			AFRH	.50			-Cr Fwd	.00
F			FAMILY SGLI	5.50			=EOM Pay	1163.93
G			TSP	112.37				
H			MID-MONTH-PAY	1164.47				
I								
J								
K								
L								
M								
N							DIEMS	RETPLAN
O							040211	CHOICE
	TOTAL	4266.70		1570.22		1532.58		

LEAVE	BF Bal	Ernd	USed	Cr Bal	ETS Bal	Lv Lost	LV PAid	Use/Lose
	25.5	25.0	11	39.5	85.5	.0	.0	.0

FED TAXES	Wage Perid	Wage YTD	M/S	Ex	Add'l Tax	Tax YTD
	2134.93	12682.36	M	02	.00	493.01

FICA TAXES	Wage Period	Soc Wage YTD	Soc Tax YTD	Med Wage YTD	Med Tax YTD
	2247.30	14402.50	892.94	14402.50	108.83

STATE TAXES	ST	Wage Period	Wage YTD	M/S	Ex	Tax YTD
	AK	.00	.00	N	00	.00

PAY DATA	BAQ Type	BAQ Depn	VHA Zip	Rent Amt	Share	Stat	JFTR	Depns	2D JFTR	BAS Type	Charity YTD	TPC	PACIDN
	W/DEP	SPOUSE	08641	.00	1	R		0			.00		

THRIFT SAVINGS PLAN (TSP)	Base Pay Rate	Base Pay Current	Spec Pay Rate	Spec Pay Current	Inc Pay Current	Inc Pay Current	Bonus Pay Rate	Bonus Pay Current
	5	.00	0	.00	0	.00	0	.00
	TSP YTD Deductions		Deferred		Exepmt			
	720.14		720.14		.00			

GRAPHIC 5.7

Pre-Tax Deductions	Post-Tax Deductions
Medical insurance premiums	Some retirement contributions (Roth IRA)
Flexible spending account contributions	Some charitable contributions
Some retirement contributions (401K)	Child support or alimony
Some life insurance premiums	

Be sure to review your pay stub. Make sure all the deductions are correct. Talk to your company's human resources department for further guidance. Refer to graphic 5.7 to see which deductions happen before and which deductions happen after taxes.

As mentioned before, about 34 percent of workers do not work directly for a business. Freelancers get paid by the job. In addition, no taxes are deducted from their payments for Social Security and Medicare, and there are no employer contributions to these taxes—as self-employed "businesses," freelancers must pay these taxes for themselves in full. At the end of the year they get a 1099 tax form to document how much money they made from a particular company. When it comes time to file taxes with the IRS, these workers must pay a self-employment tax and their payroll taxes.

Pressing Question

- What is the difference between a salaried or wage worker and a freelancer?

5E. Budget Your Money

Having a job and getting paid is rewarding. Living at home, you are usually allowed to spend most of the money on your wants, because most of your needs are provided. It is time to consider what will happen when you have to pay for everything yourself.

A budget is an estimate of your income and expenses over a period of time. When you get out on your own, make wise decisions about what you can afford. If you choose an expensive apartment, then you will lose the opportunity to use that money somewhere else. Be sensible. Take time to think about major decisions. Do not spend impulsively. For example, after you get a job try to find an apartment close by. That way, you can walk to work and save all that money on gas and car payments. If you do need a car to get to work, choosing a used car from a reputable dealer instead of a new flashy model will save you thousands of dollars. If you are disciplined, then you make wise choices and economically sound decisions. If you are single, then you can also chop all of your expenses in half by getting a roommate.

GRAPHIC 5.8

Words to Live By:
Take Time to Think
and
Respect Your Money!

Moving out on your own can be intimidating. Be sure to ask your family plenty of questions about what to expect. In the first month, create a spreadsheet that lists all of your expenses. Research their prices in your town and then estimate what you think they should cost every month. You should pick a day every month to sit down and pay your bills. Review them all and figure out which ones exceeded your estimates. Some of your expenses will be fixed costs. Others are variable costs and will change from month to month. Here are some line items for your spreadsheet:

- **Housing**—This should cost somewhere between 25 and 35 percent of your gross monthly salary. You can rent an apartment or house. Buying a house comes later in life for most people.

GRAPHIC 5.9

There is nothing exciting or glamorous about doing a monthly budget. It takes discipline and self-control. It is rewarding to have control of your finances though.

- **Automobile**—Americans love having constant access to personal transportation. Too often, people overextend themselves when buying a car. Be sure to calculate the entire cost of driving. Gas, insurance, and maintenance should be part of this category, not just the car payment.
- **Student loan**—This is the fastest-growing category of consumer debt in the United States. Some young people enter the job market more than $100,000 in debt. The monstrous payment becomes harder to justify when you are thirty-five or forty-five. Choose an affordable school.

GRAPHIC 5.10

Budgeting Tips

- Create a budget as either a written or electronic document.
- Check your budget every few months.
- Consider additions to your budget very carefully.
- Shop for the best phone plans, insurance, loans, and subscriptions.
- Watch for cost creep (some companies raise prices with little or no warning).

- **Food**—Food will account for about ten percent of your income. Be careful—carry-out food can be expensive. A $4 per day coffee habit can add up to more than $1,000 per year. Do the math ($4 × 5 days per week × 52 weeks = $1,040). A coffee grinder, a home brewer, and some gourmet beans give you the same result at about one quarter the cost.
- **Utilities**—Heating your home or apartment and keeping the lights on takes a monthly outlay. Add to these your phone bill, Internet access, and cable bill. While many in your generation do not have a land line, you may pay extra for Internet access. On the bright side, you can get rid of cable and stay entertained on the web.
- **Savings**—There are many different schools of thought on saving. One universal theme across all personal finance programs is that you must save. Saving 10 percent of your gross income is a good rule of thumb. If you start saving when you are in your twenties, then you will build considerable wealth.

GRAPHIC 5.11

A Sample Household Budget

Item	Estimate	JAN	FEB	MAR
Savings	200	200	200	200
Rent	650	650	650	650
Car payment	275	275	275	275
Car Insurance	175	175	175	175
Electric	70	62.95	59.76	77.88
Gas	100	145	105	88
Phone	75	75	75	75

As you pay your bills, enter the amounts onto your spreadsheet (see graphic 5.11). The bills should run down the left side of the sheet, and each month of the year should have its own column. Enter the amount for each month and highlight any overage. Try to figure out why the extra spending happened and fix any problems. Last, did you notice which item comes first in this household budget? The same rule applies to you. Saving is essential to your financial health. You will learn more about that in later reading.

Pressing Question

- Of all the expenses in graphic 5.11, which ones are fixed and which ones are variable?

5F. Managing Your Cash Flow

It is important that you keep track of where your money is going. The easiest way to do that is through a checking account. These accounts are extremely liquid. Checks have been around for centuries. They are widely accepted in a variety of transactions but are used less and less frequently. Technology now is allowing us to access our money in a variety of ways.

An account can be opened by visiting a local bank and making a minimum deposit. Choose a bank that is close to home and convenient for you. Once the account is activated, go home and register with your bank's website. You will then be able set up your automatic bill pay. You can give your account numbers to your employer and enroll in direct deposit.

Most accounts will come with an ATM card or debit card. Debit cards are convenient as they allow you to make purchases at the point of sale with money directly from your bank account. When you use one, remember to make sure you have money in the bank so you do not overdraw on your account. Many debit cards also carry a MasterCard or Visa logo so they can be used without typing in your account's passcode. Finally, your bank may give you some free paper checks to start using your account.

GRAPHIC 5.12

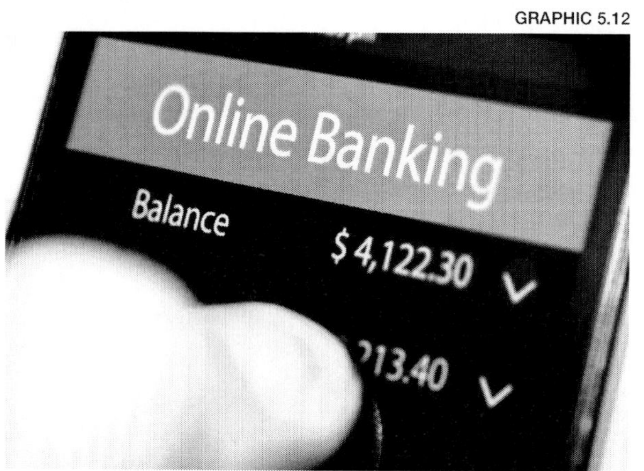

Online banking is a convenient way to manage your money. This bill paying section of a bank account allows you to enter the names and account numbers of different companies you do business with. With one or two clicks, you can send money to pay that bill. Sometimes, you can actually view the bill on your bank's site.

When you write a check to someone, that person takes the check to the bank (or sends it electronically) for deposit into his or her own account. The check will travel to the local Federal Reserve branch or other agency to be *cleared*—that is, to verify that your account has the proper funds. If you do, money will be transferred electronically between the two banks in question and the *canceled* check (or a digital equivalent) will be sent to your bank. At the end of the month, your bank will send you a summary of debits to your account, check by check. If you did not have sufficient funds in your account, the check will be sent back to the recipient's bank. This is known as **bouncing a check**. This will end up costing the writer between $25 and $75 in penalty fees.

Consider graphic 5.13. All checks will have the name of the issuer (bank or other financial institution) and usually the name of the account holder. Along the bottom, the numerical code represents the bank and the account number. When writing a check, one should include the date, name of the recipient, the amount in numbers, the amount spelled out in words, and the account holder's signature on the lower right-hand line. Checkbooks come with a convenient registry in the back in which the account holder can keep track of all the checks she writes by number, date, and description, as well as the current account balance.

When balancing a checking account, cleared checks are compared to the entries in the registry. An account holder can log into an account and compare the paid checks to the unpaid. A **debit** is registered any time money is taken from an account. Debits may be checks, cash withdrawals, paid bills, or fees. A **credit** is any deposit or addition made to an account. Credits may be deposits at banks and bank machines, electronic fund transfers, and direct deposits.

GRAPHIC 5.13

Joe Fundamentals
123 My Street
Anytown, CA 12345

5284

DATE

PAY TO THE ORDER OF $

DOLLARS

Anytown Bank
234 Main Street
Los Angeles, CA 01234

FOR

⑆2222222⑆ 123 111 555⑈ 5284

Unpaid checks and debit card purchases can cause problems. In order to avoid overdrawing the account, you can use the check register to keep a running balance of how much money is left in your account, or you can go online to keep track of the balance. At the end of the month, it is wise to make sure that checks written have cleared. This will help you determine if any check is still outstanding so you will keep that amount available for when it clears. (Most checks, however, clear immediately or at most within a couple days.)

Not too long ago, the primary way to pay a bill was to receive it in the mail, write a paper check, and mail that back to the company. Today, mobile banking allows us to manage our money from anywhere in the world. You have many options for how to pay bills. Just remember to pay them on time.

GRAPHIC 5.14

While banks used to keep huge amounts of cash deposits as their primary reserves, doors like this one in the Cleveland Federal Reserve bank were necessary. Remember that most of our savings are now kept electronically.

Pressing Question

- How does one end up bouncing a check?

5G. Saving Money in the Short Term

People save money for several reasons. They may hope to buy a car or a house, for which they need a down payment. They might save for a child's college education or for their own retirement. Some strategies are short-term, while others last for decades. Saving money wisely can bring a certain amount of financial freedom and security.

Remember from Unit 3 how banks make a profit. They make money by taking your deposits, paying you a modest interest rate, and then lending the money to other people at a higher interest rate. Because a savings account can be easily liquidated, it rarely will pay a high **yield** (or return on your money), but the more time you allow the bank to use the money, the higher the interest rate the bank will offer, through programs such as high-balance accounts or CDs (discussed later). While one should not use a bank for a long-term investment plan, these are a variety of options fora shorter-term investment. Most people, however, use banks mainly to keep their money safe and to make the withdrawals and deposits involved in day-to-day life.

The worst thing to do is to leave the money in a place where it earns nothing. Because of inflation, cash will lose value every year. Money kept at home loses value and is in danger of getting stolen or damaged. Banks offer interest and peace of mind. Remember from Unit 3 that the FDIC insures your bank deposits up to $250,000.

There are many different saving products offered by banks. Some accounts offer higher interest rates depending upon how soon the money is needed. Here are some of your choices:

- **Checking accounts**—These are convenient because a depositor is allowed to draw checks on the balance at any time. Often, no interest is paid.
- **Savings accounts**—This is a basic bank account. A low interest rate is offered because the money is still very liquid. Often the minimum deposit is higher than that of a checking account.
- **Money market accounts**—These are accounts that usually require a large balance, but the interest rates are tied to other market rates. They are relatively liquid and withdrawals can often be made without penalty.
- **Time deposits**—The most common form of this type of account is called a **CD** (or **certificate of deposit**). If you promise a bank that you will not withdraw the money before a set date, the bank will give you a higher interest rate, usually one to two percentage points higher. A minimum deposit is required and terms range from thirty days to five years. When the CD **matures** (that is the day that you can cash in the CD without penalty), you get the amount that you invested, plus the accumulated interest. There are penalties for early withdrawal.

No matter the reason for a short-term savings, it is always a good idea to maximize the interest rate you get on your deposit. You can shop around for banks and interest rates just the way people shop for anything.

Pressing Question

- With a more liquid investment, what happens to the yield?

5H. Long-Term Savings

Two main reasons to save money for the long term are to build a retirement fund or to save for your child's education. While imagining yourself at age sixty or seventy can be difficult to do, keep in mind that you will be the same person. You as an older person will want to have options, and the primary reason to save money for your retirement is to have options. Whether you want to keep working, travel and see the world, take up new hobbies, or start a second career, having enough savings will let you choose. If you live into your elderly years, you will need money if you want to stop working. Without savings, you will have no choice but to keep working.

GRAPHIC 5.15

The Wisdom of Starting Early
10% Average Rate of Return on Monthly Deposits of $100

Starting Age	Retirement Age	How Much Will You Have
25	75	$1,700,000
35	75	$632,000
45	75	$226,000
55	75	$76,000
65	75	$20,484

GRAPHIC 5.16

The Wisdom of Saving More
10% Average Rate of Return

Monthly Contribution from Age 25–75	Value at Retirement Age (75)
$ 50	$873,000
$100	$1,700,000
$150	$2,600,000
$200	$3,400,000
$250	$4,300,000

Even people who have modest incomes can retire wealthy. The secret is discipline. You need to have the ability to save money right out of your paycheck and not spend money on things you do not need. If you start saving in your early to mid-twenties, you will build a foundation of saved money that will grow over the decades, and when you can afford to save more, you should. If you save diligently and start at an early age, then you can save millions, but if you wait just ten years, you will regret it. Consider graphics 5.15 and 5.16, which are based on a 10 percent rate of return. In graphic 5.15, notice the difference between the investor who starts at age twenty-five and the one who starts at age thirty-five. In graphic 5.16, you can see that saving an extra $50 per month (or $12.50 per week) can grow into millions of extra dollars in a retirement fund.

The great benefit to all savers is **compounding interest**. Compound interest is money earned not only on the principal (main amount you invested) but also on the interest that has accumulated. For instance, on a $10,000 account in the first year, at 10 percent interest, $1,000 is earned. In the second year, the borrower will pay the same interest rate on $11,000. Ten percent of $11,000 is $1,100. After two years, the investment has grown to $12,100. After five years, the original amount has increased to $16,105. In other words, the investment grew $6,105 in five years. In the meantime, a saver just needs to be disciplined and forgo the urge to spend that extra money. Putting compound interest to work for you can make you a wealthy person.

GRAPHIC 5.17

A "nest egg" is an accumulation of assets with which someone plans to retire.

Disciplined investors will make regular contributions into their **portfolio**, their collection of various investments. Over the span of fifty years (ages twenty-five to seventy-five), the goal is to faithfully keep investing about 10 percent of your gross income (or whatever more you can afford at the time). Save early and save regularly, because the earlier you start, the greater your returns will be. The money deposited in the first few years will be the hardest-working money in the whole portfolio. Imagine the retirement you could have if you were to save $200 or even $300 per month. If your employer offers to match your contributions, you should definitely equal the match. The opportunity cost of doing otherwise could be millions of dollars.

How much will you need to retire? The answer to that question relies upon the lifestyle you wish to enjoy when you get older. The rule of thumb is to save enough to continue living a lifestyle to which you are accustomed. Ideally, a retiree should be able to live that lifestyle from the interest they get from their nest egg. Calculate 5 percent of whatever is in a retirement fund. That is the yearly total you will have to live on from the asset pool. If conditions are favorable, then retirees might be earning a 5 percent return from their safe investments. For instance, $100,000 would contribute $5,000 to living expenses. $1 million would contribute $50,000. These numbers clarify why saving is so important.

Retirees live on a **fixed income**. They know exactly what they are going to receive from Social Security and their investments every month. A person's lifestyle will be dictated by how much money he or she saved. According to the Social Security Administration, 34 percent of retired people live on those pension benefits alone. The average yearly income of those people is between $15,000 and $20,000. In 2015, the poverty threshold for a single person was $11,770. These retirees tend to struggle financially.

Remember, saving money gives you options later in life. You will still be the same person in fifty years. Most likely, you will want to stop working, but you will still have **assets** (items and investments of value that can bring income) and **liabilities** (expenses such as bills, debt, and taxes; see graphic 5.18). People who do not have the assets accumulated to retire have to keep working in order to buy food and pay rent. When you are younger it is not that difficult to save $25 per week ($100 per month). Delay your gratification for a consumer good or service, be happy with what you have, and save the extra money. Nobody has ever regretted accumulating enough money to retire comfortably.

GRAPHIC 5.18

Plus Column	Minus Column
Assets	Liabilities
Income	Expenses
• Investments • Property • Cash • Bank accounts • Salary • Stipends • Rent • Royalties • Dividends • Capital gains	• Bills • Debt • Depreciation • Taxes

Pressing Question

- What does delayed gratification have to do with retirement?

51. Some Common Retirement Fund Options

By 2033, the number of older Americans will increase from 46.6 million today to more than 77 million. Many people nearing retirement are finding out that they have not saved enough money to live comfortably. Demographically, the United States is getting older. There was a population spike, or *baby boom* in the 1950s and 1960s. These **baby boomers** are beginning to retire. As they do, they are placing an increasing strain on Social Security and Medicare programs. Many younger adults fear the bankruptcy of these programs. Young people should save money as if there will be no government benefits by the time they retire. In that way, they are assured of having enough to retire on their terms.

There are some common ways that workers put away money for retirement. These plans

GRAPHIC 5.19

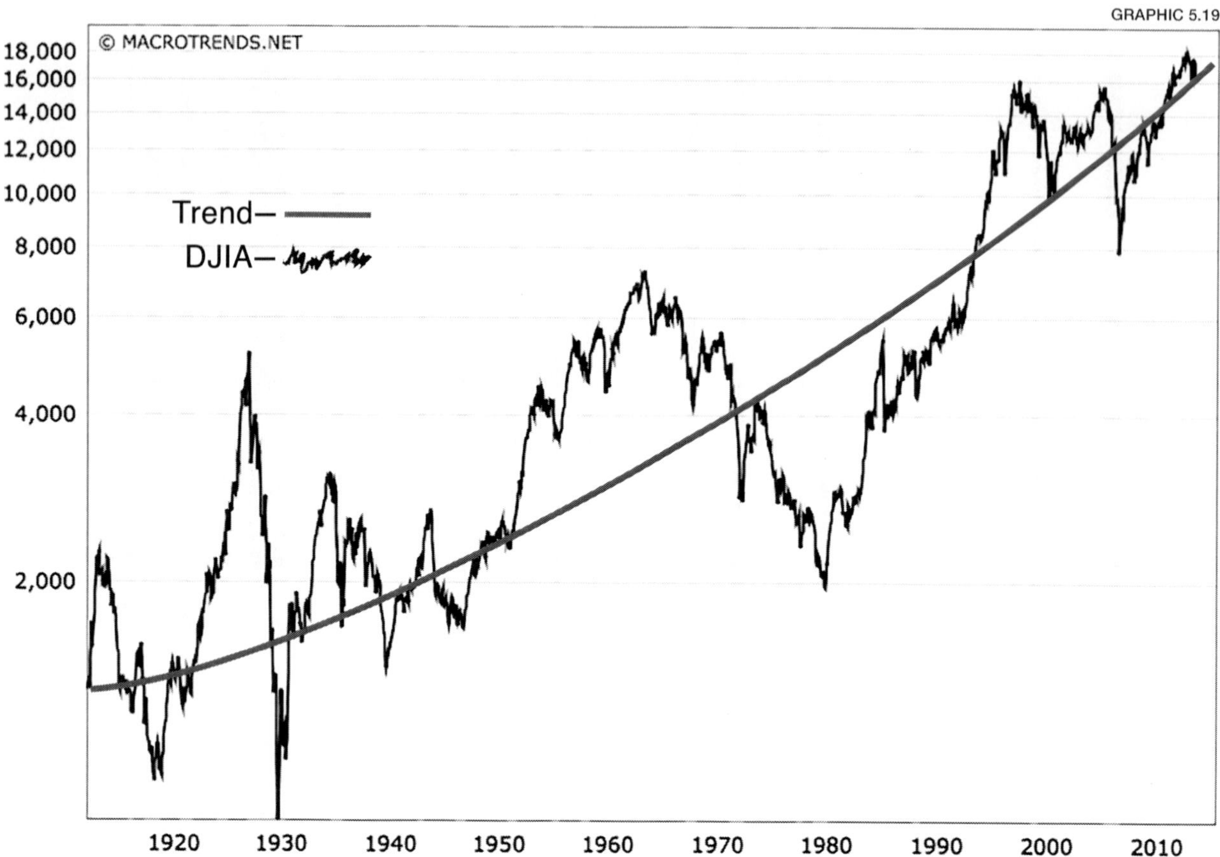

This graph shows the Dow Jones industrial average since 1980. Notice how volatile the ups and downs are. If you get greedy when the market is up and fearful when the market is down, you will lose money. If you keep investing month after month, you will take advantage of the trend line.

move their money directly from their paychecks to a financial services company. They can then choose from a variety of investments. The most common choice is a **mutual fund**. This is a pool of money that is invested by a manager in a variety of stocks and/or bonds with a particular investment strategy. The investment risk is therefore spread across the variety of different companies in the fund. By investing in a stock mutual fund, young investors can benefit from the dependable long-term growth. You do not have to pick and choose specific stocks or bonds; you can direct your money to a mutual fund. If you are looking for a return of 8 to 12 percent, then you should choose a stock fund. If you do not like to see your nest egg drop by 20 percent in value from time to time, then bond funds offer 2 to 6 percent generally. Recall that graphics 5.15 and 5.16 show savings growth based on a 10 percent return rate.

Regardless of where your money goes, remember to always be saving. The old motto is "pay yourself first." Saved money is for your future self. Your nest egg will lose in some years and gain in others. Some people have difficulty seeing their savings drop in value during "down years," but recall that saving and investing every month lets you take advantage of **dollar-cost averaging** (refer to graphic 5.19). Over the decades, when markets are down, your contributions buy more shares in your mutual funds. When the markets rally and grow, you benefit from the increased value. By following a long-term strategy, you benefit from the overall upward climb in the market. If you panic and sell at some point, you will lose out on all that growth potential.

By the time you are in your mid-twenties, you should open and establish an account with a financial services company to begin your life savings.

There are thousands of companies from which you can choose. Chances are your employer will have a relationship with one or more. Not only are there a lot of companies to choose from and mutual funds to research but also many ways to save money. Here are some of your choices:

- **Individual retirement accounts (IRA)**—There are many types of IRAs. Some are set up by employers while others are started by individuals. Contributions to some IRAs are deductible from your taxes. A **Roth IRA** contribution is not tax deductible, but it has other advantages. Once you reach the age of 59½, the money you withdraw is exempt from taxation.
- **401(k)**—This is the most common investment vehicle today. Most employers offer this investment type as a benefit. The company will match what the employee gives up to a certain dollar amount. Contributions to a 401(k) are also pre-tax investments. This means that the contribution is subtracted from your gross income before taxes are taken. This allows you to save more and lower your taxable income. Because the employer informs the worker exactly what the match will be, a 401(k) match is called a **defined contribution plan**.
- **Pension plans**—Pensions are usually a perquisite or "perk" (benefit) offered by older companies and unions. The organization will contribute money to a pension fund in the name of the employee. The money is pooled together and invested. Upon retirement, the worker will receive a predetermined amount of money each month. Because the workers know how much their income will be in advance, pensions are **defined benefits plans**. Pension plans are not as common as they were decades ago.
- **Universal life insurance**—More of an old-fashioned savings plan, life insurance pays your beneficiary a set amount of money when you die. Before that sad day, payments into the policy in excess of your premium help build cash value. Upon retirement, you can make withdrawals from the plan.
- **Annuities**—These are designed to provide a predictable monthly cash payment to the holder. These are sometimes funded by employers or individuals. Commonly, people fund these as they approach retirement, when they want to keep their nest eggs safe.

No matter how you save, remember how important it is to start early. Last, be sure to **diversify** your investments. This means to spread your money around among multiple mutual funds, stocks, and bonds. It is also a good idea to put your money in different types of savings accounts with different financial institutions.

Pressing Question

- Why do financial advisers tell their clients not to "put all their eggs in one basket?"

5J. Investing in Stock

In economics, the word *investment* is used in a couple of different ways. Companies buying machines and governments building bridges are making *capital investments*. An investment that creates a new business is called a *real investment*. In this section we will learn how people invest, saving money for the future in mutual funds, stocks, and bonds. These are *financial investments*. They do not create anything new or help economic growth, but they do help investors build wealth.

Stocks are sometimes called **equities**. As you learned in Unit 2, owning stock gives you partial ownership of a company. Big companies sometimes have billions of pieces of themselves for sale on stock markets. Owning one share of stock gives you a very small part of the corporation. Nevertheless, that share sometimes gives you the right to vote on how the company is run and maybe even receive a part of the profits.

Since 1929, the stock market has earned returns around 10 percent for investors. Consider graphic 5.19. During the late 1990s, there was enormous growth in the stock market overall. Companies become more valuable as they earn profits and sell more products. Stock is an attractive investment because it offers the investor two different ways to make money. First, the holder can buy low and sell high as the company grows. The amount earned when the stock is sold is a **capital gain**. Second, investors sometimes get a share of the profits in the form of **dividends**.

Investors must decide on their financial goals when investing. For older investors who are retired or close to retirement, they might consider **income stocks**, which are from large companies with a long track record of paying dividends. Sometimes called **blue chip stocks**, they belong to prominent and notable companies. People who buy **growth stock** expect a large capital appreciation. Young investors can take a loss if the newer company struggles, but they hope that the growth will bring large returns. Sometimes companies will offer an issue of **preferred stock**. This is stock that gives the investor a fixed share of the profits before common shares.

GRAPHIC 5.20

Bloomberg terminals appeared on trading desks decades ago. They cost tens of thousands of dollars per year to lease but provided traders with comprehensive and real-time data.

Most people who own stock do so by owning shares in mutual funds. More experienced investors may actively manage their portfolios. This means that they are choosing companies by doing their own research. Wealthy investors have financial advisers who actively trade on their behalf. Regardless of the method, stock transactions must be done through a financial services company or website. These companies own a seat on an exchange. A seat is a license for a company to buy and sell stock on an exchange. For each buy or sell order, the company gets a **commission**, a percentage of each transaction as a fee for service. The Internet and mutual funds have democratized investing to the point where people with modest incomes can build considerable wealth.

There are three major stock markets in the United States. If you decide to buy one hundred shares of IBM, it will be bought for you on the New York Stock Exchange (NYSE), the oldest in the country. When you do, you will be buying stock that has already been issued and held by several other investors. Because IBM is available to any investor, it is known as **common stock**. Microsoft's stock is exchanged on the NASDAQ, a market founded in 1971. It has surpassed the NYSE in both number of shares traded (volume) and dollar value (capitalization). Finally, the American Stock Exchange (AMEX) focuses on securities called *exchange traded funds*.

GRAPHIC 5.21

XYZ Corporation ★ Watchlist

A 149.62 ↓1.52(1.01%) 4:02PM EDT **F**

After Hours : **149.17** ↓0.45 (0.30%) 4:52PM EDT - Nasdaq Real Time Price

B	Prev Close:	151.14	Day's Range:	**G**	149.18 - 150.78
C	Open:	150.78	52wk Range:	**H**	140.56 - 185.72
	Bid:	149.00 x 100	Volume:	**I**	3,915,682
	Ask:	149.78 x 100	Avg Vol (3m):		4,226,730
D	1y Target Est:	158.53	Market Cap:	**J**	146.56B
	Beta:	0.880051	P/E (ttm):	**K**	13.16
E	Next Earnings Date:	19-Oct-15	EPS (ttm):	**L**	11.37
			Div & Yield:	**M**	5.20 (3.41%)

151.5
151.0
150.5
150.0
149.5
149.0
Yahoo!
10am 12pm 2pm 4pm
Previous Close
1d 5d 1m 3m 6m 1y 2y 5y max

As discussed in Unit 2, companies sell their stock to raise capital for expansion. Remember that selling stock for the first time is known as an initial public offering. By "going public," a company can raise money for expansion. It will offer the public a set number of shares at a given price. The company files papers with the Securities and Exchange Commission, which then notifies the public. On the day the company goes public, most of the shares are bought by mutual funds and financial institutions. After that, the public will start buying and shares of the company's stock.

Owning a share of company stock, investors keep track of how the company is doing. The company may contact you periodically to keep you up to date. It will send you a copy of the annual report every year. If you want deeper information, the company's 10-K is available online. This document, which is submitted to the SEC, details the profits, costs, debt, and future considerations of the company. Investors watch their holdings in stock charts and on websites. These can tell a savvy investor something useful about the company's stock. Investors should do voluminous research before buying into a company.

Simple stock charts can be found all over the Internet. Go to a search engine, find out what the company's "ticker" symbol is, and type in a search. The stock chart should be one of the top results. They are not very hard to understand. Refer to graphic 5.21. The key data points are explained below:

A. The current price and the change since yesterdays close. The stock is down from the day before by $1.52.

B. At the end of trading the day before, that was the price. The markets are open from 9:30–4:00 on most weekdays.

C. $150.78 the first price that the stock sold for today.

D. Analysts think the stock will hit $158.53 this year.

E. The company will announce how it performed on October 19th.

F. XYZ is the company's symbol.

G. The price varied $1.60 during the trading day.

H. The stock price varied about $45 in the last twelve months.

I. Volume is the number of shares traded during the day.

J. All of the company's stock added together is worth $147 billion. Stock price multiplied by the number of shares.

K. This is the current stock price compared to the earnings per share. The lower this number is the better.

L. Earnings per share is the company's net revenue divided by the number of shares. If this number is "N/A," then that means the company lost money in the last fiscal year.

M. Dividends are the portion of the profits given to each share. The yield is the dividend divided by the stock price. If the stock stays at $149.62, then the $5.20 per share is 3.41 percent return on your money.

GRAPHIC 5.22

Component Companies of the Dow Jones Industrial Average

1929	1956	2015
Allied Chemical	Allied Chemical	3M Company
General Foods	General Electric Company	American Express Co
Paramount Publix	Procter & Gamble Company	Apple
American Can	American Can	Boeing
General Motors Corporation	General Foods	Caterpillar
Radio Corporation	Sears Roebuck & Company	Chevron
American Smelting	American Smelting	Cisco Systems
General Railway Signal	General Motors Corporation	The Coca-Cola Company
Sears Roebuck & Company	Standard Oil of California	DuPont
American Sugar	American Telephone and Telegraph	ExxonMobil
Goodrich	Goodyear	General Electric
Standard Oil (NJ)	Standard Oil (NJ)	Goldman Sachs*
American Tobacco B	American Tobacco	The Home Depot Inc
International Harvester	International Harvester	Intel
Texas Company	Texas Company	IBM
Atlantic Refining	Bethlehem Steel	Johnson & Johnson
International Nickel	International Nickel	JPMorgan Chase
Texas Gulf Sulphur	Union Carbide	McDonald's
Bethlehem Steel	Chrysler	Merck & Co.
Mack Truck	International Paper Company	Microspoft
Union Carbide	United Aircraft	Nike Inc.
Chrysler	Corn Products Refining	Pfizer
Nash Motors	Johns-Manville	Procter & Gamble
U.S. Steel	U.S. Steel	The Travelers Companies
Curtiss-Wright	E. I. du Pont de Nemours	UnitedHealth Group
National Cash Register	National Distillers	United Technologies
Westinghouse Electric	Westinghouse Electric	Verizon Communications
General Electric Company	Eastman Kodak Company	Visa
North American	National Steel	Walmart
Woolworth	Woolworth	The Walt Disney Company

People who do not actively manage their stock holdings do not need to watch stock prices every day. Most adults like to know how the stock market is doing overall, however. Each of the markets has an indicator that states how part of the market or the market overall did that day. The most quoted index is the Dow Jones Industrial Average. It is a gauge of thirty large industrial companies on the NYSE (graphic 5.22 shows how the Dow has changed with the American economy). The NASDAQ composite tells investors how that market fared. The S&P 500 lets the public know how 500 of the largest and most important companies across multiple markets performed. Aside from these three, there are hundreds of indicators that show how different sectors of the market did. There are thousands of indexes around the world that tell global investors how each country's market performed.

Pressing Question

- What makes a stock go up in price over time?

GRAPHIC 5.23

This is an old stock certificate for Loudon Park Cemetery Company. Investors once received paper copies that proved they owned a "piece" or "share" of a company. Today, shares are traded electronically.

5K. The Bond Market

If you have money, somebody somewhere will pay you to use it. This is why bonds exist. The bond market is huge. It is many times bigger than the stock market and plays a vital role in the health of our banking and financial industries. Unlike stocks, which offer ownership in a company, **bonds** are loans that investors make to governments and corporations. For instance, a bond issued by the Treasury Department is a loan to the US government. The government promises to pay interest over time. By going straight to the investor instead of a bank, the borrower gets a lower interest rate and the lender gets a higher return. Bonds are the foundation of finance.

Since bonds are loans, if you buy a $10,000 bond at an interest rate of 6 percent, then you will be paid $600 per year. If it is a ten-year bond, the same sum is earned every year. When the bond matures, the bond will be worth $16,000.

Depending on the bond, you can get your money in a variety of ways. Sometimes you pay a fraction of the face value of a bond and the full amount is paid upon maturity. Sometimes you get an interest check in the mail once a month, quarterly, or annually. If you can think of an arrangement, it is probably being done. It is all about accessing someone else's capital so it can be put to use.

There are several types of bonds. Some are issued by governments and others are issued by corporations. Like stocks, some bonds are riskier than others. Ones that are issued by the federal government are very safe and referred to as **investment grade**. Others have more inherent risk, because the issuer is less likely to pay the lender back. Risky bonds are called **speculative grade**, or **junk bonds**. Lending and borrowing money in the bond market comes in many different forms. A few of the more common types of bonds are:

- **Savings bonds**—These can be bought for as little as $50. They have maturities of ten to thirty years. They are bought at a fraction of face value. They make great gifts.
- **Treasury bonds**—The minimum investment is $1,000. The average investment duration is five years.
- **Treasury notes**—Investment amounts can range from $1,000 to $5,000. Maturity ranges from two to five years.
- **Treasury bills**—These require a minimum investment of $10,000. They are held for a range of three to twelve months.

- **Corporate bonds**—When a company needs to raise money, it might choose to sell stock, but it can also sell bonds. They too are loans that pay interest over time.
- **Municipal bonds**—These are sometimes called "munies." They are bonds offered by local governments. To encourage investors, they are especially enticing, because they are exempt from federal taxation. They are commonly offered by school districts and communities to fund local projects.

Bonds offer businesses and governments an alternative to borrowing money from a bank. The bond market lets borrowers go directly to investors. Many people use them as a means of saving. As it turns out, bonds are a safe place to park your money.

When issued, bonds are given a credit rating just as an individual is rated when applying for a mortgage. Companies, institutions, and governments employ investment bankers when they wish to issue bonds. A credit agency rates the bonds according to the borrower's ability to pay back a loan. Large companies with many assets and high profits are a safer bet. Younger companies with no track record and bleak prospects may also issue bonds but will have to pay a higher interest rate. Different companies rate bonds. Moody's and Standard & Poor's, two of the world's largest credit rating agencies, rate bonds from AAA to C (graphic 5.24).

GRAPHIC 5.24

Bond Rating	
Investment Grade	**Speculative Grade**
AAA - Low Risk	BB
AA	B
A	CCC
BBB	CC - Very High Risk

Because the United States has a credit history that is more than two hundred years old, it has an AAA rating. This means it has to pay less for the use of the money. Old, solid companies may have ratings of A, as do some dependable local governments. Companies on the brink of failure will have a lower rating.

Like stock, bonds can be traded on markets. When they are issued for the first time, bonds are sold on a **primary market**. However, someone who has held a bond for a certain length of time may decide to sell it before it matures. If held to maturity, bonds offer a guaranteed return unless the issuer defaults. They are a much safer investment than stock, but if a bond is taken to a secondary market to be sold to another investor, then the seller might get less than what it is worth. Look to graphic 5.25 which describes the situation.

GRAPHIC 5.25

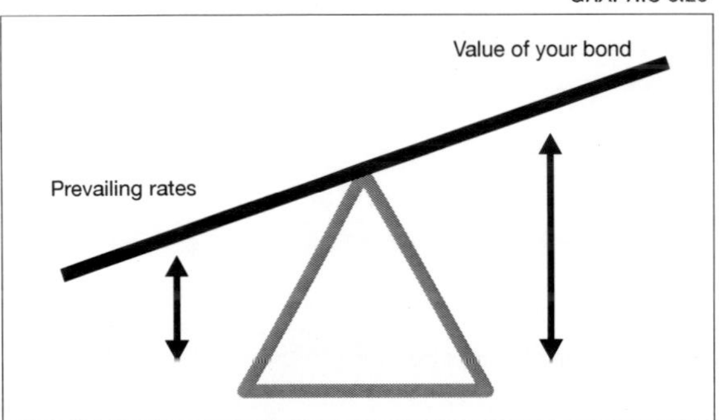

If you hold a 10 percent bond and want to sell it before maturity, the price you get will hinge upon prevailing interest rates. For instance, if people can buy 12 percent bonds when you hit the market, then you will get less than face value for the bond. On the other hand, if rates fall to 8 percent, then you may get a premium for your bond. If you hold the bond to maturity, then you should get the interest promised and your original investment back.

Pressing Question

- What motivates people to sell their bonds early?

5L. High-Risk Investments

Are you the gambling type? While some stocks and speculative grade bonds are considered risky, there are investments that can double in value in minutes. At the same time, they can become worthless just as quickly. These investments might be difficult to understand, but they are deals that require the investor to speculate on the future. Alternately, these investments might be a bet on a company's stock going down instead of up. This type of investment can be confusing, and most investors would never dream of holding one of these securities. To be clear, risky investments are best left to professionals.

For example, **futures** offer investors the right to buy a contract to take shipment of something not yet produced. Commodities like agricultural products, metals, coal, petroleum, and natural gas are traded. Why on earth do people do this? In the 1800s, farmers would experience wild fluctuations in price as harvest time came closer. All would rush to get their goods to market to garner the highest price. As time passed and more products arrived, prices would plummet.

To avoid this dilemma, farmers would sell their product to commodity traders months before harvest. The traders would then take the futures to commodities exchanges. Depending on the weather, world harvests, political conditions, and thousands of other factors, the unharvested product's price would fluctuate. This process continues on a grand scale in numerous places around the world. In the United States, the largest markets are in New York City and Chicago. **Hedgers** are people who hold options for several months to secure a modest gain. They work for companies that need the commodity like a corn chip company that needs tons of corn. On the other hand, **speculators** buy and trade futures trying to make a quick buck in the short term.

GRAPHIC 5.26

Savings bonds are good gifts for high school and college graduates. The buyer pays a fraction of the face value. Thirty years later, the bond is worth face value.

Stock options are contracts that convey to its holder the right, but not the obligation, to buy or sell shares of stock at a specific price on or before a given date. Options that give the holder the right to buy a stock are referred to as **calls**. If the value of the stock in question goes up and you have the options at a low price, you can "call" your options in and get a discounted price. **Puts**, in contrast, give the holder the right to make another party buy the holding.

For instance, you hold XYZ stock that has climbed to $110 per share, and you wish to lock in your capital appreciation. When someone approaches you to sell you some puts, you agree. She sells you 1,000 puts of XYZ at 110. You pay her $2,000. This transaction benefits you, because you have guaranteed you can sell your shares for at least a predetermined price. The risk for the seller of the options is the chance that XYZ falls in price and the holder of the options "exercises the option." This forces you to buy a stock at a higher than market price.

If you own 1,000 shares of XYZ that you bought at $100 per share, and the price has risen to $115, you may want to "lock in" your profits at the new price. In this case, you could sell options on your stock at the current price. If the price went down, then the buyer would not want your stock; if the stock goes up, however, the buyer could take your stock at a discount price and you would lose the additional capital gain. It can all get quite confusing. When it comes to investing in futures and options, it is best to leave that job to the experts.

The last category of risky investment is the practice of **selling short**. If you believe stock is going to go down in value, then you can borrow someone's stock for an agreed-upon time period (you pay the lender a commission). Then, you sell those shares right away. When the stock goes down, you buy it back at the lower price and keep the difference, but, if it goes up, then you will lose those extra dollars. "Selling short" is very risky, as the investment might be worth less than you invested. If you have ever heard the expression,

"Don't sell me short," now you know that it means to bet that the value of a stock will go down.

Pressing Question

- At what point in one's life is it safest to try a risky investment, closer to or farther from retirement? Explain your logic.

5M. A Credit to Your Name

Credit is your ability to borrow someone else's money. For instance, a fifty-year-old man who has bought several cars, two houses, and other items with borrowed money has an established track record. He has good credit and can access money easily. **Creditors**, or money lenders, would be more than willing to lend him money. On the other hand, someone who has a history of paying late or not paying at all will have difficulty borrowing money. Just think, To what sort of person would you be willing to lend money? Some of your friends might have a reputation for borrowing money and not paying it back. Are people willing to give them more?

Banks and other creditors depend on credit agencies to evaluate everyone's borrowing habits. These agencies keep track of every dollar that is borrowed. They also track whether payments are made on time, criminal history, places of residence, and legal problems. All of these factors are compiled on a credit report. If you apply to borrow money, the lender will ask your permission to look at your report. When considering someone's credit health, financial institutions consider four factors: These are known as the 4Cs:

- **Credit history**—When was money was borrowed in the past, and how faithfully was it paid back? Every debt a person has is followed month to month. They "paid as agreed," sent in late payments, or did not pay at all.
- **Character**—Does the borrower have a criminal past? Perhaps there are legal judgments against him or her. These details are public knowledge and are gathered by the major credit agencies.
- **Capacity to pay**—What is the borrower's monthly income and can he or she handle a monthly payment schedule? Someone who makes $70,000 per year can afford the payment on a $100,000 house but not on an $800,000 house.
- **Capital**—How much money does the person have in the bank? Most banks expect a down payment on a loan. Does the person have capital resources that could be considered **collateral** (objects or investments of value that can be handed over to the bank in the event that you do not repay the loan)?

GRAPHIC 5.27

Credit Ratings

Score	Approximate Grade
770-850	A+
720-769	A
670-719	B
620-669	C
570-619	D
569 and below	F

Sometimes, people borrow more money than they can afford to pay back. Perhaps they do not take the time to think and delay their gratification. They are driven by consumerism and buy what they want with **credit cards**. These cards allow the holder to borrow money for a purchase at the point of sale. The money is lent at high interest rates, usually between 15 and 20 percent. Credit cards are issued through and managed by banks. They operate through a massive computer system operated by companies like MasterCard, Visa, and Discover. While credit cards do afford holders a certain amount of financial freedom, they can get people into financial trouble.

What happens to people who overborrow? When they stop paying a debt, it is called a **default**, and creditors then have the right to repossess the item that the lent money bought. If someone is unable to pay a mortgage (recall from Unit 3 that a mortgage is a loan that buys land, buildings, or houses), a lender is then allowed to **foreclose**, or take back, the property. Sometimes, people will be unable to pay back any of the money they have borrowed. If this is the case, then they are able to go to court and ask to have assets protected from their creditors. This legal declaration of one's inability to pay one's debt is known as **bankruptcy**. While most credit information follows us for seven years, a bankruptcy will be on our credit record for ten years. Bankruptcy is a last resort for people in serious financial trouble.

GRAPHIC 5.28

Maintain good credit by paying debt and bills on time; this way you will get the lowest interest rates.

All of your 4Cs are taken into consideration by the three major credit agencies: Experian, TransUnion, and Equifax. They use this information about you and your past behavior to calculate a FICO score, issued by Fair Isaac Corporation, a major data-gathering company. Creditors will use one of the three main agencies or use an average of each credit score to determine a borrower's creditworthiness. Scores typically range from 350 to 850. Higher scores are better. Consider graphic 5.27, which translates credit scores into letter grades. To whom would you lend money? Graphic 5.29 breaks a credit score down into different components.

You should check your credit report two or three times per year. Set a schedule for yourself. The three major agencies charge you for access to your report. They even do so through websites that claim to be "free." They are not. To get a truly free credit report, go to AnnualCreditReport.com. This is the site that Congress mandated be set up by the three agencies. There the reports are indeed free of charge.

Pressing Question

- What are behaviors that get some consumers into financial trouble?

5N. Major Purchases

Young people just out of school tend to rent apartments or houses. The landlord will usually want a renter to sign a **lease**, a contractual agreement to pay rent every month for a given period of time. Contained within this lease are obligations to pay for damages to the property caused by you, the tenant. Here are some of the basic considerations to keep in mind when choosing a rental property:

- Is it in your price range? You can always cut your rent and bills in half or more by getting a roommate.
- Is it close enough to where you work that you could possibly avoid driving a car?
- Does the landlord pay for any utilities (trash, water, gas, electric)?
- Do you like the neighborhood? Are there things to do nearby?

GRAPHIC 5.29

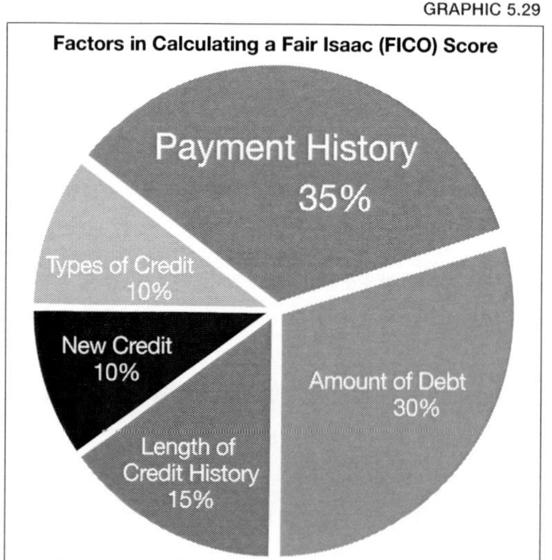

At some point in your life, you might want to buy a house. Americans see houses as not only a place to live but also a good investment. However, the Great Recession of 2008 shook that notion and led to the collapse of the American housing market. Many people questioned the merits of home ownership, especially when their home values went "under water" (they owed more to the bank then the house was now worth). Throughout the United States, some streets filled with foreclosed and empty homes. As the economy corrected, people recovered from the panic. Their outlook began to brighten, and despite the 2008 bubble, Americans still take out mortgages to buy houses.

So is a house a good investment? That answer depends on whether you plan to stay in a house for a long time and truly need the space for a growing family; if so, a home mortgage, and even and the expense it brings, makes sense. If you are young and do not plan to live in the same city for a long time, purchasing a home and taking on a mortgage may be a bad financial decision. Take time to think and ask for advice from family and friends.

Choosing the right house should start in the place where most big purchases should start, the Internet. Search sites like Zillow.com and Realtor.com to help you locate homes in your area that are listed for sale. You can narrow your search by criteria you select and then decide if they are fairly priced. American consumers often overspend and overextend themselves when buying a house. Use one of the many online mortgage calculators when trying to figure out what the payment will be. Other costs to consider are:

- **Downpayment**—This is usually 20 percent of the value of the mortgage.
- **Monthly payment**—This will be your principal and interest every month.
- **Taxes**—Property taxes usually cost several hundred dollars per month. Collected by the county, they are usually added to a special escrow account at your bank, which will dispense those funds every six months.
- **Home insurance**—Homeowner's policies are required by most banks. Often, these funds are added into your monthly payment and dispensed by the bank, just like your taxes.
- **Mortgage insurance**—Some lenders require certain borrowers to pay additional insurance if they are considered to be at higher risk of defaulting the loan.

Think about it. When you first buy a house, what you are really doing is giving the bank 5 to 20 percent of the value of the sale price and borrowing the rest. You will then spend the next fifteen to thirty years paying the bank back its money with interest. The bank is able to lend you tens and even hundreds of thousands of dollars, because the house and land itself have a market value that the bank can sell in case you default on your mortgage. Remember, a borrower must qualify for the loan based on a bank's set policies.

GRAPHIC 5.30

Before you even think about purchasing a house, you will probably buy a car. No single big-ticket item gets the young adult into as much financial trouble as a car. The United States is a country of people who love personal transportation. Getting your first job and paycheck will make you feel flush with possibilities. You might tell yourself that you deserve or need a new car, but before you run off to the dealership you need to take a lot into consideration.

There are options! Consider a few. Before you buy a car, find a job; then choose an apartment or room to rent in a house that is close to where you live. If you are going to live in a big city, you can use public transportation or a car share program. If you insist on buying a car, try looking for a used car that has a good record of upkeep and maintenance. Expenses that come with a car add up quickly. Here are a few things to consider before you sign on the bottom line:

- **Payments**—Find the best interest rate you can using the Internet. You can borrow money from a bank or from the manufacturer. Use a loan calculator to figure out your payment. Be sure to shop around for the best rate available. Creditors are competing against one another for your business.
- **Insurance**—Young people pay a lot for car insurance (as will be discussed in a later section). Keep in mind that insurance companies may charge lower premiums for used cars—call them to find out what your make, model, and year will cost per month to insure. You might find that your monthly insurance costs are greater than your car payment.
- **Gas**—Fuel economy should be part of your purchase decision. Figure out what it will cost to fill your whole tank. Then figure out what it will cost to drive to and from work every day.
- **Maintenance**—You will need to get regular service in order to make sure you get your money's worth out of your purchase. If your car breaks down, it can cost thousands of dollars to get it running again.

Ultimately, cars get you from one place to another. Consider every cost when purchasing. Take your monthly payment, monthly insurance, estimated gas cost, and maintenance and add them together. Divide that number by thirty. This is your daily cost of ownership. Then take the monthly cost and multiply it by twelve to calculate the yearly cost of ownership. This might change the type of car you want to buy.

If you decide that you need a car, do research on the Internet. When you go to the dealership, take a parent or elder with you. Do not sign papers on your first visit to the dealership. If you leave your number, the salesperson will call you back the next day with a better deal. Shop for a car toward the end of the month. Auto dealers have quotas they must reach every month in order to receive their full compensation from the manufacturer. If they need to sell lots of cars to hit that quota, then you might get a good deal. Be humble when you shop. Dealerships sell hundreds of cars per month; consumers buy one every few years. Nice people often get better deals too.

The last consideration in getting a car is the option to lease a car. Car lease payments are lower than the purchase payments. A lease has a more affordable monthly payment, because it finances the amount that the car will depreciate during the duration of the lease. For example, an $18,000 car will depreciate around 50 percent in three years. Therefore, $9,000 is financed over thirty-six months (around $300 per month). Buying the car would cost more than $500 per month in the same time frame. On the other hand, at the end of a lease that has cost you almost $11,000, you have nothing to show for your money. In effect, a lease is a long-term rental, so the value of the asset is zero at the end of the term.

Try to remember that cars are transportation. If you buy one for status the decision could cost you the hundreds of thousands you would eventually accrue if you saved that money with compounding interest. Remember to take the time to think.

Pressing Question

- What costs do most consumers forget to add in their monthly payments when they are about to buy a car?

50. Good Debt or Bad Debt?

For some people, the only good debt is no debt at all. Others see debt as a tool to improve their lives in the short term and to build wealth in the long term. Too many Americans assume debt that gets them into financial trouble. Borrowing any amount of money will affect your credit history and your financial future. Remember, a debt is a contractual obligation to pay back money over time, and almost always with interest.

Debt should not be entered into lightly, but some debts are necessary. Some are even advantageous. For instance, if you are single and expecting a job transfer, purchasing a home might be a bad idea. Renting is probably for you. If you have children and plan to live in the same city for five years or more, however, a home mortgage might prove to be a good deal for you. Your home should go up in value in that time and can be sold for a capital gain (which is tax exempt for a primary residence). In the meantime, you will have a place to live as well as certain tax advantages (mortgage interest is tax deductible).

In general, if a debt can add value, wealth, or benefit to your life, it is good debt. A modest student loan that helps you jump-start a lucrative career is beneficial. A home mortgage that gives your family stability also becomes an asset that increases in value. A loan that helps you start a new business can help you earn income for decades in the future. Sometimes, debt can make financial sense.

Trouble ensues when you take on debt to satisfy your immediate wants. Remember that delayed gratification in your financial life means you put off your short-term wants in order to create financial security in the future. Bad debt usually comes from purchases meant to satisfy our immediate desires. We often believe that ownership of a certain item will bring added status in how others see us. For Americans, these purchases usually come in the form of auto loans and credit card bills. Loans for expensive cars and high-interest credit card debt are bad debt.

Most consumers who have to declare bankruptcy can pinpoint their downfall to a hefty credit card debt. As you get older, you will begin to experience the barrage of credit card deals. After finishing school, you may be offered thousands of dollars in credit and enticing introductory rates. As with any contract, make sure you read the fine print, especially regarding the interest rates, fees, and penalties.

GRAPHIC 5.31

People and businesses can go to court and get help in restructuring debt. Oddly, the one type of debt that never gets erased is student loans.

The problem with credit cards is that they let the consumer get immediate gratification. Instead of having to save for that computer or big-screen TV, they can get it right away. A consumer can make a purchase, but credit cards operate on the concept of revolving debt. When a transaction is made on a credit card, the entire balance does not have to be paid off at the end of the month. A bank has transferred money to the seller's bank. In the meantime, the holder will be charged the high interest rates according to the credit card contract. This interest adds up very quickly. Some credit cards start at 20 percent and can go even higher.

Banks and other credit card issuers discovered that people who are bad with credit could be good sources of revenue. Late fees are charged for payments that are not sent in on time. These fees have steadily increased over the past fifteen years from an average of $15 to more than $50. A card user could be penalized for spending more than their limit, using a foreign ATM, or getting a cash advance. Banks make millions in profits from the extra fees.

If you do not wish to carry large amounts of cash and still want the convenience that a credit card offers, there are two alternatives. A charge card like American Express will let you spend whatever you want interest-free but requires the entire balance be paid at the end of the month. Another option is to pay cash with an ATM or debit card. Many banks offer cards that are tied to your checking account that also feature a credit card logo on them. This means that transactions can use the company's electronic network to move money from one bank to another. Using an ATM card is the same as using cash, because the money is immediately transferred from your checking account.

Keep in mind, not all checking accounts have this flexibility. Here are some useful pieces of advice when it comes to credit cards:

- High-interest debt is bad debt. You get only short-term satisfaction with most credit card purchases. Mortgages and student loans are good debt. They improve your financial well-being in the long term.
- Buy only what you can pay off at the end of the month.
- Only buy goods that will last. Dinners and entertainment are fleeting. A TV, for example, can be enjoyed for years.
- Avoid carrying a balance. Even the best card rates are higher than you should be comfortable with.
- Get a card in college if one is offered. Buy a few small things for which you already have cash (like your school books). Pay off the balances right away. By doing this, you will establish a credit history of being a good risk. This will help once you get a job and go to make a major purchase.

Credit cards might be a major part of our financial culture. They offer freedom and convenience. Just remember to use them prudently.

Pressing Question

- What is the yearly and monthly interest charge to someone who has a $5,600 balance on a credit card that charges 17.5 percent APR?

5P. Insurance Basics

Young adults are very aware of car insurance. If you know what your insurance costs every year, you understand how frustrating such an expense can be. Sometimes, insurance can cost more than the car payment. Meanwhile, your parents probably pay a fraction of what you pay. While it seems unfair, there are good reasons for the expense.

Life is full of choices, for example deciding to drive a car. There is a chance that something bad could happen while you do. If you are going to take chances, it can help to get guidance from an **insurance agent**, a person who sells coverage on behalf of a company. Insurance can help minimize the financial risk we take. People buy insurance in order to reduce risk. In particular, businesses and individuals are responsible for their actions by law. They are **liable**. Every time you drive to school, you go out to dinner, and you buy something, bad things can happen. Insurance allows us the opportunity to control our chances. Most of the time, however, bad things do not happen.

GRAPHIC 5.32

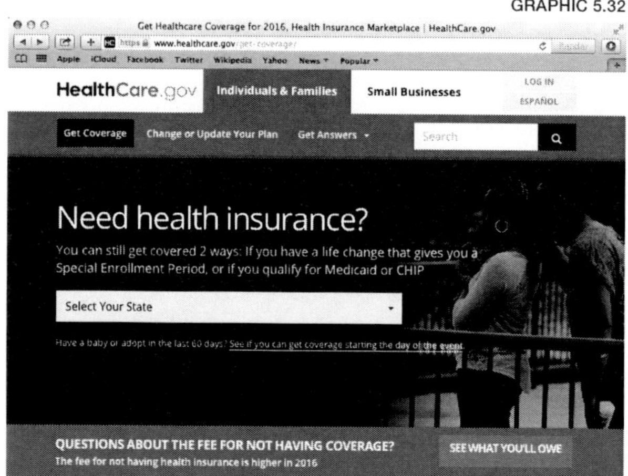

The graphic above comes from HealthCare.gov. If you are self-employed or are between jobs, then you will need to get health care. It makes financial sense to have coverage, and the law now mandates it. One hospital stay can bankrupt you quickly.

Insurance companies take in **premiums**, the cost consumers pay for an **insurance policy**. A policy is the contract that spells out what the company will pay for should something unfortunate happen. They collect premiums and pool that money just in case customers make a claim, a request for money to pay for some damage incurred. Insurance providers have to estimate the likelihood that a client will make a claim for money. In order to do this, they use massive amounts of data and statistics. The mathematicians who make these complex calculations are called **actuaries**.

With all these statistics, insurance companies have become adept at predicting human behavior. They cannot base the cost of a policy on a hunch. Rather, researchers gather all the data they can to accurately estimate a premium. It comes down to a simple formula: frequency times severity. The likelihood that somebody will make a claim is called the **frequency**, while the average cost of a claim is called a **severity**. Premiums are calculated by multiplying the probability (a percentage) of a claim by the dollar amount that would be paid.

For young people, auto policy premiums are expensive. Insurance companies use two tools to calculate their figures. First, **demographics** classifies people in groups according to age, income, gender, location, and past behavior. Insurance companies gather huge amounts of data to better gauge the probability that a customer will make a claim. Young people get into more car accidents than any other demographic group. When they do, the accidents tend to be very expensive. Their accidents are more frequent in addition to more expensive. Hence, their premiums are high. When you reach the age of twenty-five, your car insurance will drop considerably. If you get married, then it will drop more. Married people over the age of twenty-five are a better statistical risk. Agents would rather young adults wait until after their twenty-fifth birthday to get a policy.

If it is any consolation, young people can get very affordable life insurance. As mentioned in the last section, life insurance pays a beneficiary a sum of money when the policyholder dies. Different from universal life, **term life insurance** is not used as a savings; rather, it is merely for the death benefit. It tends to be more affordable than universal life. Premiums are calculated according to the health and age of the policy holder. A young person is less likely to die than an old person (frequency). Other factors include the health and behavior of the customer. A young, nonsmoking, person who does not ride motorcycles or skydive will get a lower premium than a chain-smoking, fifty-five-year-old daredevil. Any potential financial loss to the insurance company is also considered its severity.

Young people also pay less for health insurance. They rarely get sick and do not need to see doctors as often. In the United States, the Affordable Care Act (also known as Obamacare) requires that all adults be covered by health insurance. The program depends upon young people paying into the insurance policies to help defray the cost of insuring older people.

If you have a job, most employers provide coverage. This is about half of all people in the United States. Those who do not have a job might be on Medicaid or Medicare (30 percent). The remaining 20 percent who must buy their own policies can start at HealthCare.gov From there, they can log onto the site and research available plans. Insurance companies offer four levels of coverage (bronze, silver, gold, and platinum). The better the policy, the more expensive it will be.

What makes some policies expensive and others affordable? There are many reasons. Regardless of the type of insurance, there are words you need to know.

- **Deductible**—This is the amount the customer must pay annually before the health insurance benefits begin to cover the customer. (Some types of expenses may not be applied to the deductible or exempt from this requirement.) With a $500 deductible, a policyholder must pay the first $500 of the claim and the insurance company pays a percentage of the rest after the deductible has been met. With high-deductible medical insurance, the insured person must pay more before the insurance company's payments kick in.
- **Copayment** (or **copay**)—This is a flat fee that has to be paid each time you make a claim. Common in medical insurance, copays are sometimes required when a customer sees a doctor or fills a prescription.
- **Coinsurance**—Also common in medical insurance, this requires the insured to pay a

percentage of every claim. For instance, if a visit to the doctor costs $200, the insurance company might pay 80 percent ($160), and the patient pays 20 percent ($40).

- **Network**—In medical insurance, this is the list of doctors and hospitals with which your provider has negotiated prices. Your coverage is much better when you stay within your network. Prices go up considerably if you go "out of network."
- **Flexible spending account**—This is money that you can set aside from your paycheck before taxes are taken out. These accounts are funded by employers and must be spent within a certain amount of time.
- **Health savings accounts**—Employers may also contribute to an HSA. These are different, because anybody can contribute to your account. Also, these funds can grow without limit and can be spent any time. They are usually used to help pay for a high-deductible medical plan.

GRAPHIC 5.33

HealthCare.gov

The American insurance industry is massive. People buy health, life, and homeowner's insurance. Businesses need policies for liability. Banks sometimes require insurance in case a borrower does not pay a mortgage. Film studios take out policies in case one of their stars cannot finish a film. Even insurance companies buy policies to insure them against potentially large losses.

Pressing Question

- How many insurance policies are you covered under right now? List them.

GRAPHIC 5.34

Health care insurance premiums have been rising faster than inflation for decades.

5Q. Identity Theft

While the Internet has transformed the way we work, get entertained, and access information, it has come with some consequences. Before the Internet and electronic commerce, identity theft was rare, limited to stolen credit cards and forged checks. Starting in the 1990s, however, criminals became increasingly sophisticated. Today, they can steal vital personal information from you without your knowing it. They can then defraud you of thousands of dollars.

According to the Federal Trade Commission, "identity theft occurs when someone uses your personally identifying information, like your name, Social Security number, or credit card number, without your permission, to commit fraud or other crimes." If a thief can discover personal information about you, that thief can then open up lines of credit in your name, siphon money from your bank account, or hijack your computer. In each instance, victims rarely know what has happened until well after the crime is done. The problem is so pervasive that the FTC and police departments across the country have divisions dedicated to investigating these cases.

How do thieves perpetrate the crime? It is simple. They acquire our personal information when we are not careful. Some of the practices include:

- Dumpster diving
- Stealing wallets
- Credit card skimming (using a machine to steal your numbers)
- Stealing and diverting mail
- Computer hacking and malware
- Phone theft
- Document forgery (especially checks)
- Phishing phone calls and e-mails

Once your personal information is stolen, many different types of fraud may occur. Credit cards can be misused or opened in your name. Check fraud may help the thieves take money from your account. False identifications using your Social Security number may allow them to get medical services, borrow great sums of money, and travel under your name. It seems that the thieves are getting cleverer—are you ready?

There is good news, however. There are simple ways for you to protect yourself. This starts with knowing what is important. Anything with your Social Security number on it should be guarded carefully, and the same goes for any contract, financial statements, and checks. Limit the number of credit cards you carry, and watch your financial statements once per week online. Here are some other helpful hints:

- Shred important papers every month.
- Be careful what you put in the mail.
- Never give financial information over the phone or by e-mail, especially your Social Security number.
- Never open or respond to an e-mail from a bank or business if you are not already a customer.
- Update your computer virus software every month.
- Choose really good passwords (use caps, numbers, hyphens, and unpredictable character strings).
- Keep important papers locked up at home.
- Hire an online service like LifeLock or Identity Guard. They monitor your information and help fix any problems.

GRAPHIC 5.35

Words to Live By

Delay Your Gratification
Always Be Saving
Money Is Hard to Earn
Take Time to Think
Money Is for Saving
Pay Your Bills on Time

How will you know if your identity has been stolen? Sometimes your credit card company or bank will call to ask about suspicious charges. You may notice these charges first. You also might start getting calls from creditors with whom you have never dealt. Maybe you get denied for credit for no good reason, or your bills have stopped arriving. Be on guard and snap into action.

If you suspect that your identity has been stolen, consult your panic list. This is a list of all the phone numbers of your bank(s), credit card companies, and the major credit agencies in the United States. Keep this list in a guarded document on the cloud. When you call your creditor and credit agencies, put a **fraud alert** on your name. This gives you extra protection and the credit agencies will watch your data closely. This alert will also allow you to get free copies of your credit reports all at once. Inspect them closely and dispute all charges and debts you did not make. If you suspect the worst, then request a full **credit freeze**. This stops any accounts from being opened in your name. Then, file a police report as soon as possible. This creates a paper trail that you can present to skeptical banks or creditors who doubt your word. Last, file a report with the Federal Trade Commission. This may help them investigate and prosecute crime rings.

Remember, a little bit of caution can prevent most of the trauma and hassle of identity theft. Be cautious and aware, and, if you do suspect a problem, then be sure to take action as quickly as you can.

GRAPHIC 5.36

Your Social Security number is the key to your financial kingdom. Do not give it to anyone you do not know as legitimate. Do not carry it in your wallet. Be careful where you use it on the Internet especially.

Pressing Question

- In your opinion, what are the three most important things to remember about personal finance?

Name:

Vocabulary Crossword

Directions: Complete the puzzle using the vocabulary from your reading and the clues below.

Clue Sheet

Across

2. When a bond or loan contract ends
3. Stock that offers assured dividends
5. The interest rate for best customers
8. A subtraction
10. An investment that makes something new
11. Cards that operate on revolving debt
13. Future investors who lay off risk
15. IOUs from business or government
16. The amount in your account
17. Your share of the profits

Down

1. What a check with insufficient funds does
2. Local bonds
3. Cost of getting an insurance policy
4. Turning an asset into cash
6. A commodity contract
7. What happens when you do not pay your mortgage
9. Someone who sets up deals
12. Cost of using someone else's money
14. Piece of ownership in a corporation

Name:

Career Research and Web Exercise

Directions: In the following tables, choose two careers you might possibly pursue. Afterward, start with the Bureau of Labor Statistics and find the Occupational Outlook Handbook. You should explore and look to see what other information is out there. Record what you learn in the tables and cite any new sources below the tables.

<table>
<tr><td>Possible Career 1</td><td rowspan="2">BLS Info Outlook</td><td>Good Schools</td><td>Professional Organizations</td><td rowspan="2">Possible Upside</td><td rowspan="2">Possible Downside</td></tr>
<tr><td>Starting Salaries</td><td>Sample Classes</td><td>Possible Internships</td></tr>
</table>

Additional Sources:

<table>
<tr><td>Possible Career 2</td><td rowspan="2">BLS Info Outlook</td><td>Good Schools</td><td>Professional Organizations</td><td rowspan="2">Possible Upside</td><td rowspan="2">Possible Downside</td></tr>
<tr><td>Starting Salaries</td><td>Sample Classes</td><td>Possible Internships</td></tr>
</table>

Additional Sources:

Name:

Household Budget

Directions: In column 1, write down your best guesses as to what these line items would cost a young person in her twenties out on her own right now. In column 2, write the actual estimate provided by your teacher. In column 3, list what your household (your parents/guardians) pays for each of those items. List the totals in the last row.

Monthly Expenses	**1** **Your Estimate**	**2** **Class's Estimate**	**3** **Your Folks' Estimate**
Housing			
Electric bill			
Gas bill			
Water			
Sewer			
Cable			
Internet access			
Phone			
Cell phone			
Car			
Car insurance			
Gas for car			
Groceries			
Fast-food meal			
Health/hygiene			
Medical insurance			
Savings			
Clothes			
New stuff			
Student loans			
Entertainment			
Totals			

1. Total the second column. _______________
2. Multiply that number by 12. _______________
3. Multiply line two by 1.30 to account for taxes. _______________
4. This is what you need to make every year. _______________
5. What items on this list were not part of household budgets twenty or thirty years ago?

6. What line items could be eliminated altogether?

Name:

Checking Account

Directions: While a bank balances your bank accounts automatically online (just log on and see what you have in there), it is good practice to learn the old-school methods. Fill out the check register below with the information provided. The dates are not in order, so you must rearrange them and place them in accordingly!

Initial balance = $512.11

April 22	Service fee of $1.50
April 25	check 576 made to BMV $178.99
April 12	ATM fee of $1.00
April 19	Auto debit for water bill $28.66
April 13	check 578 for electric bill $56.98
April 11	cash deposit of $700
April 12	check 580 for gas bill $44.67
April 5	paycheck direct deposit $1,344.11
April 6	ATM fee of $1.50
April 25	POS $11.40 Food Mart
April 22	check 577 for car payment $184.79
April 4	cash withdraw $60
April 22	Pizza shop POS (point of sale debit purchase) $23.79
April 2	check 579 for car insurance $356.77

Check Number	Date	Description	Debit	✓	Credit	Fee	Balance

Name:

Changing How We Roll

Directions: For each of the following activities, indicate how people used to do them. In the last column, explain how we do them today. The first activity is completed as an example.

Old School	Activity	New School
You would drive to the bank and deposit a live check in person.	Deposit a paycheck	Use direct deposit.
	Sit down once a month to "balance" the checkbook	
	Save all of your old checks	
	Shop for a new camera	
	Pay bills	
	Get postage for a package	
	Look for a place to live	
	Look for a new job	
	Play a video game	
	Rent a video	
	Go to the music store	
	Save money for retirement	
	Shop for a new mortgage	
	Read the news	
	Phone someone overseas	
	Find out where your son is	
	Stay in touch with friends	

Name:

The True Cost

Directions: Many consumers hesitate to think about the long expense of a major purchase. Thinking carefully about what things really cost can greatly influence your cost-benefit analysis (and therefore your purchase decision). It may change the way you see things.

Tale of Two Cars: Jo works 14 miles from home. Find the price of two cars on the Internet, calculate a loan payment, and estimate the other costs.

Expense	Car Model #1:__________	Car Model #2:__________
A. Monthly payment		
B. Monthly insurance		
C. Registration fee		
D. Maintenance		
E. Gas cost per month based on car's mileage		
F. Sum: A + E		
E. Cost per day (F/30)		
G. Cost per year (F ×12)		

Cell Phone Swap: Jill wants the latest high-end phone. Which is the cheaper way to go? You can find the cost for lines A–D on the Internet.

Expense	High-End Phone	Low-End Phone
A. Purchase price		
B. Monthly plan cost		
C. Sales tax per month		
D. Monthly cost (B + C)		
E. Yearly plan cost (D × 12)		
F. True two-year cost (D × 24) + (A)		

Name:

Reading a Stock Chart

Part 1

Directions: Using Google Finance, Yahoo Finance, or another financial website, choose two companies, and fill in their stock information below.

52-Week High	52-Week Low	Stock	Div	Yield	PE Ratio	Volume	High	Low	Last/ Close	Change/ CHG

52-Week High	52-Week Low	Stock	Div	Yield	PE Ratio	Volume	High	Low	Last/ Close	Change/ CHG

Part 2

Directions: Using your online financial site or investopedia.com, define the following terms:

1. Dividend:

2. Earnings per share:

3. P/E ratio:

4. Market cap:

5. Annual report:

6. Yield:

7. Target:

8. Analyst:

Part 3

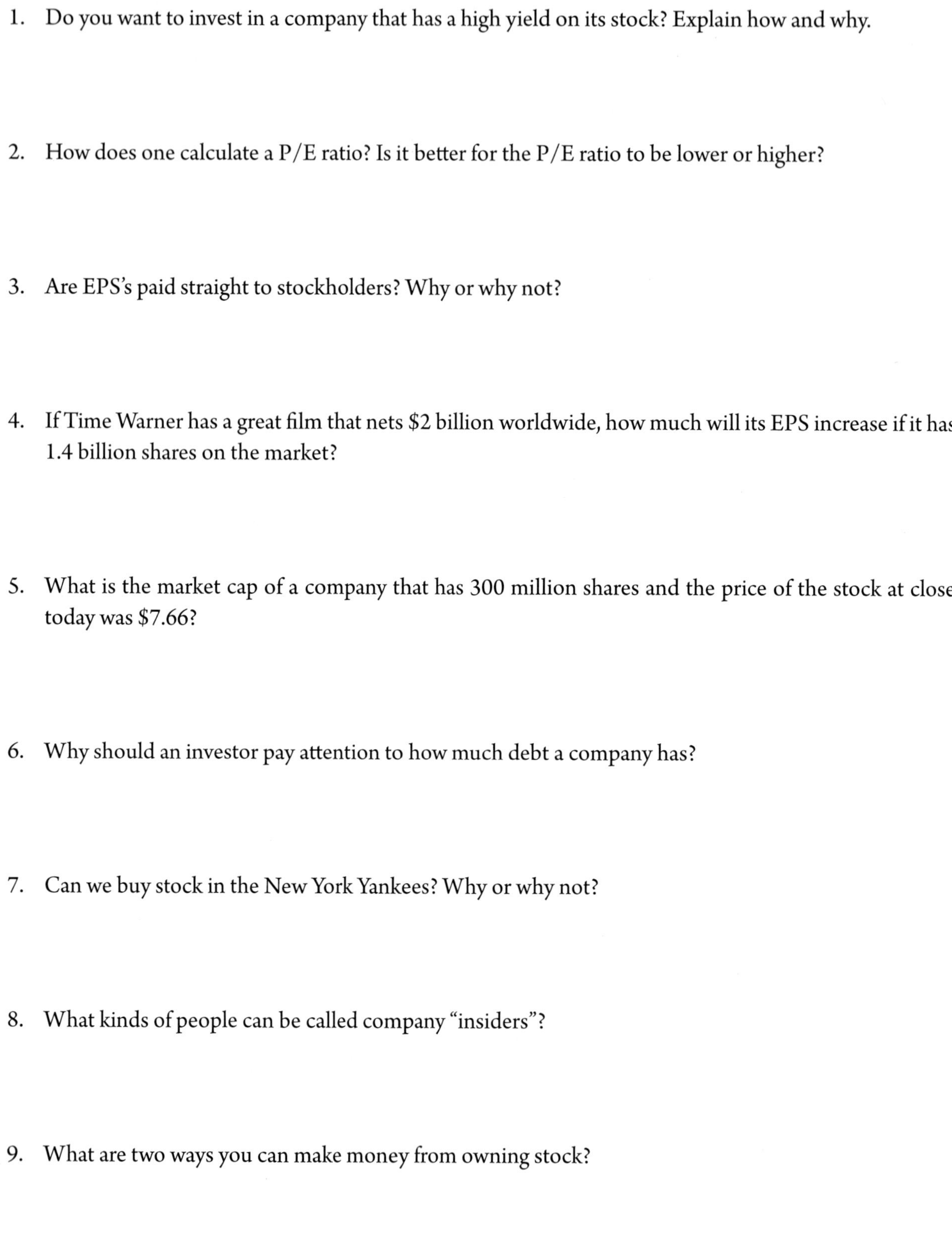

1. Do you want to invest in a company that has a high yield on its stock? Explain how and why.

2. How does one calculate a P/E ratio? Is it better for the P/E ratio to be lower or higher?

3. Are EPS's paid straight to stockholders? Why or why not?

4. If Time Warner has a great film that nets $2 billion worldwide, how much will its EPS increase if it has 1.4 billion shares on the market?

5. What is the market cap of a company that has 300 million shares and the price of the stock at close today was $7.66?

6. Why should an investor pay attention to how much debt a company has?

7. Can we buy stock in the New York Yankees? Why or why not?

8. What kinds of people can be called company "insiders"?

9. What are two ways you can make money from owning stock?

Name:

Stock Web Exercise

Directions: Using your reading and the Internet, fill in the chart below by choosing a company in which you are interested. Try Google Finance or Yahoo Finance to start. Investopedia will have some good definitions, too.

Name of the company	
Location (main HQ)	
CEO biography	
Product and market description	

Statistics	Definition	Company's Current Number
Volume		
Change in $$ (from the previous day if market is closed)		
Percent change (for the day or from pervous day)		
52-week high and low		
Dividend per share		
Earnings per share		
Price/earnings ratio		
Shares outstanding		
Sales		
Div date		
Market capitalization		

On the back: Find five current news articles regarding this company. Create a chart that shows the title of the article, the author or news service, the date, and a two- or three-sentence explanation of the article's information.

 Name:

Understanding Bonds

Part 1

Directions: In this situation you have a friend who borrowed lunch money from you. In the top part of the table, put the behaviors and actions from the right-hand side of the page into the appropriate left-hand columns.

Trustworthy Behavior (good credit)	Suspect Behavior (bad credit)	Behavior Bank
		He paid you back on the day that he said he would.
		He ducks down the stairs when he sees you.
		He borrowed money from three other people in the meantime.
		He paid back other people to whom less money was owed.
		He said thank you.
		He bought you lunch as a gesture of gratitude.
		He told other kids she did not plan to pay you back.
		He bought a new iPod since you lent him the money.
		He gave you half the money ahead of his agreed payment date.

Part 2

Directions: Answer the questions.

1. How can a business establish good credit?

2. For what reasons might a business borrow money?

3. For what reasons might a government borrow money?

4. What happens to the interest rate for a bond issuer with good credit?

5. What happens to a bond issuer with a bad credit history?

6. Who probably gets a better interest rate, the US government or AT&T?

Part 3

Directions: Using your reading or a website such as Investopedia, define the following:

1. Savings bond:

2. Corporate bond:

3. Municipal bond:

4. Treasury bond:

5. Yield:

6. Maturity:

7. Default:

Name:

Portfolio Basics

Part 1

Directions: Place the investments in the appropriate spot on the risk pyramid. Then answer the questions that follow.

- Junk bonds
- Mutual funds
- Stocks in large, proven companies (blue-chip stocks)
- Money market funds
- Futures
- Treasury bonds
- Options
- Growth stocks
- Corporate bonds
- Municipal bonds (munies)
- CDs
- Rental real estate (per label in answers)
- Speculative and penny stocks
- Savings bonds
- Short-sold stocks

High Risk

Medium Risk

Low Risk

Part 2

Directions: Answer these questions to the best of your ability:

1. What would you invest in if you had a(n):

   a. aggressive investment strategy

   b. conservative investment strategy

2. Use the two circles to the right to create pie charts for the same investor at two different times in her life. What should she be investing in?

   Age 25 **Age 75**

3. Are futures a good way to save for a retirement? Why or why not?

4. Why should an employee take advantage of the employer's 401(k) programs?

 Name:

Borrowing Money

Part 1

Directions: Find a "payment calculator" online. Fill in the tables below as you figure out the estimated monthly payment in each of these scenarios.

Mortgage Payments			
Amount Borrowed	**5% 30-Year Fixed**	**6.5% 30-Year Fixed**	**8% 30-Year Fixed**
$100,000			
$140,000			
$180,000			
$225,000			

Auto Payments			
Amount Borrowed	**6.5%—5 Years**	**8.5%—5 Years**	**6.5%—4 Years**
$14,000			
$18,000			
$22,000			
$35,000			

Part 2

Directions: Answer these questions with a sentence or two each.

1. What does it mean when a commercial talks about "5.9 percent financing"?

2. How long does the typical car loan last? Home mortgage?

3. What is an ARM (adjustable rate mortgage)? What is the upside and downside of this type of loan?

4. Why are interest rates higher for car loans?

5. What are the current average rates for a home mortgage, auto loan, and credit card?

6. Realtors speak of PITI: principal + interest + taxes + insurance. What type of taxes and insurance do they mean?

7. *Equity* is the amount of value you have invested in your house, expressed as a dollar amount. (It is not the same as the total you have paid, which includes interest paid to the lender.) What is the equity if you have paid half of the principal on a $150,000 mortgage and the house is currently worth $220,000?

8. What is a home equity loan?

9. How much do lenders expect you to have as a down payment for an auto loan and a mortgage?

Mortgage Jargon

Directions: Using vocabulary words from the unit reading or from the Internet, fill in the blanks with the appropriate jargon.

Mortgage Words to Locate on the Internet
lien, gross, property taxes, insurance, fixed, adjustable, escrow, commission, Realtor, Realtor.com, point

Paul and Dana are a young couple looking for a starter home. They visited a reliable real estate site, ____________ (1), to choose a house they can afford. It has all the homes for sale in their area that are listed on the "multiple listing service." They have also consulted with a ____________ (2), a professional who helps people buy and sell homes. The person who sells them a home will have to pay their realtor a ____________ (3).

They have a ____________ (4) monthly income of $3,600 minus all their other debt payments. Therefore, according to their agent, they can afford a payment that is 36 percent of that monthly income, or ____________ (5) (calculate). They do, however, need to worry about additional monthly expenses like ____________ (6) and homeowner's ____________ (7). Their bank, or ____________ (8)-holder, will most likely put that extra money into a third-party, separate ____________ (9) account.

Because interest rates are low currently, they opted for a ____________ (10) -interest-rate loan that would provide security for them in case interest rates go up in the future. They know that an ____________ (11)-rate loan can go up with market rates. They might consider giving the bank some cash called a ____________ (12), which would get them an even lower interest rate.

 Name:

A Closer Look at Credit

Part 1

Directions: In the table below, put the behaviors in their proper box to match up with one of the "4Cs" of credit. Then, answer the questions at the bottom with the help of your reading or the Internet.

Match the Behavior to the Right 4C		Behavior Bank
Character	Capacity to pay	- He made car payments on time for forty-seven months straight. - He was convicted of check fraud. - Has gross monthly income of $3,200. - He has savings of $12,000. - He missed a credit payment last year. - A judge ordered him to pay a contractor. - He has twelve credit cards.
Capital (money)	Credit history	- He owns a lot of stock. - He makes income from stocks and bonds. - He is over the limit on one of his credit cards. - He has four giant car loan payments. - He has never had any legal trouble. - He was convicted of a felony four years ago. - He just got a huge raise. - He paid off three mortgages in ten years. - He has only one debt, for a car lease.

Part 2

Directions: Using the Internet, your reading, or a robust class discussion, answer the questions below.

1. What are the three best pieces of advice you could give a young person out on her own for the first time when it comes to establishing good credit?

2. What is the name of the website you can visit for a credit report free of charge?

3. List two sites below that give you a credit report but require you to pay for them.

4. What are the benefits of having good credit?

5. Complete the sentence: ______________ is your ability to ______________ someone else's money.

6. What are the three main credit agencies?

7. The line below represents credit scores. Put a letter grade (A–F) at different spots of the scale.

350 400 450 500 550 600 650 700 750 800 850!

Name:

Insurance Jargon

Directions: Choose the words from the box and write them in the appropriate blank.

Insurance Words to Locate on the Internet
actuaries, agent, claim, copay, coinsurance, deductible, demographics, liability, policies, premium, severity

Bill, my insurance ________ (1), suggested I needed to review my coverage. I have three ________ (2) with his company including life, homeowner's, and automobile insurance. I was a little upset that the cost of my auto policy, or ________ (3), went up when I moved into the city. He told me that insurance rates are based on statistics and calculated by mathematicians called ________ (4). They study large groups of people, using ________ (5), to determine people's behavior. They help companies predict the likelihood of paying a ________ (6) to a policyholder. Premiums are calculated when the frequency of claims (chance) is multiplied by the average ________ (7) (cost). The most expensive part of the auto and home policies goes to cover people's financial responsibility for their actions or negligence. This is called ________ (8). If a claim is made, the initial amount of money paid by the policyholder is called the ________ (9). This is not to be confused with a ________ (10), which is the amount that someone pays of each claim, such as the $10 I pay when I visit the doctor's office. I have a friend whose medical insurance requires him to pay a ________ (11) of 20 percent of every claim.

 Name:

Insurance in Depth

Part 1

Directions: Fill in the chart below using the reading from your chapter. If the formula for calculating an insurance premium is frequency × severity, then what factors do you think fit into each category for a variety of different policies? For example, what could make a car accident more likely? More severe?

Insurance Policy	Frequency?	Severity?
Auto	*How often does this particular group get in accidents and then to make claims?*	*The average cost of repairing damages in property or people.*
Homeowner's		
Life		
Flood		
Business		

Part 2

Directions: Answer the questions.

1. What is a demographic group? What describes your demographics?

2. Why do teenagers pay more than any other demographic group for auto insurance?

3. Why do insurance companies rely on actuaries in determining the cost of a premium?

4. What are some of the costs to consider when buying an insurance policy?

5. How do insurance companies make profits?

6. Define the following:
   a. Claim:
   b. Agent:
   c. Premium:
   d. Deductible:
   e. Policy:

 Name:

Changes in Health Insurance

Part 1

Directions: Write the words from the box in the appropriate blank.

Health Insurance Terms
premium, copay, preventative, coinsurance, Medicaid, flexible spending account, employers, deductible, Medicare

_______________ 1. I pay $22 every time I go to the doctor's office, $100 if I go to the emergency room.

_______________ 2. My grandmother is more than sixty-five and gets government insurance called . . .

_______________ 3. I have to pay $12,500 per year for my family coverage.

_______________ 4. I have to pay 20 percent of every dollar that a doctor or hospital charges me.

_______________ 5. I have to pay a $2,500 out-of-pocket maximum every year.

_______________ 6. To pay my medical bills, I use a debit card that is tied to money that comes out of my paycheck prior to taxes being deducted.

_______________ 7. While governments in Europe typically provide health insurance, these provide insurance to people in the United States.

_______________ 8. The poor and unemployed may qualify for government insurance called . . .

_______________ 9. These are services that I receive when I think I am healthy but tell me of potential problems.

Part 2

Web exploration: The law has a "Patient's Bill of Rights." What are some of those rights for these groups? Use www.healthcare.gove and www.medicaid.gov for your research.

1. Young people:
2. People with preexisting conditions:
3. The elderly:
4. Business owners with more than fifty employees:
5. Small employers:
6. Poor people:
7. Young people who do not make a lot of money:

Part 3

How Much Will Insurance Cost Me? Use the "Find Insurance Options" tab on www.healthcare.gov to see what you would have to pay for insurance if you were on your own.

 Name:

Identity Theft

Part 1

Directions: Use the Internet to define the words below. You should be able to find much of the information at www.consumer.ftc.gov.

Theft Method	Definition
Skimming	
Dumpster diving	
Diverting mail	
Phishing	
Vishing	
Forging documents	
Shoulder surfing	
Data breaching	
Malware	
Overlay	

Part 2

Directions: Fill in the blanks based on your reading of Section 5Q.

1. Incidents of identity theft are becoming ______________________ common.
2. The three major credit agencies are ______________________, ______________________, and ______________________.

3. The key to borrowing money in my name is my ________________ ________________ number.

4. If I suspect that my identity has been stolen, I should call the major ________________ agencies.

5. At that time, I can put a ________________ alert on my credit reports.

6. If I am sure that my identity has been compromised, I should request a credit ________________.

7. I should also file a ________________ report.

Part 3

Directions: List some best practices to prevent identity theft.

What are some best practices to prevent identity theft?

Unit 6
Globalization

Questions to Consider

1. Why is there poverty?
2. Why are some countries poor and the United States so rich?
3. Is free trade a good thing for the global economy or our economy?
4. How will the United States do economically in the next one hundred years?
5. What is the difference between capitalism and socialism?
6. Does our economy distribute wealth evenly and fairly?
7. Is socialism a more humane form of economy?

Terms You Need in Order to Read

Capitalism
Economy
Ethics
Free trade
Globalization
Poverty
Productivity
Socialism

Globalization

6A. The United States in the World Economy

One hundred years ago, the most powerful nation in the world was the United Kingdom (Great Britain). It had colonies all over the world, the biggest economy per person, and a currency, the pound sterling, that functioned as the world's medium of exchange just as the dollar does currently. Today, the UK's economy ranks thirty-ninth. What happened? Does it mean that people in the United Kingdom are poor now? No, they are not. It just means that the world economy has changed dramatically.

The amount of goods and services that the world produces has grown to levels that would have been unimaginable one hundred years ago. Scores of countries that did not exist back then have become global players. Many of these new nation-states are former colonies of the UK and other European countries. While the world economy is many times larger than it was a hundred years ago, Western countries now have to compete with rising economic powers like China, India, and Brazil. This does not mean that the United Kingdom is poor or that it is a bad place to live. In fact, it is modern and advanced economically and socially. The UK is not the richest nation in the world, but that does not mean it is not a livable country.

The United States has less than 5 of the world's population but produces about 23 percent of total global products. Many people believe that the United States is in economic decline and losing ground to other countries. Statistics do not support that assumption. Since the Industrial Revolution, our economy has grown at around 2 percent per year. Sustained over decades, the size of our economy doubles every thirty years or so. No other country in the world has sustained that consistent level of growth. The fact remains that the United States has the world's second largest economy. Major technological innovations like automobiles, airplanes, alternating current, refrigeration, computers, and the Internet began with our entrepreneurs. The economy has its ups and downs, but, on average, steady growth is expected.

This economic growth can be attributed to a few characteristics. First, historically the United States has had plentiful natural resources. Entrepreneurs started businesses to capitalize on that abundance. Second, it is relatively easy to form and start a business in the United States. Forming a corporation only takes a few days, and capital is easily accessible. Third, our democratic system strikes a balance between allowing businesses freedom and protecting the rights of the consumer. For instance, AT&T grew into a monopoly, but the government split the company up to ensure greater competition. Fourth, the US population is largely literate. Education gives people the knowledge needed to be innovative and start businesses. Finally, the United States is a country of immigrants. People of diverse cultures and experience bring new ideas and ways of thinking into the marketplace. These are among only a few reasons that explain the incredible story of US economic growth. Contrary to the views of some pessimists, competition from other countries has not eroded our place in the world but strengthened it. As it turns out, trading with other countries can benefit everyone.

GRAPHIC 6.1

Since 1990, cities like Shanghai, China, have grown dramatically. While many people see this as a threat, expanding trade has boosted global productivity and reduced the amount of conflict in the world.

Many people believe that the United States is powerful because of its military. A government can only fund the armed forces with tax revenue, and because the US economy is so large, the IRS collects trillions of dollars per year. Logically, the United States is not powerful because it has the largest army. The United States is powerful because it has one of the world's largest economies.

Recall Unit 3, Section 3G, the reading about gross domestic product (GDP). Our country's ability to produce goods and services at an ever-expanding level helps to increase our disposable income. When there is more produced every year, people can save more and wealth is created. This will translate into a higher **standard of living**, or the overall level of wealth, luxury, comfort, and well-being of a population. Because there is more produced, there is more to be divided among the populace. If we did not produce as much, there would be less for us to have and our standard of living would diminish. Considering our access to food, energy, comfort, health care, and entertainment, the United States has a very high standard of living

Pressing Question

- Go through your closet and look at the tags on your clothes. How many items can you find that were made in the United States?

6B. Globalization

Globalization is the increasing interconnectedness and integration among the people, companies, and governments of different nations. It is driven by international trade and investment. Computers, the Internet, and communication technology have accelerated the process over the past fifty years. While people are more connected than ever, the change from a world of isolated and feudal societies to our modern, global world began centuries ago.

China once traded with the Roman Empire more than 2,000 years ago. The Great Silk Road connected Asian markets with kingdoms in Russia, the Middle East, and beyond. Brave sailors and traders boarded small wooden ships with cloth sails and traveled across uncharted waters. You probably recall the Renaissance and the Age of Exploration from your history classes. By the 1500s, European countries had established colonies all over the globe. Some explorers were motivated by religion, but most were propelled by the untold riches they expected to find. In their home countries were merchants who risked vast fortunes on the promise of a remarkable return. Investors bought ships and hired crews in the hope that the holds would return loaded with gold and spices. Expeditions could take years, and investors had to wait until, "their ships came in."

Through the 1600s and 1700s, nautical technology improved and countries fought one another over valuable trade routes and colonies. On the ships, people also carried books. This helped scientists and philosophers exchange information and expand humanity's knowledge base. In the 1800s, the development of powered engines shrank the time it took to cross an ocean from months to weeks. The invention of the telegraph allowed communication across and between continents with no wait at all. As communication and travel became easier, the pace of technological improvement quickened. This was the **industrialization** of the world.

The Industrial Revolution changed the way people lived forever. For most of human history, almost everybody worked, lived, and died on a farm. After industry changed how things were produced, people began to move to cities, work in factories, and migrate around the world. In fact, of the nearly 8 billion people who live on planet Earth today, more people live in cities than in the country. Urban living did not surpass rural living until 2009, but billions of people still live and work on farms using centuries-old technology.

As the twentieth century progressed, the pace of technological change quickened further. Air travel became common. Shipping overseas

GRAPHIC 6.2

In the 1800s, ships got bigger and faster as they added engines to turn paddle wheels or propellers. The ship above still kept mast and sails as a backup source of power.

and overland got more cost-effective. Telephones and radios quickly made their way into people's homes. Mass communication allowed information to move between researchers and scientists and to the general public. The advent of clean water in cities and modern medicine cut death rates and infant mortality rates by incredible margins. In countries that were developing, citizens enjoyed an ever-increasing standard of living. While the twentieth century was marred by two world wars and a global depression, the process of globalization has brought great benefits to humanity.

Two technologies have accelerated the pace of communication and change more than any other. First, microchips brought the power of computers into every business and home. Before 1975, there were no personal computers. They were the size of buildings and school busses, not to mention expensive. Today, people walk down the street with supercomputers in their pockets (smartphones). Second, the Internet can connect all the computers in the world together. This seems normal to young people today, but it could be humanity's greatest invention. The Internet is transforming every industry, connecting all people, and propelling new inventions in previously unimaginable ways. The convergence of all these technologies has enabled a new era based on telecommunications and information. The future might be uncertain, but it is certainly bright.

We are undergoing a change called the **Information Revolution**. It is a time of rapidly advancing technology in which data, money, and knowledge race across the globe at the speed of light. Human beings now have access to great computing power and much of the world's accumulated information. These connections can greatly enrich our lives.

While the pace of globalization accelerates and brings great benefits to people, it does have a darker side. Increased trade has prompted some developing countries to sacrifice human rights and environmental protection for economic growth. People work in sweatshops for little pay, breathe smoggy city air, and drink tainted water. Increased movement of people around the world has also allowed for more human trafficking and slavery.

Even harder to prevent, cybercrime and hacking have endangered our retail, banking, and government computers. Our private information can be stolen and sold across the world. Despite these new, terrible realities, the Information Revolution has benefited humanity greatly.

GRAPHIC 6.3

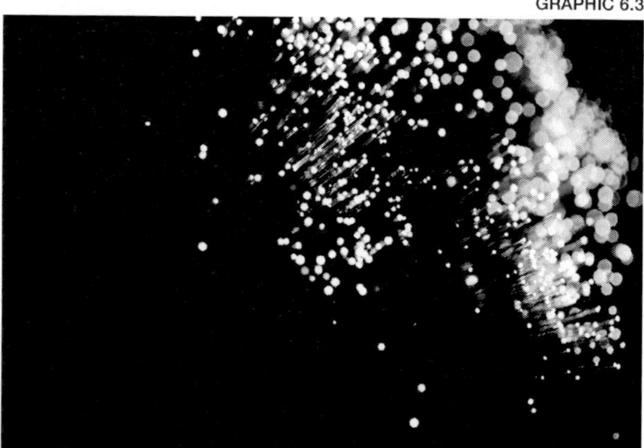

Communication has been the key to the faster pace of technological change. Playing video games against people in other countries and teleconferencing across the globe is made possible by millions of miles of glass fibers, ten times thinner than a human hair, transmitting information as electronic signals.

On the upside, the modern global economy has lifted billions of people out of abject poverty across the globe. Information now reaches the most isolated places. All accumulated human knowledge and education can be accessed by a farmer's children in the developing world, allowing them to be educated and *enlightened*. This adds to the global **human capital**, that is the skills and knowledge that a person or group of people has. These young people can then contribute their ideas and productivity to the rest of the world. This added competition not only helps the once isolated parts of the world develop but grows the whole world economy, allowing everybody to benefit.

Pressing Question

- What do you think the expression "all boats rise with the tide" means?

GRAPHIC 6.4

The United States and North Vietnam fought a war that killed millions of people. Today, a reunited Vietnam is thriving economically. Even though Vietnam's per capita GDP is a small fraction of that of the United States, people there are relatively happy.

6C. Global Economic Comparison

Think about the average American teenager for a moment. She is currently attending a school at an annual cost that is greater (more than $10,000) than some people in the world will see in a lifetime. She wakes up every day in a dwelling that is climate controlled, relatively safe from crime, and furnished with an assortment of electronic conveniences. In the morning, there is a refrigerator full of food and a closet full of clothes. If there is a car for her to drive to school, life is that much more convenient and luxurious. Weekends are filled with movies, games, and the company of friends. Best of all, she can choose her own future. While it is true that about a fifth of US kids live below the poverty line, by the standards of the world life for American teens is relatively pleasant. How close do you come to the scenario above? Remember that many people in the world do not have adequate housing, electricity, or even clean water.

Recall from Unit 3 the term *gross domestic product.* This refers to the dollar value of every good and service produced in our economy in one year. It is not helpful to compare one country's GDP to another, since GDP does not account for population. Also, recall that if GDP is divided by the number of people who live there, it reveals a country's *per capita* GDP. This helps an economist compare the productivity of one citizen to another. The poorest countries in the world have a per capita GDP of $2,500 and lower. Keep in mind that the number does not represent income, but the amount of goods and services produced by one citizen. Developing nations around the world may have per capita GDPs of $5,000 to $15,000. At the same time, in the United States, the per capita GDP was more than $46,000 in 2014—three and a half times the world average.

This does not mean that people in developing countries are unhappy. In fact, as long as a person has enough food and does not live under an oppressive government, that person is usually content. People who live with much less are statistically happier than the average American. Apparently, money is not everything.

Aside from calculating per-person productivity, there are other ways to gauge the standard of living of another country. They are very helpful tools in discerning the quality of life in a country very different from our own.

- **Total fertility rate**—This is the total number of pregnancies a woman will have in a lifetime. In the Western world, it is around two and under. In places with higher poverty, the numbers can sometimes climb above six. Wealthier countries have women who choose to have fewer children. This difference comes from the education and economic opportunities available to women in the developed world.
- **Infant mortality rate**—This is calculated as the number of babies who die before reaching the age of twelve months. It is stated as a

number out of one thousand. For example, the United States has a rate of around 6/1,000. The lowest rates exist in Europe and East Asia, which can fall below 2/1,000. The highest rates are from the poorest countries. Sometimes these are as high as 180/1,000. Countries with lower birthrates, education for girls, and universal medicine have the healthiest babies.

- **Life expectancy**—People in the developed world will live well into and past their eighties. This number has been climbing steadily for the past one hundred years. It doubled in US cities quickly after clean water systems began using chlorine to sanitize water.

GRAPHIC 6.5

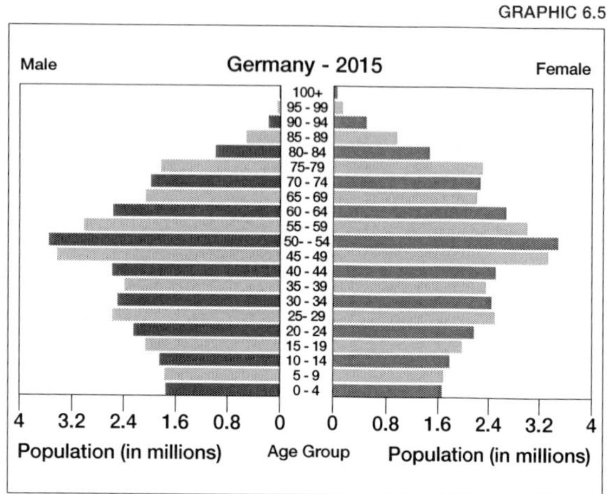

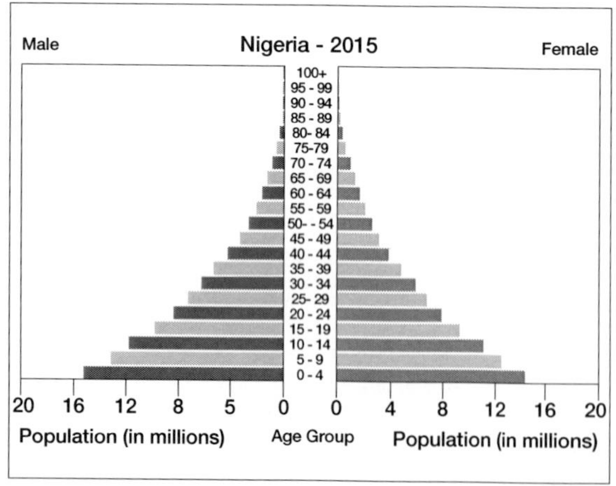

According to CIA.gov, the populations of Germany and Nigeria tell two very different stories. Nigerians are much younger than Germans overall.

- **Purchase power parity (PPP)**—Because of the lower labor costs in some countries, necessities like food and shelter are less expensive. A full meal in Hanoi, Vietnam, might cost you 75 cents, whereas the same meal will cost $20 in Manhattan. PPP takes a basket of basic goods in a country and uses that to create a ratio that illustrates what its per capita GDP truly reflects. For instance, a country may have a per capita GDP of about $750 as a raw number but a per capita GDP of $3,100 when PPP is considered.

GRAPHIC 6.6

Waterborne illnesses are a major source of childhood death around the world. This well was built in Kenya by the US Navy. A healthy population is more apt to be productive.

- **Literacy rates**—Most developed countries have compulsory education until the age of eighteen. Citizens have access to libraries and the Internet. Participation in the national and global economies is within reach of average people. The poorest countries tend to restrict education, particularly the education of women.
- **Net migration**—Some countries are gaining population. This gain would give them a positive migration rate per 1,000 people. If this number is negative, people are leaving. It is difficult for a country to lose population and have a growing GDP.
- **GDP composition**—Developed countries have small percentages of their labor force working on farms. In the United States, less than 1 percent of people work on farms. Ranching and farming constitute a small percentage of the GDP.
- **Age distribution**—Consider graphic 6.5. Economists also look at the breakdown of age groups in a country. With their declining birthrates, Germany and Italy have decreasing

populations. The United States has a growing population because of immigration. The poorest countries in the world have disproportionate numbers of young people. Birthrates are high, because children are a source of labor and social security.

- **Human Development Index (HDI)**—This is an index of life expectancy, education, and income used to rank countries into four tiers of human development. It is published by the United Nations. It offers a simple way of gauging how a country is developing without researching each of those individual statistics.
- **Corruption Perceptions Index**—A think tank in Germany annually ranks countries by people's perception of corruption levels through surveys and analysis. **Corruption** is loosely defined as the misuse of public power for private benefit. This index currently ranks 177 countries on a scale from 100 (noncorrupt) to 0 (highly corrupt). Many underdeveloped countries suffer from governmental corruption, including government officials siphoning money from their economies.

The statistics for the United States indicate its economic place in the world. The United States has a high per capita GDP, high literacy rates, and long life expectancy. All of these statistics are available on CIA.gov in the World Factbook (graphic 6.7). It is the book of record when it comes to international statistics and research. Here, all the countries are ranked to all the previously listed statistics. Many Americans might be surprised to find out that the United States is not number one in any of these areas.

Pressing Question

- What two distinct patterns do you notice in graphic 6.5? What future problems might they cause?

6D. Problems in the Developing World

The term **developing world** refers to nations that have yet to experience a transforming industrial revolution, that have relatively low productivity, and whose populations disproportionately live in poverty. These countries can be found in Latin America, Africa, Eastern Europe, and Asia. The term **underdeveloped country** refers to a nation that lacks industry, infrastructure, and economic resources. These countries also contain more than 75 percent of the world's population. In the past, these countries were referred to as the "Third World," ranking the United States and Europe as being the "First World." However, just because a people live in a developing nation, it does not mean that they are not making advances. It also does not mean that all people cannot benefit by increased trade, interaction, and continuing development. As the century progresses, poorer countries will grow economically and become valuable allies and trading partners.

GRAPHIC 6.7

The CIA World Factbook is the gold standard of international research.

Why can they not develop? Why do they not industrialize like Western countries and prosper? The answers are not simple. The solutions are even more difficult. There are several reasons that so many countries in the world lag behind the West:

- **Lack of capital**—Poor countries do not have much capital. Without capital, a country cannot produce goods and services efficiently. The government lacks the money to build the roads, power plants, water systems, and airports necessary to allow the economy to grow. This lack of infrastructure will not allow businesses to start or expand. People do not have money to save or invest. Foreign investors shy away, because they fear political instability or the lack of infrastructure needed to conduct business. The citizens of El Salvador work long hours to produce agricultural goods. Most manufactured, higher-value goods have to be imported from more developed nations.

- **Lack of natural resources**—Many countries simply do not have the natural resources to develop. The geography in countries like Mali or Oman is largely arid. Widespread agriculture cannot be sustained. They also lack sufficient mineral resources to produce new goods. Unlike the surrounding countries, they do not have oil to export.
- **Overpopulation**—In many countries, children are a necessary source of labor. Families rely on **subsistence agriculture**. They must eat what they grow to stay alive. Most of their time is spent tending to a farm. Children can be a great help, but food is sometimes scarce. There is little time to produce other goods, which leaves the family with little hope for economic improvement. Education and literacy rates are low. The government of Indonesia has encouraged citizens to resettle from the island of Java (which is overpopulated) to other islands in the nation. The hope is that the overcrowding on one island will dissipate while more inhabitants on isolated islands will bring development.
- **Lack of skilled workers**—People in poor countries lack access to education. Because of this deficit, the country will lack the skilled workers needed to produce goods that can be sold to other countries. Human capital, expertise, and know-how are vital components of a developed economy. Mongolia is geographically isolated. The citizens have had little contact with the outside world. The majority of the population still lives live a seminomadic life outside cities. People are skilled herders, but they do not produce products that are particularly valuable on the world market. Educated people become more valuable in the modern world as they specialize in highly technical fields. This requires education and training.
- **History**—Many disadvantaged countries are former colonies of a Western power. India spent hundreds of years under British rule. Most economic development benefited England, not India. Wealth did not get reinvested in the country's infrastructure. While India's economy has grown considerably in the last few decades, its per capita GDP is a small fraction of that of the United Kingdom.
- **Political instability**—The Democratic Republic of the Congo used to be a colony of Belgium. After it gained independence, foreign powers conspired to place a dictator, Mobutu Sese Seko, in charge of the country. This led to decades of brutal oppression. After his ouster in the mid-1990s, the country suffered a series of crippling civil wars. History can hobble a country's economic development. The people in power siphoned money from the economy and padded their own bank accounts. The DRC has yet to recover from these decades of instability.

GRAPHIC 6.8

Gandhi with Lord Pethick-Lawrence, British secretary of state for India, after a meeting. India gained its independence in 1947.

- **Social obstacles**—In some countries, society is structured according to strict social or class divisions. Ultraconservative religious practices restrict girls from going to school, holding jobs, and even driving cars. This shrinks the labor force by half. Tribes and clans jockey for power and control over meager resources. Foreign investment and economic growth are rare. Saudi Arabia is a monarchy with a strict segregation of men and women. Women need permission from a male relative to travel, go to school, get a job, open a bank account, or get surgery. These restrictions keep most women out of the workforce. Keeping half of a country's potential wage earners out of the economy dramatically inhibits productivity.

- **Corruption**—After the fall of the Soviet Union, the bloc of countries in Eastern Europe became independent nations. Since then, countries like Russia have struggled with organized crime. Payoffs and protection money must be paid to criminals and government alike. It is a serious deterrent to new business. The government then chooses to funnel meager resources to friends and relatives. This **crony capitalism**, as it is called, is so common in some countries that foreign investors refuse to conduct business there.

Growth in underdeveloped countries benefits the whole world. While the previous factors are daunting, any country can become a valuable trading partner. Trade can benefit both countries involved. US citizens may partake in new imports and the smaller country may get investments and technology. This increased interaction also makes war less likely.

GRAPHIC 6.9

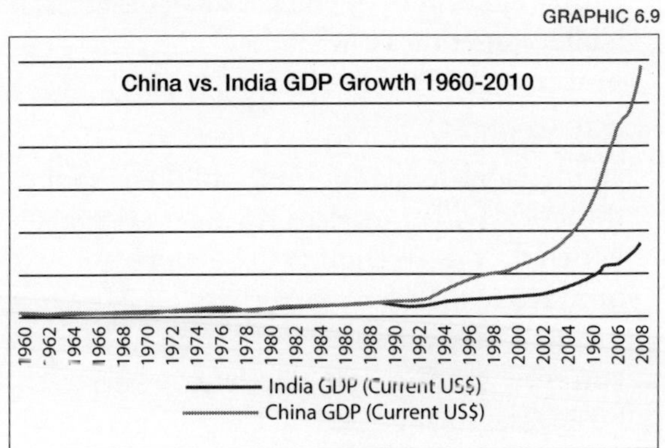

After World War II, India gained its independence from the United Kingdom, and China ended two decades of civil war. By 1950, both countries had isolated themselves from world trade and global interaction, and both tried different forms of socialism. After the breakup of the former Soviet Union in 1991, a new wave of political thought moved around the globe. China and India reemerged onto the world stage in the early 1990s. Today, China has an authoritarian capitalist society. Citizens enjoy free markets but have limited political rights outside the Communist Party (recall graphic 6.10 from Unit 1). India is the world's biggest democracy and enjoys a rapidly growing economy. Like the United States and China, it has a free-market capitalist economy. (Refer to graphic 6.9.) All countries can benefit by increasing trade and cooperation. Trade breeds competition, raises wages, and improves standards of living. Best of all, people who interact and communicate are less likely to go to war.

GRAPHIC 6.10

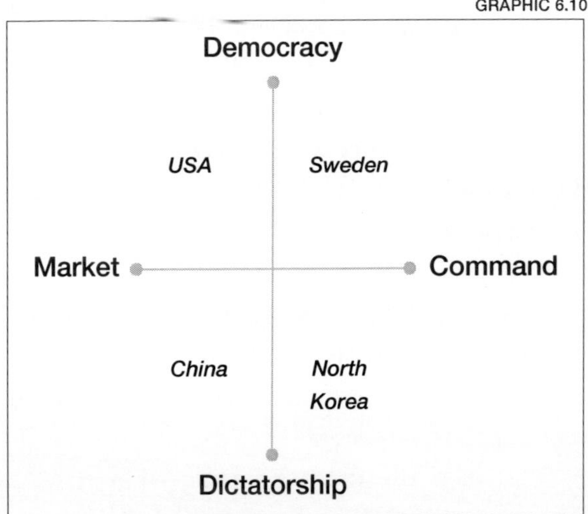

Pressing Question

- If you were in charge of helping an underdeveloped country develop, what are the three best pieces of advice you would offer?

6E. How to Help the Developing World

While it might seem that the world is a dangerous and desperate place, analysis of economic data shows some promising trends. Life spans across the globe are lengthening. Billions of people have been lifted from abject poverty. Conflict is on the decline, despite the perception portrayed on the news. Economic development is reaching the farthest corners of the planet, and people are benefiting. Mass starvation and famine, common throughout the twentieth century, have been largely eliminated. One hundred years ago, there were only a handful of democracies in the world. Today, there are more than one hundred. All of these are reasons to celebrate, but it does not mean that developing nations are ready to compete with Western countries economically.

For the decades following World War II, organizations like the International Monetary Fund (IMF) and the World Bank made large loans to governments to help build their countries' infrastructures (roads, airports, and ports, for example). This money, however, did not address some basic issues and problems facing a poor country. In fact, money often disappeared into the hands of corrupt government officials. Even worse, a poor country had to accept the terms of opening their markets to free trade. This often pitted a poor farmer against a multinational corporation or large agribusiness. Metaphorically, it was like tossing a novice swimmer into the deep end of a pool. These countries did not have the tools to compete. After all of those loans, many nations were hopelessly in debt.

With all of the disadvantages listed in the previous section, developing countries face significant obstacles to continuous economic growth. In order to help them overcome these difficulties, the United States, other developed countries, and nongovernmental organizations (NGOs), focus on the following issues:

- **Keep people fed**—Malnourished people cannot hunger and thirst for freedom until they get food and water. Starving people are rarely productive. History has shown again and again that an undernourished population is apt to rebel and cause political instability. Organizations like Water.org encourage market-based ideas about getting fresh drinking water to people around the world.

GRAPHIC 6.11

Muhammad Yunus of Bangladesh founded Grameen Bank, which specializes in microloans to small businesses in the poorest places in the world. For this work, he won a Peace Prize in 2006.

- **Keep people safe**—People need to have confidence that when they go to a market to partake in economic activity, they will not be attacked. Markets are powerful. In places savaged by war, the first signs of normality that often appear are markets. People have a natural urge to trade and interact. Violence quickly quiets that urge. The United Nations has peacekeeping forces that attempt to provide security to war-torn areas.
- **Get people capital**—When people can borrow small amounts of money, they can start small businesses. These businesses require employees. People work, get paid, and are then able to buy the essentials. **Microloans** (loans of a few hundred dollars or less), first seen in the early 1980s, give the world's poorest people a means of opening a small business, which sometimes can lift them and others out of abject poverty. (See graphic 6.11.)
- **Get people educated**—With more connections to the Internet, children around the world will have access to great teaching. When they learn enough to be more productive than the average worker in their country, they can make more money. With entrepreneurship training, they can start businesses. Countries like Rwanda in central Africa now require all students to learn how to be entrepreneurs. This knowledge can lead to economic growth, technological innovation, and even good governance.
- **Get rid of corruption**—Organized crime and government corruption stifle develop-

ment. People need the knowledge and assistance to rid their governments of crony capitalism. This type of systematic theft of public resources by governments has been named **kleptocracy** by world economists.

- **Establish a democratic government**—Only after people are fed, literate, and vested in their own economy can a democracy be healthy. Political systems built upon poverty, tribalism, religious strife, and corruption are doomed to fail. The United States saw this pattern as it tried to establish democracies in Iraq and Afghanistan with mixed results.

The United States gives more money away to foreign countries than any other on the planet. Some countries get close to four billion dollars from the State Department. Others get less than $1 million. In all, foreign aid is far less than 1 percent of the federal budget. Most of the money is spent in humanitarian projects and aid for economic development. Strategically, this foreign aid gives the US government leverage in trade negotiations or times of crisis.

Pressing Question

- Of all the ways to help a poor country develop listed in this section, which one is most important in your opinion? Why?

6F. Free Trade?

Globalization can be a controversial subject. Some people associate increasing trade with jobs leaving the United States for other countries. This has been the case in many industries. In the 1970s and 1980s, a great number of manufacturing and textile jobs left for countries like Mexico. In the 1990s, many companies shifted their production facilities to China. Since the Internet boom, thousands of back office jobs and customer-service jobs in call centers have gone to India. It does seem like a threat to our way of life. Can free trade really be good for everybody?

Consider graphic 6.12. S_{USA} represents the domestic supply of steel. S_{World} represents the supply of the steel around the world. The world supply curve is more elastic, because there are many more substitutes available. Absent of free trade, US citizens have to pay a price at point A. If trade is opened up, the price will be reduced to point B. The lower price increases the amount of steel used in the United States through higher demand. It also frees up money for consumers of steel to spend on other products, which may bring them more utility. The added competition will affect domestic producers and their workers. From point B, follow the price back toward the y-axis and to point C. Notice where it hits the S_{USA} curve. This indicates a lower quantity supplied than existed before free trade. The lower production almost always means a loss of jobs in that industry, and this is when free trade becomes controversial.

GRAPHIC 6.12

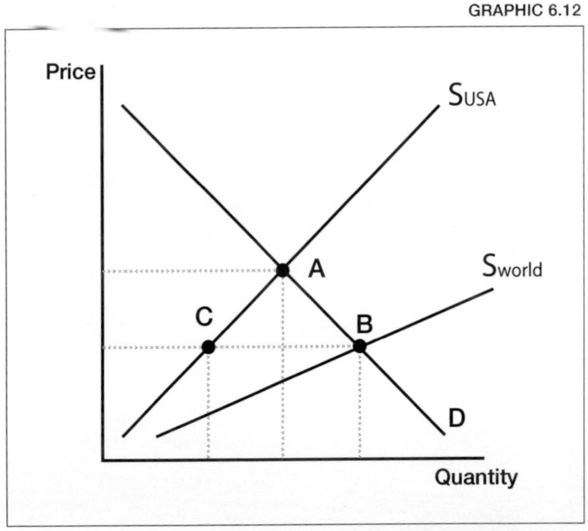

The Internet will increase the pace of globalization and free trade. According to the United Nations, 40 percent of people in the world have access to the Internet. As that number gets larger, it will be easier for companies to access the human capital in distant countries. Talent no longer knows boundaries. Young people now have to compete with workers around the world. College graduates could very easily lose a job to someone who lives in another country. Using the Internet, people can meet face to face, exchange documents, and deliver services across the globe.

GRAPHIC 6.13

North American Free Trade Agreement
Central American Integration System
Union of South American Nations
Caribbean Community
European Union
European Free Trade Association
Central European Free Trade Agreement
African Union
Eurasian Economic Community
Arab League
South Asian Association for Regional Cooperation
ASEAN Free Trade Area Agreement
Pacific Islands Forum

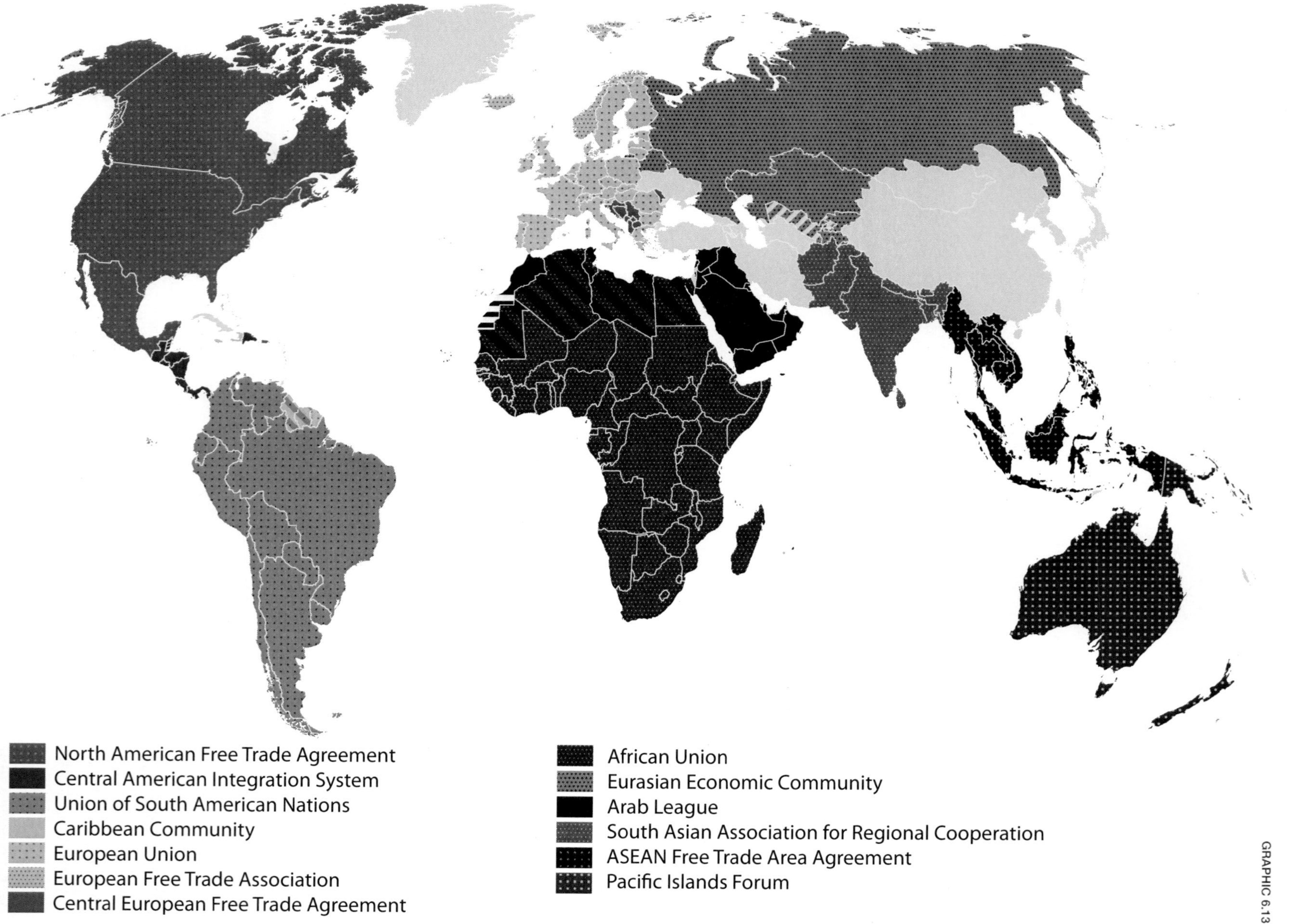

GRAPHIC 6.14

Free Trade Agreements

The United States has free trade agreements in force with twenty countries. These are:

- Australia
- Bahrain
- Canada
- Chile
- Colombia
- Costa Rica
- Dominican Republic
- El Salvador
- Guatemala
- Honduras
- Israel
- Jordan
- Korea
- Mexico
- Morocco
- Nicaragua
- Oman
- Panama
- Peru
- Singapore

The United States has many free trade agreements. Consider graphic 6.14. One of the most influential is the **North American Free Trade Agreement (NAFTA)**. In this treaty, Canada, Mexico, and the United States agreed to do away with the economic barriers between them. Since its inception in 1994, NAFTA has had mixed results for the United States. Some jobs have left, but the lower prices of our products in Mexico have created higher sales and increased profits for some domestic industries. Our region is not the only to adopt freer trade. Refer to graphic 6.13. Almost every country in the world engages in some form of free trade.

Increased trade does reduce the prices of goods in the United States, as graphic 6.12 illustrates, but what about the lost jobs? What does it mean economically? If the steel industry in the United States is less efficient than in another country, then economists would argue that resources should be allocated to more efficient industries. Some countries are better than others at producing certain goods.

For instance, Brazil can produce coffee more cheaply and efficiently than the United States. Brazil has an **absolute advantage**. This is the ability of a country to perform particular economic activities more efficiently than another. It is better for Brazil to grow coffee.

Nations must also consider the **comparative advantage** to producing a specific product. This refers to the ability of one nation to produce a good at lower opportunity cost relative to the same products in another country. For instance, Brazil and the United States have the ability to produce both coffee and computers. If Brazil moves resources from coffee to computers, then it will increase computer production by 20 percent. If the United States moves the same amount of resources from domestic coffee production to making computers, it can produce 50 percent more computers. The United States has a comparative advantage in producing computers. This does not mean that Brazil should or will stop producing computers; it merely means that the United States can do so more efficiently than growing coffee.

It is in the best interest of a country to export its products to other nations. This can help expand domestic industries. The people of the United States can buy only so many cars, but by opening new markets our auto industry can prosper and hire more people. An **export** is a good or service that is sold to someone in another country. An **import** is a good or service that is produced in another country and brought to the United States. If more goods are exported than imported, there is a **trade surplus**. For decades, the United States has imported more than it exports. This is called a **trade deficit**. Recall from Unit 3 the formula for calculating GDP. A trade deficit must be subtracted from a country's productivity, because the goods were made in another country. In the end, it is best to have a balance between exports and imports.

Sometimes to protect jobs or a particular industry, a government may place a **tariff** on imports. This is a tax and makes the good more expensive. While this could be a good source of revenue for the government and can help to protect some industries, other countries may respond by doing the same to our products. This could result in a **trade war**, with nations escalating their tariffs in order to restrict any trade among countries. In the case of an international dispute, one country may place an **embargo** on the other. This means that the two countries have cut off all trade with each other.

Today **trade sanctions**, or restrictions on particular markets of specific countries, are used as a means of coercion by the international community.

Free trade continues to expand around the globe. While some countries have difficulty competing, the trend is clear. It is also conceivable that a world without trade restrictions could exist in this century (see graphic 6.15). Economically, a country that produces a good less efficiently should allocate more resources to its more efficient industries. This can increase the wealth and well-being of the citizens of that country. The increased interaction and dependence on one another will also make it very unlikely that there will be a World War III. Young people play video games together, sing one another's songs, and eat one another's food. This interaction means world peace is more likely.

GRAPHIC 6.15

Principles of Free Trade
(Source: World Trade Organization)

Free trade should be:

without discrimination—a country should not discriminate between its trading partners (giving them equally "most-favoured-nation" or MFN status); and it should not discriminate between its own and foreign products, services or nationals (giving them "national treatment");

freer—barriers coming down through negotiation;

predictable—foreign companies, investors and governments should be confident that trade barriers (including tariffs and non-tariff barriers) should not be raised arbitrarily; tariff rates and market-opening commitments are "bound" in the WTO;

more competitive—discouraging "unfair" practices such as export subsidies and dumping products at below cost to gain market share;

more beneficial for less developed countries—giving them more time to adjust, greater flexibility, and special privileges.

Pressing Question

- Why are imports subtracted from a country's GDP?

6G. Socialism in the World Today

When Mikhail Gorbachev dissolved the Soviet Communist Party in 1991, the Soviet Union ceased to exist and a democratic Russia emerged. This ended 50 years of icy relations and mutual military buildup between the United States and the Union of Soviet Socialist Republics (USSR). This "cold war" not only created a constant threat of nuclear conflict but also pitted the economic theories of socialism against capitalism. All the countries and people who fell under the sphere of the USSR were isolated from the world economy. Economists in the West generally view the various attempts at communism around the world as a disaster.

In the mid-1800s, when the Industrial Revolution was taking hold in Europe, Karl Marx and Friedrich Engels were dismayed at the widening gap between the rich and poor. They believed that history was a story of the struggle between those who own the factors of production and those who do not. They wanted a society where everyone had roughly the same amount of goods, where there was an absence of class differentiation, and where the government worked to create an equitable economy. They wrote down their ideas in ***The Communist Manifesto***, calling for "working men of the world" to unite in a revolution.

While Marx never envisioned that his ideas would grow into a nation like the former Soviet Union, he did believe that after the socialist uprising there would need to be someone to guide the country into a future that promised equality of status and wealth for all people. What actually happened in Russia in 1917 was a prolonged civil war that devastated its people and eventually led to the brutal dictatorship of Joseph Stalin. Marx did not intend that.

Marxism is a worldview and way of thinking that focuses on class relations as the major source of historical trends. It also stresses that the disproportionate distribution of wealth causes social strife. Marx thought that economic classes—those who control the factors of production and the workers who produce goods and services—caused problems and that there should only be one class, a class of workers. Communists in Russia used a dictatorship to impose this outcome on the people. Many other countries have supported Marx's idea of the equality of material wealth. A few socialist systems, such as the one in Norway, have created the world's most proportionate distribution of wealth.

GRAPHIC 6.16

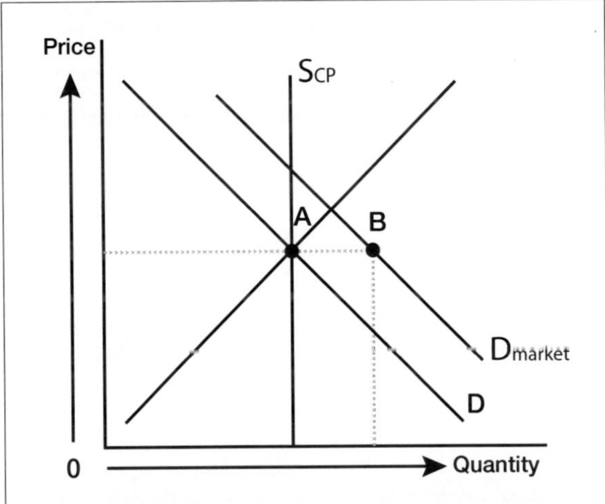

As explained in Unit 1 some countries, including Cuba, China, and North Korea, have attempted **central planning.** This notion is a key component to most authoritarian socialist governments. In essence, central planners dictate to the public how much of each good and service should be produced, how resources are utilized, and how citizens should live. They ignore market forces for the most part and try to guess at what society wants. Look at graphic 6.16. Assume this graph shows the market for cars in a North Korea. The S_{CP} (central plan for supply) curve shows how many cars the government chose to make this year. The demand curve marked D indicates where the government believes the demand for cars should be. The D_{market} curve shows the actual market demand. The distance between points A and B indicates a shortage of cars. During the mid-twentieth century, most if not all communist countries experienced chronic shortages of goods and services.

Some economies have fared well with socialist distribution of wealth. In Sweden, for instance, people retain the basic rights of free speech and democratic elections while the government plays a key role in planning the economy. This is called **democratic socialism**. The Swedish government controls about 10 percent of the country's industry while private interests own the rest. Swedes pay a high level of taxation. More than one-half of the country's income is handed over to the government. With this money, the government provides social programs like health insurance, free education, subsidized housing, and retirement benefits. Because of this, Swedes enjoy one of the highest standards of living in the world.

Some economists argue that democratic socialist countries lack a vibrant entrepreneurial culture and that this has stifled innovation. Statistics do show that many countries with this type of economy have flat levels of growth and chronic high unemployment. Economist Milton Friedman wrote that there is a trade-off between equality and freedom. Consider graphic 6.17. To get more equality in society, some freedom must be sacrificed. On the other hand, a freer society will be less equal. In raw numbers, countries like the United States have exceeded the economic growth of socialist countries. Conversely, those countries tend to have lower social numbers like infant mortality and poverty.

GRAPHIC 6.17

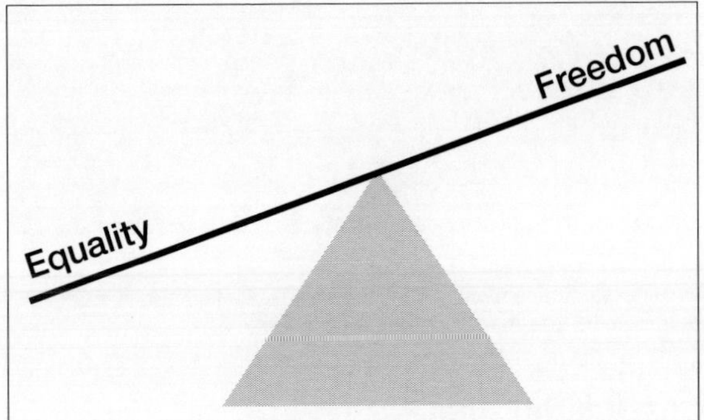

As a lesson in the stark difference between command and market economies, consider the Korean peninsula at night (graphic 6.18). To the north of the border, North Korea lacks the money and infrastructure to provide enough electricity at night. To the south, people live in a vibrant, productive, and modern economy. The primary difference between the two is merely who gets to make most economic decisions. Central planners call the shots in North Korea while in South Korea private citizens, with greater control, enjoy private property and economic freedom.

GRAPHIC 6.18

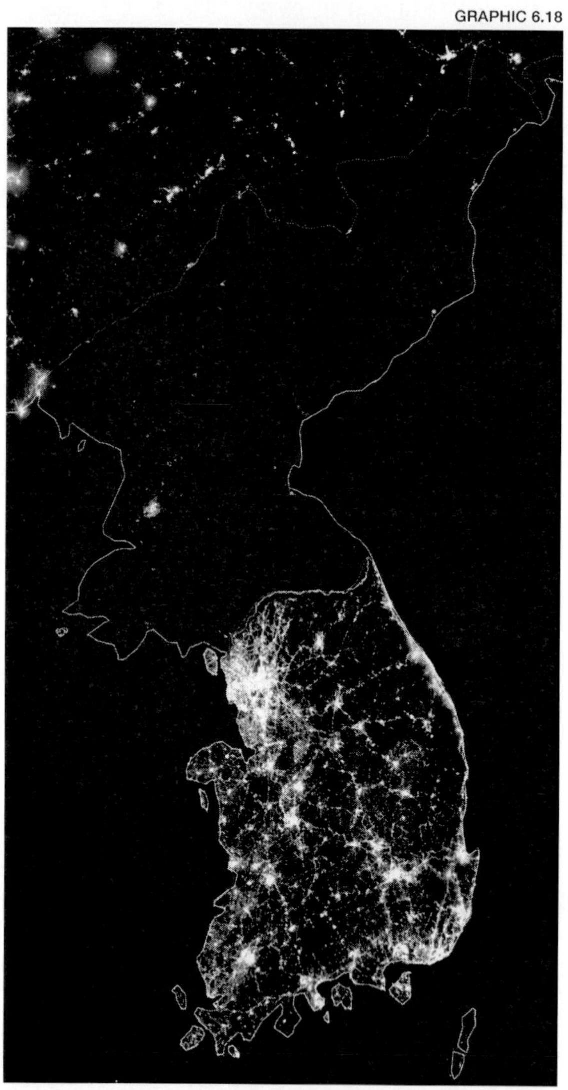

A satellite view of North and South Korea at night. Command-market North Korea can be seen almost completely blacked out, in stark contrast to its free-market cousin to the south.

Pressing Question

- Explain the trade-off between equality and freedom in a society.

6H. Poverty

As you have read in an earlier section, the United States has the world's second biggest economy. It leads the world in innovation and technology. Its economy grows dependably decade after decade. Why then is there poverty in the United States? With so much being produced and so much being consumed, one would think that there would be enough prosperity for everyone. For decades, 12 to 15 percent of the people in the United States lived under the poverty line. This translates to tens of millions of people.

Poverty simply means to be extremely poor. There are levels of material goods that most Americans consider to be socially normal. For instance, if somebody lacks enough money to afford food and adequate shelter, that person lives in poverty. The Census Bureau sets the poverty threshold. This is the level of annual income under which an individual or household is considered to be impoverished. It is around $12,000 for an individual and $25,000 for a family of four.

Poverty touches every part of a person's life. Children who are born into poverty are likely to remain in poverty the rest of their lives. They typically have less than adequate nutrition, education, and household stability. They are more likely to be incarcerated at some point in their lives. People in poverty suffer a greater incidence of disease, mental illness, and crime. Americans believe in **social mobility**, or the ability of someone to earn a higher income than did their parents. Many people in poverty do work at full-time jobs. They are called the "working poor." For these people, social mobility is rare and difficult. For the poor outside the United States, the absence of modern capital, social stability, and education makes economic advancement almost impossible.

To help ameliorate the impact of poverty, the United States government has a host of programs. The Supplemental Nutrition Assistance Program (SNAP), sometimes called "food stamps," provides debit cards that poor families use to buy staple foods. WIC (Women, Infants, and Children) provides additional nutritional assistance to families with children under five years old. Lunches and breakfasts are served in more than 100,000 schools across the country to tens of millions of children.

GRAPHIC 6.19

Economic shocks and structural changes to the economy can reduce some people into poverty. During the Great Recession, these homes in Detroit were abandoned and fell into ruin.

The government also provides funds in the form of welfare. This money provides minimal level of well-being and social support for all citizens. It includes unemployment insurance, social security survivor and orphan benefits, supplemental income assistance, and a host of other entitlements. These programs do help people in need, but they have not eliminated poverty itself.

Poverty in the United States is different from poverty in undeveloped countries. Poor Americans have access to popular culture, TV, and the Internet. Psychologically, however, poverty in the United States can still be worse than in other countries. **Relative poverty** is the condition of a person when a comparing lifestyles of people within the same country. With mass media, people are exposed to images of what money can buy and how other people live. This situation can increase the emotional impact of poverty. Seeing others live in comfort and luxury as you are in a dire situation will breed feelings of inadequacy, discontent, and resentment.

Across the globe, poverty can be inhuman. There are places in the world where people live on garbage dumps with their children. Perhaps their country is in the midst of conflict. Maybe they have survived a natural disaster. Whatever the case, the extremely poor in the world live with vermin, suffer from constant illness, and are chronically malnourished. This lack of basic human necessities is **absolute poverty**. People need access to clean water, proper food, and basic education.

According to the estimates, approximately 14 percent of the world's people in 2010 lived at or below $1.25 a day—down from 43 percent in 1990 and 52 percent in 1981 (see graphic 6.21). In 2011, more than 1 billion people lived on less than $1.25 a day compared to the 1.93 billion in 1981. At the current pace, fewer than one billion people will still live in extreme poverty in 2020.

It is evident that there are fewer people in the world who live in abject poverty compared to a few decades ago. This is a remarkable achievement of the modern market economy. With capitalism, however, money tends to gather in one place. In some countries, people live in horrible conditions with little hope of social advancement while others live lavish lifestyles. This is a matter of distribution of wealth.

GRAPHIC 6.20

These women in India scavenge for anything of value in a garbage dump.

A term that comes into many discussions about poverty is **living wage**. This is the minimum income a person needs to earn in order to afford basic needs like food, shelter, and medicine. Often the working poor in the United States receive some additional form of public assistance like food stamps, Medicaid, or subsidized housing.

Advocates for the poor point to this as an argument to raise minimum wage and improve educational systems. A living wage is usually less in developing and underdeveloped countries, because of the lower cost of living. To help families across the globe, some organizations advocate "fair trade" policies. This means that they will buy products (such as coffee) only from merchants who pay their vendors a living wage.

GRAPHIC 6.21

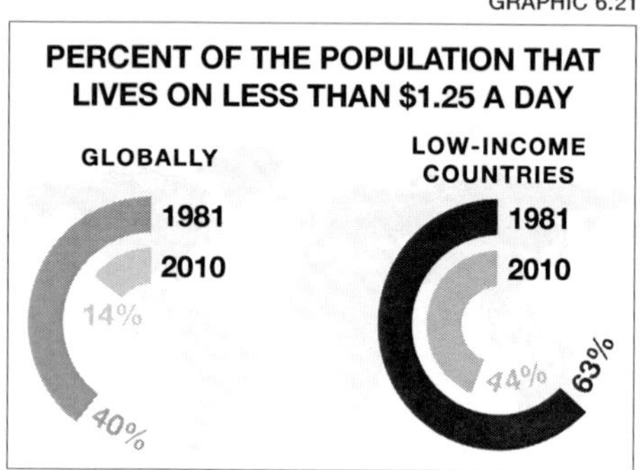

Pressing Question

- What makes poverty worse in countries in the developing world?

6I. The Increasing Wealth Gap

People have the right to spend their money the way they wish. It is a fundamental right people should have. With that in mind, overspending is a problem in the United States. People are often not using their own money to buy consumer goods. Instead, they are borrowing it. People are borrowing money for wants. Economists know that mounting debts are unsustainable. People are driven to buy items that are beyond their means. They are driven by **consumerism**, an ideology and philosophy that encourages an ever greater accumulation of goods. Businesses know this and influence people with advertising.

Sometimes people buy a consumer good believing that it will improve their standing with others and publicly display their economic status. This is called **conspicuous consumption**. It was first written about more than one hundred years ago by sociologist Thorstein Veblen. Recall from Unit 1 that utility is the satisfaction that a good or service gives the user. A luxury car bought by someone who cannot afford the payments is a good example. Any car can take someone from one place to another. If a consumer believes that a more expensive car improves his place in the community, that car purchase is the result of psychological misperceptions. After all, purchases bring only a temporary satisfaction. It is important to understand why people consume.

In the United States, the public is bombarded with advertising showing how consumption elevates status and well-being. It has a huge impact on how people spend their money. The fact remains that there are fewer wealthy people in the United States than most people think. This does not stop people from consuming beyond their means.

In measuring a person's economic status, the two yardsticks most often used are income and wealth. While **income** refers to the total amount of money earned during a given period, **wealth** is someone's total amount of accumulated assets. A salary of $75,000, bank account interest, and stock dividends get added together into income. Equity in a home, stock, mutual funds, and bank deposits are typical forms of wealth. Saving part of an income every year helps people build wealth.

GRAPHIC 6.22

On the left, the *favelas*, or slums, of Rio are crowded into a very small area. On the right, high-value apartments accentuate the disparity of wealth in Brazil.

Remember that the distribution of wealth is a comparison of the accumulated assets of various

GRAPHIC 6.23

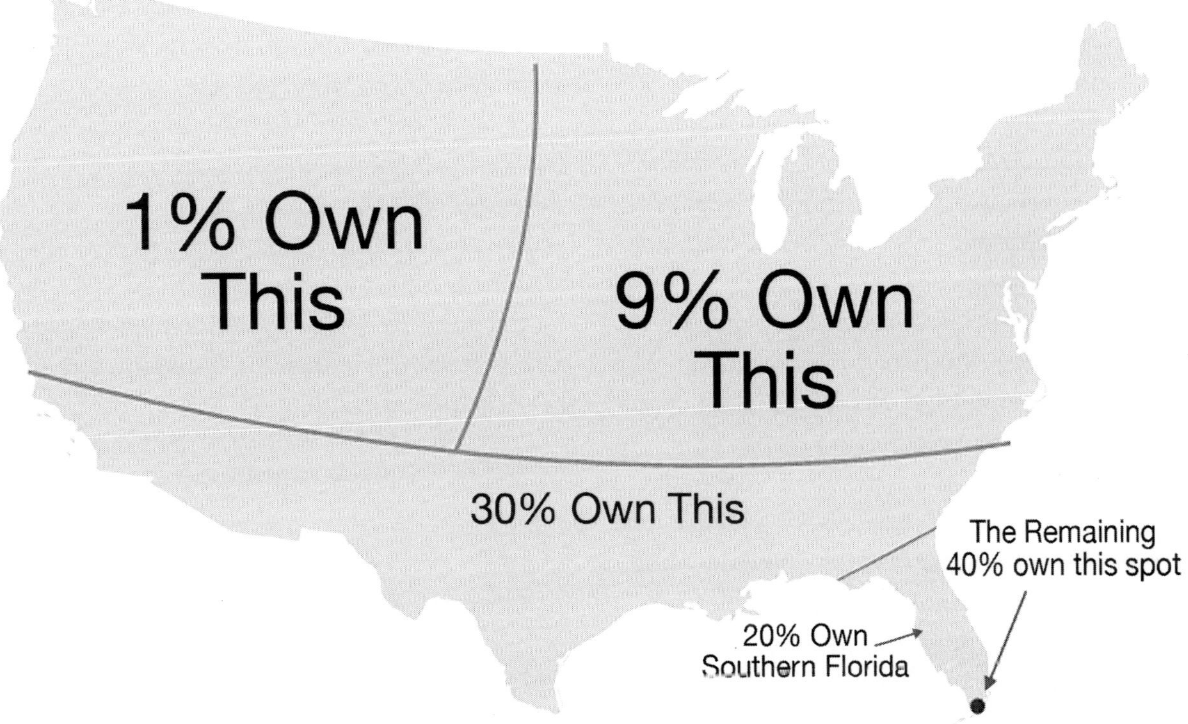

members or groups in a society. In the United States, the total net worth is measured in tens of trillions of dollars. In graphic 6.23, the total US wealth is divided among groups and compared to a map of the country. Notice the disproportionate amount of money that has accumulated in the top 10 percent of the citizens. The top 20 percent of the country owns 94 percent of the wealth. The bottom 80 percent of people in the United States, about 264 million people, own 6 percent of the wealth. Capitalism tends to accumulate wealth in one place. In the United States, this certainly holds true.

One way that economists use to demonstrate the distribution of wealth in a society is the **Lorenz curve**. Refer to graphic 6.24. All the people in society are divided into five groups called quintiles. The first quintile covers the poorest people and the fifth quintile is the richest. The 45-degree line that bisects the graph shows a completely equal distribution of goods. The third richest quintile would control 60 percent of the wealth, and 80 percent of the population owns 80 percent of the wealth.

GRAPHIC 6.24

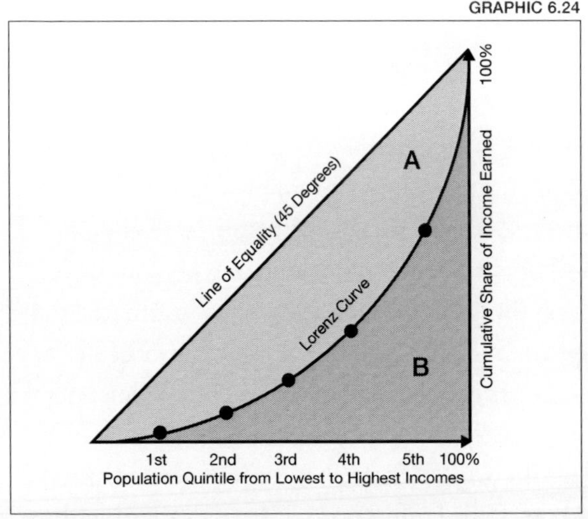

Notice the curved line marked “Lorenz curve.” The poorest quintile owns a very small amount of the country’s wealth. The second quintile does not own that much more. The richest fifth quintile owns close to 70 percent of the wealth. This

Lorenz curve is indicative of a country that has an uneven distribution of wealth. In a country with a wide disparity of wealth, the deeper curve moves away from the line of equality. A country with more equality will have a curve that is shallow and closer to the 45-degree line. Countries in northern Europe like Norway and Denmark have a relatively even distribution, while developing nations in Africa and South America have uneven distributions.

To be strong economically, nations need a large middle class. Modern economies are dominated by consumption. If most of the income rests in the hands of a few people, they do not provide enough buying power to sustain economic growth. A few very rich people buying yachts certainly helps the yacht industry, but it does not power the overall economy. A large middle class with disposable income will buy wants and needs in abundance. In a real way, this strong middle class can actually make the rich people richer by supporting the businesses they own.

While the Lorenz curve is helpful in analyzing disparity of wealth, a small calculation called the **Gini coefficient** clarifies matters further by enumerating the data. To get the Gini percentage, simply take the entire area shaded A and B, then divide it by area A. The entire area adds up to 100, and if A is 49 percent of the area, then the Gini coefficient is .49. The number will be between 0 and 1. Zero is a society with complete equality and one is a society in which one person owns everything. The Gini coefficient is estimated to be around .68 for the entire globe. This indicates a highly unequal distribution. Rich people control a vast share of the planet's wealth.

The United States has a coefficient of around .41, and this is after taxes are imposed upon the incomes of the upper classes. The pretax Gini coefficient is about .56, on par with most of the Western world. When all these other countries charge their taxes, however, the number falls from .20 to .28 in countries like Norway, Denmark, and Luxembourg. As mentioned in previous sections, countries with a democratic socialist system tax rich people heavily and then provide a wide array of social services. This counts as redistribution of wealth and lowers the coefficient.

Countries in Africa and South America have the world's highest Gini coefficients, some of them more than .70. These countries have seen wealth accumulate for an ever-smaller group of people. In fact, these countries often have few social services for the poor. These developing countries need a massive overhaul of their tax systems to diminish the disparity of wealth.

GRAPHIC 6.25

The Bitexco Financial Tower is the third tallest building in Vietnam. It stands as testament to the country's modernization and emergence into the global economy.

Over the years, a progressive tax has proven to be the only way to create a more equal society. In the United States, taxes can be raised only by Congress, and tax law is especially hard to change.

Where you stand on the question of equality and taxation is largely the core of your political beliefs. Recall from Unit 4 that liberals tend to favor progressive taxes and conservatives tend to favor flat taxes, conservatives do not.

The primary problem with an unequal distribution of wealth goes to the core of economics. If a tax system or economic system funnels money into a few hands, less benefit goes to a vast majority of the people. Wealthy people will consolidate most of their money into financial assets, not in capital (or new businesses). In essence, their money is locked up and not creating utility. On the other hand, if workers have higher wages and/or better education, they tend to increase their own utility with that money. Millions of people spending disposable income is better economically than dozens of people accumulating wealth. The broader distribution allows for more entrepreneurship, business growth, and prosperity. More people benefit overall.

Pressing Question

- Should Congress raise the marginal tax rates on the rich in the United States to address income and wealth inequality?

6J. Regional Breakdown

World population (over 7 billion) is expected to surpass 9 billion people by 2050 and then plateau. Some sociologists speculate that it might even shrink after that. This trend is already playing out in some countries like Germany and Italy. As more women become educated and join the workforce, economies grow and enhance standards of living. Couples postpone having children until later in life, and the size of the average family shrinks. Most developing countries have yet to see this trend. With the eradication of major diseases, more people are making increasing amounts of money, living longer, and having smaller families.

Modern medicine and technology are slow to reach some parts of the world. Demographically, the families who live in those parts tend to be larger and their life spans shorter. As mentioned previously, there is measurable progress. Here are brief descriptions of the different economic regions of the world:

- **Western world**—The United States, Canada, and Western Europe developed the world's first modern economies. People in these countries have long life spans and governments with low rates of corruption and stable economic growth. Europe is largely connected by the European Union and the Eurozone currency. The economies have moved beyond heavy industry and are primarily service based.
- **Latin America**—Mexico, Brazil, and Chile are the major economic forces in this part of the world. Since World War II, however, several economies in this region, including those of Brazil and Mexico, have been derailed by currency crises. These former colonies of Portugal and Spain have political systems that struggle with corruption. The disparity of wealth is the highest in the world in some countries, exacerbated by ethnic and social divisions. Despite many obstacles, these countries are poised to become major players in the global economy.
- **East Asia**—After its defeat in World War II, Japan spent decades building itself into a global economic leader. China emerged from a prolonged period of isolation in 1990 and until recently has experienced growth of 8–12 percent annually. A third testament to the power of capitalism in creating economic growth is South Korea. Its cars and electronics are staples in American homes. As these countries continue to grow economically, tensions will arise over territory, shipping lanes, and markets. As China begins to shift from an export-based to consumer-based economy, it may struggle with political changes. In any case, these three countries are a true global force.
- **Southeast Asia**—Vietnam, Cambodia, Thailand, and Indonesia have emerged from colonial control into thriving economies in the process of modernization. Vietnam

survived a ten-year war with the United States in which more than 2 million of its citizens died. Cambodia experienced a civil war in which an oppressive regime executed more than a million people. Since then, open trade deals with the West have spurred investment, and market reforms have kindled new businesses. These countries are quickly moving from agriculture to industry. Even Burma (Myanmar), once the most reclusive country in the world, opened up to trade in 2010.

- **South Asia**—The seven countries directly below the Himalayan mountains surround India geographically and economically. Formerly British colonies, India and Pakistan used to lead the regional economy. Both countries now lag behind in development because of pervasive socio-cultural issues. Like China, India emerged into the world economy by connecting to the Internet, providing cheap labor, and opening markets to foreign products. Sri Lanka and Bangladesh are both key players in the world textile industry. Steady growth appears to be the norm for South Asia, but the specter of conflict between Pakistan and India looms.
- **Sub-Saharan Africa**—Many countries that suffered from conflict were left alone by colonial powers from the 1950s to 1970s. A pattern of corrupt governments led by dictators became the dominant political theme. Civil wars and tribal conflict continue to devastate economies and stunt growth. However, political reform is taking hold in some countries and foreign investment is finding its way in. This has led to increased manufacturing as some textile manufacturers have found friendly business environments and cheap labor. This aside, southern Africa contains 11 percent of the world population but accounts for only 1 percent of the global product.
- **Russia and Eastern Europe**—After the fall of the Soviet Union, industry lagged decades behind the West as a result of ineffective central planning. Since then, countries from the Baltic (Lithuania and Estonia) to the Balkans (Croatia and Slovenia) have thrived. Some cities are now hubs of Internet innovation, and tourism flourishes. Russia remains suspicious of the United States and Western Europe and will try to maintain a sphere of influence over these countries; Russia has vast mineral resources and deposits of oil. It does, however, struggle with corruption and organized crime. These countries should continue to experience steady economic growth and assume a prominent place on the world stage.
- **Central Asia**—Most Americans are unfamiliar with the Central Asian nations Kazakhstan, Uzbekistan, Tajikistan, and Turkmenistan. Over the next few decades their presence will be felt as new deposits of oil and other minerals make their way to world markets. They struggle with geographic isolation and cultural tension. The area between the Black and Caspian Seas (sometimes called the Caucasus) remains largely under Russian influence. As pipelines are built to transport Caspian oil to the Black Sea, expect these countries to become more familiar.
- **Southwest Asia**—Commonly called "the Middle East," these countries—which stretch from Iran across the Arabian peninsula to Egypt, north to Turkey, and east to Israel—share (with the exception of Israel) share a similar cultural and religious past. The petroleum exports from Iran, the United Arab Emirates, and Saudi Arabia have made them global forces. Beneath the surface, political divisions, including a cold war between Iran and Saudi Arabia and religious extremism, have put a damper on economic growth. Israel leads the region in productivity but remains politically isolated based on cultural differences. Political upheaval and regime change that emerged from the 2011 "Arab Spring" have opened some markets and closed others. Economists speculate what the region will do once oil reserves are depleted and in the face of challenges posed by terrorism perpetrated in the name of religion.

Despite the impression that most people get from the news, the world is indeed becoming a better place. Major diseases that once killed millions have been eradicated, major global conflict is largely avoided with diplomacy, and the Internet connects businesses across the globe. People now face the major challenges of their countries modernizing.

GRAPHIC 6.26

Dubai, located on the shores of the Persian Gulf, has opened markets and created friendly business environments that have spurred massive investment. It looks like this today despite being a small desert city thirty years ago.

Pressing Question

- What foreign country would you most like to visit? Why?

6K. How Does the Future Look?

Technology continues to transform the world. Medicine will progressively lengthen life spans, and new products will excite consumers and open new markets. Half the world now accesses the Internet, and there exist 7 billion cell phone plans (just over the past twenty-five years). New technology is adopted more quickly, disrupts accepted business practices, and will continue to transform human life in unpredictable ways.

Futurists are people who consider current trends and try to extrapolate what life will be like in the next decades and centuries. Some predictions include a world without disease in which tiny robots swim in our bloodstream and repair cells. They predict that people will implant devices in themselves to access the Internet just by thinking about it. Some even envision that your entire brain will be downloaded into a computer. What they propose is a world where death is rare and all human beings are connected.

This seems like science fiction, but forms of these visions are already being tested in labs. What seemed like fantasy only thirty years ago appears ordinary today. Decades ago, nobody in the general public envisioned supercomputers that fit in a pocket (smartphones), a global accumulation of all human knowledge (the Internet), self-driving cars, smashing protons together at the speed of light, or commercial space travel. All of these ideas have been or are about to be transformed into reality—and much faster than was anticipated. The only sure thing that can be said about future technology is that it will be incredible.

GRAPHIC 6.27

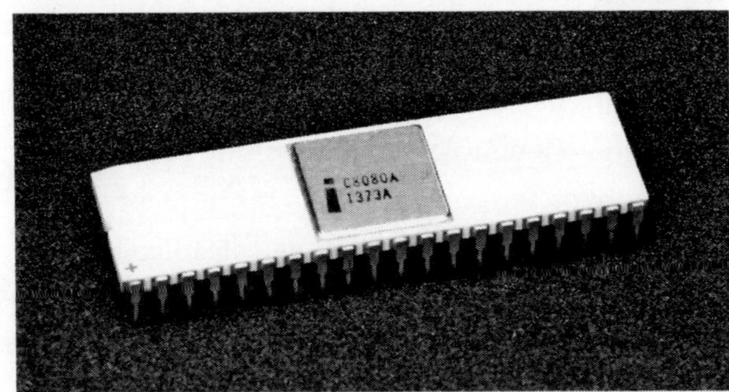

When it was introduced, this Intel 8080 chip made computers affordable enough to have in the home. From the mid-1970s on, computers have transformed business, education, and entertainment.

The pace of change is not arithmetic; rather, it is exponential. More than fifty years ago, one of the founders of Intel, Gordon Moore, posited that the number of transistors on a microchip (the on/off switches that translate instructions to a computer) would double every one and a half to two years. His prediction has held true since the 1960s. In 1975, the 8080 chip had 6,000 transistors and sparked the personal computer revolution. Today's chips have billions of transistors that all fit onto a silicon chip smaller than a fingernail. Assembled into one computer, these chips allow the fastest computers in the world to perform quadrillions (petaflops) of calculations per second. Other areas of science and technology also seem to follow Moore's framework. Medical breakthroughs happen every week. Stars and planets are discovered every day. The pace is astonishing.

Amidst the wonder are concerns. Doctors are concerned about viruses and bacteria that are immune to our medicine. Politicians worry that some rogue state or terrorist group will get hold of a nuclear weapon. Climatologists fear destructive weather patterns and rising sea levels. Water shortages are beginning to plague some parts of the world. Poverty and injustice still seem like insurmountable problems. All of this sounds frightening, but believe in the ingenuity of the human race to solve these biggest problems. Despite all of these challenges, young people should be optimistic about their future.

As you have learned, chances are that the younger generations will have to change jobs more than their parents or grandparents ever did. Shifting technology will continue to change the nature of work and require a more adaptive workforce. International trade will steadily increase the amount of competition among countries. Manufacturing will shift from people to robots to 3D printing. The future workforce will need to have multiple technological skills, rudimentary programing experience, and the ability to retrain quickly. Young people will live longer lives than any previous generations, raising the retirement age but increasing the window to save for retirement.

Within the next one hundred years, computers will get so fast and so sophisticated that they will become artificially intelligent. Imagine a world where computers invent the next computers. There may be a day when computer thinking will be indistinguishable from that of humans. Combined with robot technology, this will pose some exciting, yet alarming, possibilities. Cars can drive themselves, and people talk face-to-face from opposite sides of the globe. Wild ideas once confined to science fiction are already coming true.

Regardless of the future, one fact remains true. More than ever before, people need to know how the economy operates. No matter how technologically advanced the world becomes, markets will still work in the same way. There will still be supply and demand. The government will still collect taxes. People will still need to invest and budget their money. Those with a basic understanding of economics will have a significant advantage making their way in our economy.

Pressing Question

- What is your boldest prediction for technology one hundred years from now?

 Name: ______________________

Vocabulary

Directions: Using your reading, place the words from the word bank in the appropriate blanks.

Globalization Word Bank
5, 23, Corruption, deficit, democratic, distribution, down, embargo, expectancy, export, Gini, Globalization, import, kleptocracy, Marx, micro, mobility, mortality, NAFTA, poverty, standard, subsistence, tariff, war

While the United States has less than ______(1) percent of the world's population, it is responsible for ______(2) percent of the world's productivity. Because of this, citizens have a high ______(3) of living. People here have disposable income, high life ______(4), and a low infant ______(5) rate. In the developing world, many problems create obstacles to wealth. The ______(6) Perceptions Index rates many governments as corrupt. People in developing nations eat what they grow using ______(7) agriculture. Leaders systematically steal from the people, so sociologists call the government a ______(8). Most countries in the developing world are growing economically. Some banks offer ______(9)-loans, small amounts of money meant to help impoverished people start businesses.

The general direction in the world is toward more free trade, not less. ______(10) is the increasing interconnectedness between people, countries, and businesses. The United States, Canada, and Mexico are in a free trade agreement called ______(11). Trading with other countries tends to make prices go ______(12). A good brought into your country is called an ______(13), and one you send out is called an ______(14). Trading freely makes both countries more efficient. Sometimes, countries will put a tax on an import called a ______(15). They want to protect their own markets or help shrink their trade ______(16). If too many tariffs are charged, it causes a dispute called a trade ______(17). Even worse, one country might completely cut off trade from another in an ______(18).

People in developing nations struggle with the state of being extremely poor—called ______(19). Because of the ______(20) of wealth, people in this condition have little chance of moving up the socioeconomic ladder. If the money was spread around more evenly, perhaps there would be more social ______(21). Economists like Karl ______(22) advocated a worldwide revolution to make a pure socialist state. Countries like Cuba still have a socialist system. Denmark and Norway are countries with a low ______(23) coefficient, which means that they have a relatively even distribution of wealth. They are not communists but ______(24) socialists.

Name:

Where Does the United States Rank?

Directions: On the table below, define all the terms in the appropriate boxes. Then, using CIA.gov, find the current data for the United States. Include the world rank for the United States in the data category of the last column. How do these data shape your view of the United States?

Statistic	Definition	US Current Data	US World Rank
GDP			
Per capita GDP			
Population			
Total fertility rate			
Net migration			
Infant mortality			
Life expectancy			
Government spending			
Age distribution			
Corruption Perceptions Index			

Statistic	Definition	US Current Data	US World Rank
Human Development Index			
Primary imports			
Primary exports			
Trade balance			

Name:

Regional Research

Part 1

Directions: Using the World Factbook at CIA.gov and your reading from section 6J, find the data for three countries. Choose those countries from the list of regions in your reading.

Item to Find	Country #1 - ________	Country #2 - ________	Country #3 - ________
Current head of state			
Geography			
Main exports			
#1 industry			
GDP			
Per capita GDP			
Current population			
Type of economic system			
Currency name			
Currency in US dollars			
Total fertility rate			
Life expectancy			
Infant mortality			

Part 2

Directions: Below, black out the countries you researched and circle the region in which it is found. Then, circle the rest of the regions mentioned in Section 6J on the map.

Name:

Developing Economies

Directions: For each of the following statistics, describe the average data values for developing countries and developed countries, and then answer the question at the bottom.

Developing Countries	Statistic	Developed Countries
	GDP	
	Per Capita GDP	
	Total Fertility Rate	
	Net Migration	
	Infant Mortality	
	Life Expectancy	
	Government Spending	
	Age Distribution	
	Corruption Perceptions Index	
	Human Development Index	
	Primary Imports	
	Primary Exports	

Part 2

Directions: Refer to your reading. What are some ways that developing nations can grow their economies and improve the lives of their citizens?

 Name:

Free Trade Analysis

Part 1

Directions: Follow the directions below to fill in the graph. Use the reading in Section 6F as a guide if you need extra help. Answer the questions as you go along.

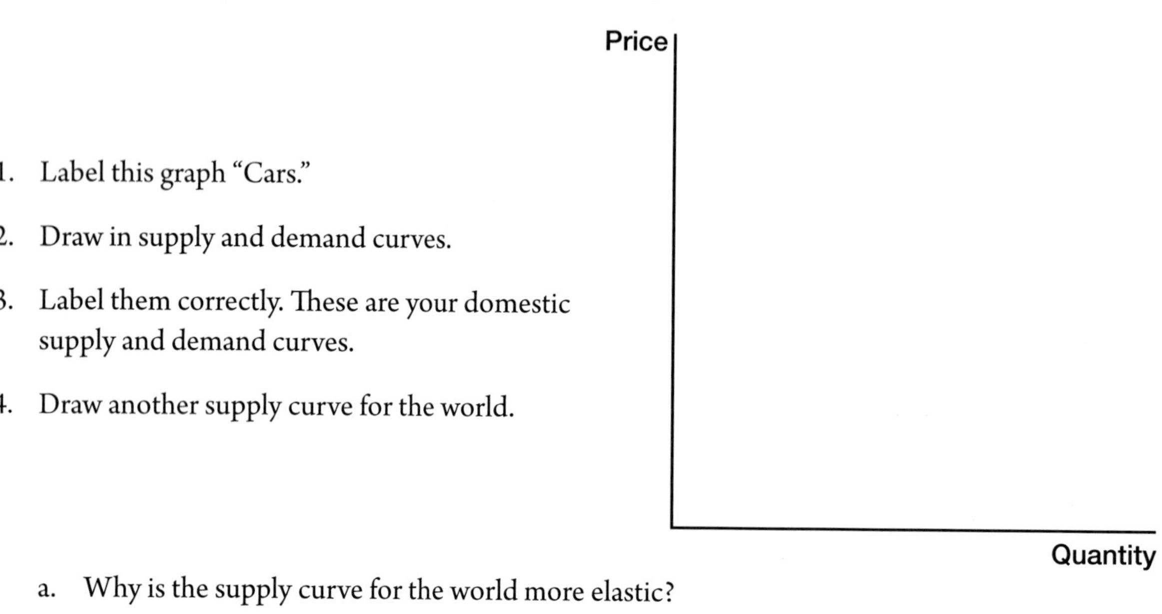

1. Label this graph "Cars."
2. Draw in supply and demand curves.
3. Label them correctly. These are your domestic supply and demand curves.
4. Draw another supply curve for the world.
   a. Why is the supply curve for the world more elastic?

   b. What happens to prices if trade opens up?

   c. What happens to the quantity consumed?

   d. What is a tariff?

5. Draw in a price that represents a higher tariff price than the equilibrium from world trade. Draw a line that cuts across the graph from that higher price. How does the tariff affect the amount consumed?
   a. Prices?

   b. Foreign producers?

   c. Domestic producers?

Part 2

Directions: Using your reading, answer the questions below.

1. What are the principles of free trade? Explain their importance with an example.

2. List five free trade agreements in the world.

3. Go to trade.gov:

    a. What is the mission of the site?

    b. What agency manages this site?

    c. What services does this agency provide?

4. Which countries are the five biggest trading partners of the United States? What do we trade?

Name:

Poverty

Directions: Using the Internet, gather data and fill in the blanks.

______________________ The current poverty rate in the United States.

______________________ The poverty line for a single person.

______________________ The poverty line for a family of four.

______________________ The number of households that collect food stamps.

______________________ The number of people who benefit from Medicaid.

______________________ The current budget of Social Security.

1. Define:
   a. Living wage:

   b. Social mobility:

   c. Relative poverty:

   d. Absolute poverty:

   e. Fair trade:

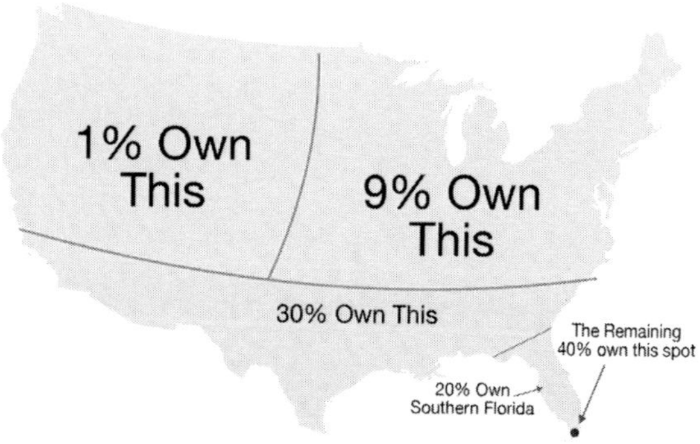

2. What does the map on the right illustrate?

3. Estimate the figures for wealth distribution:
   a. Bottom 20 percent:
   b. Second 20 percent:
   c. Third 20 percent:
   d. Fourth 20 percent:
   e. Top 20 percent:

4. Name five disadvantages a person born into poverty faces in the United States.

5. Draw a Lorenz curve for your estimates from the map.

Name:

Research a Vacation

Directions: Choose one country within each region where you would like to travel. Using a search engine and travel sites, fill in the tables and blanks below with the appropriate information.

In Southeast Asia:

Cost of the Flight	Cost of Lodging/Night	Cost of Food/Day	Cost of Entertainment
Exchange Rates	Primary Language	City to Visit	National Dish

- State Department travel warnings (state.gov):
- Places to visit:

In sub-Saharan Africa:

Cost of the Flight	Cost of Lodging/Night	Cost of Food/Day	Cost of Entertainment
Exchange Rates	Primary Language	City to Visit	National Dish

- State Department travel warnings (state.gov):
- Places to visit:

In Eastern Europe:

Cost of the Flight	Cost of Lodging/Night	Cost of Food/Day	Cost of Entertainment
Exchange Rates	Primary Language	City to Visit	National Dish

- State Department travel warnings (state.gov):
- Places to visit:

In Latin America:

Cost of the Flight	Cost of Lodging/Night	Cost of Food/Day	Cost of Entertainment
Exchange Rates	Primary Language	City to Visit	National Dish

- State Department travel warnings (state.gov):
- Places to visit:

Name:

Game-Changing Technology

Part 1

Directions: For each of the following technologies, describe how people lived before the invention. Then describe how people benefit from the technology today.

Before	Invention	After
	Glass	
	Clocks	
	Chlorinated Water	
	Refrigeration	
	Vaccines	
	Anesthetic	
	Electric Light	
	Alternating Current	

Before	Invention	After
	Antibiotics	
	Internal Combustion Engine	
	Computer	
	Cell Phone	

Part 2

Directions: Consider the technologies in Part 1. Of all these technologies, which three are the most important? Why?

 Name:

The Internet

Part 1

Directions: Locate definitions of these terms on the Internet and write them below.

Internet Term	Definition
HTTP	
HTML	
Browser	
Web	
Internet	
Search engine	
Server	
URL	
IP address	
Download/upload	
Malware	
E-commerce	

Part 2

Directions: Answer the questions below with a few sentences:

1. Describe how a website gets to your phone when you use the Internet.

2. What industries have been most changed by the Internet?

3. Find and list five jobs that did not exist twenty-five years ago.

4. What mistakes do young people make on the Internet?

5. Where did the Internet come from?

6. Place the milestones listed below in chronological order:

- Google
- Gore Bill
- first microchips
- Apple's first PC
- Colossus, ENIAC
- Mosaic
- Arpanet
- Windows 95
- first cell phone

1940 1950 1960 1970 1980 1990 2000 2010

Glossary

1040: This is the standard federal return form. This form allows the filer to account for deductions.

1040EZ: A short form for young people who do not have major deductions or income.

1099: This is proof of income for freelance workers. No payroll or withholding tax was deducted from that income, so a self-employment tax will need to be paid.

401(k): The most common investment vehicle today. Most employers offer this investment type as a benefit. The company will match what the employee gives up to a certain dollar amount. The contributions to 401(k)s are also pretax investments.

ability-to-pay principle: The idea that those who make more money should pay a larger portion of their income or wealth to the government. People who believe in this idea believe that the government should take an active role in achieving more income equality.

absolute advantage: The ability of a country to perform particular economic activities in higher volume than another.

absolute poverty: A lack of basic human necessities.

accounting: The process of keeping track of an person's or business's money.

actuary: A mathematician who makes complex calculations about insurance data and statistics, particularly for the insurance industry.

adjusted gross income: Total income calculated from wages, salaries, tips, dividends from stock, interest earned from banks, and royalties from published works.

age distribution: The breakdown of age groups across a country.

allocative efficiency: A situation in which consumers are all paying the lowest prices possible and all the producers capable of supplying at that price are doing so.

American Federation of Labor (AFL): Founded in 1886 by Samuel Gompers, the AFL was a federation of smaller craft unions— mainly for *skilled* workers. Gompers and his followers were most noted for their support of "bread and butter unionism." This meant that they pursued the basic issues like an eight-hour workday, no child labor, safer working conditions, and higher wages.

amortization: The process of calculating a schedule of periodic payments (principal and interest) for a loan over a specific term (such as 30 years for a house).

annual percentage rate (APR): The annual interest rate charged for borrowing money, expressed as a single percentage number that represents the actual total yearly cost of funds over the term of a loan, which includes fees and other costs.

annuities: These financial products are designed to provide a predictable monthly cash payment to the holder. They are sometimes funded by employers or individuals.

Anti-Federalists: A faction of early leaders of the United States. Led by Thomas Jefferson, they had a fundamental distrust of government.

assets: Things that a business, government, or individual owns.

authoritarian socialist: The economic system in which the government controls most of the resources and makes most economic decisions.

automatic stabilizers: Economic policies and programs designed to offset fluctuations in a nation's economic activity without government or policymaker intervention.

average total cost (ATC): The number found by dividing your total cost by the number of units you produce or provide.

baby boomers: People born after World War II, roughly between the years 1946 and 1964.

balance: Money left in an account.

bank: A business that holds and lends money to people.

bankruptcy: A legal declaration of one's inability to pay one's debt.

barter: An exchange of goods and/or services without the help of money.

basket: A sample of goods and services (currently about 80,000) purchased by households in the United States that represents a larger number.

behavioral economic theory: First appearing in the 1960s, this field combines psychology and neurology with economics and challenges the idea that people are always rational. Consumers often make decisions that go against the classical model. Economists who use this theory try to show how this behavior affects the overall economy.

benefits-received principle: The idea that those who get more government services should pay more for them.

bias: The inclination the Fed has to fight either inflation or recession.

blacklist: Historically, a list of union members that a company made and distributed to the other companies to discourage their employment by others in the industry.

blue-collar job: An occupation that requires physical labor.

bonds: Loans that investors make to governments and corporations.

bouncing a check: Writing and submitting a check for payment when the account on which the check is written has insufficient funds to cover the amount. The check written to the recipient will be returned to the recipient's bank. The writer of the check will usually pay a penalty fee.

boycott: A protest wherein people refuse to buy a company's products.

break-even state: The state of neither earning a profit nor suffering loss.

budget surplus: Revenue that exceeds spending.

business organization: An antiunion organization established by business owners to exchange ideas about keeping workers happy or breaking strikes more effectively through vehicles like the chambers of commerce.

business plan: A document that provides an introduction to the business, a description of the market, an analysis of the start-up costs, and a prediction of when the business hopes to break even.

call: An option that gives the holder the right to buy a stock.

capacity to pay: A monthly income that demonstrates that a person can handle a monthly payment schedule.

capital: Tools, machinery, and other equipment used in the production process.

capital gains: Money earned on an investment (such as stocks, bonds, or real estate) when the investor buys low and sells high.

capital gains tax: The tax applied to earnings distributed on an investment that has increased in value.

capital goods: Goods that allow people to become more efficient, such as new machines, roads, and technologies.

capitalism: An economic system that favors the individual's freedom in the marketplace.

career: A job that requires specialized education and training, typically becoming the focus of one's life's work.

central planning: The method whereby a government controls the economy by deciding how goods will be produced, how many are made, and how they are distributed.

certificate of deposit (CD): An investment of cash in a bank account that allows the bank to keep the funds for a set term, typically ranging from thirty days to five years. Longer terms yield higher rates of return, yielded to the investor when the term is up.

character: The details about a person's criminal past or legal judgments used to calculate a credit score.

checking account: An account that is convenient because a depositor is allowed to draw checks on the balance at any time. Oftentimes, no interest is paid.

chief executive officer (CEO): A common title for the chief administrator of a company.

choice: An act of selecting or making a decision when faced with two or more possibilities.

claim: A request for money to pay for some damage incurred.

classical economic theory: Dominating economics through much of the 1800s and 1900s, it primarily holds that markets and economies self-regulate and that individuals make rational decisions based on what they believe to be in their best self-interest. Its prominent thinkers include Adam Smith, David Ricardo, and Milton Friedman.

Clayton Antitrust Act: Passed in 1914, it strengthened the Sherman Act by prohibiting price discrimination, exclusive contracts, local pricing, and interlocking directorates.

coinsurance: This requires a policyholder to pay a percentage of every claim.

collateral: Objects of value or other assets that can be handed over to the bank in the event of that a person does not pay the loan.

collective bargaining: Negotiations for compensation (wages, benefits, hours, and the like) between workers in a union and their employer, usually conducted by representatives who bargain on their behalf.

collusion: The conspiring of companies to fix prices.

command economy: An economy that relies on powerful government officials using central planning to make economic decisions. The individual citizen plays little or no role in economic decisions.

commercial bank: The most numerous, profitable, and stable type of bank. Unlike a credit union, it is a for-profit business.

commission: A part of the proceeds earned by the brokerage firm from buying or selling stock.

commodities: Items of value that can be stored and transported.

commodity money: A form of exchange consisting of an item of value, or commodity, that can be stored, transported, and used like money. Examples include shells, precious metals, grain, seeds, cigarettes, and salt.

common stock: Stock that is available to any investor.

communist: *See* **authoritarian socialist.**

Communist Manifesto, The: A political pamphlet written by Karl Marx and Friedrich Engles in 1848 that presented the problems of capitalism and suggested the alternative, socialism.

comparative advantage: The ability of one nation to produce a good at lower opportunity cost relative to another country's ability to do so.

competition: The efforts of two or more companies to secure the purchase power of consumers, which is naturally limited by scarcity of resources.

complements: Two or more products or services that are used together.

compounding interest: Interest earned on the combined principal and interest earned over a preceding period.

conglomerate: A merger of two or more companies that offer different goods or services.

Congress of Industrial Organizations (CIO): The first successful union for unskilled workers, founded in 1935. Started by John L. Lewis, it successfully unionized the auto industry and influenced the US Congress to write key legislation favorable to average workers.

conservative: A person who, economically, wants lower taxes, less spending by the federal government, more power to the state governments, and fewer regulations placed upon business.

consolidation: The reduction of the number of firms in a market that happens as companies go out of business and other businesses merge.

conspicuous consumption: The purchase of a consumer good in the belief that it will improve one's standing with others and publicly display an affluent economic status.

constituents: A group of people who are represented by an elected official.

consumer confidence: The amount of confidence a consumer has to make a purchase in the economy.

Consumer Financial Protection Bureau (CFPB): Founded in 2011 in response to the 2008 economic meltdown, the CFPB alerts consumers about scams and questionable financial practices.

consumer preferences: A shifting tendency for consumers to buy more of one product or another.

consumer price index (CPI): A measure of the changes in the price level of a market basket of consumer goods and services purchased by households. It allows economists to measure the health of the economy.

Consumer Protection Safety Commission (CPSC): Founded in 1972, the CPSC regulates the safety of consumer products. For instance, when a car has a safety issue, they will inform the public and might suggest a recall.

consumerism: An ideology and philosophy that encourages an ever greater accumulation of goods.

contract: An agreement between two or more people to perform a service or to provide a good.

contractionary policy: The raising of taxes for the purpose of lowering spending and thereby slowing the economy. When the government raises taxes and lowers spending.

cooperative: A not-for-profit business that provides a service to a group of members.

copay: A flat fee that has to be paid each time you make an insurance claim.

corporate bonds: Bonds that corporations can sell to raise money. They are loans that pay interest over time.

corporate income tax: The tax on corporations according to their net income. Many expenses, such as capital improvements and charitable contributions, are deducted from corporations' taxable revenue.

corporation: A business that has filed a corporate charter with its state of origin.

corruption: The misuse of public power for private benefit.

Corruption Perceptions Index (CPI): An index generated by the nongovernmental organization Transparency International that annually ranks countries by people's perceived levels of government corruption through surveys and analysis.

cost-benefit analysis: The assessment of how much a decision will cost the decider weighed against the benefits gained.

cost-of-living increase: A pay raise that matches inflation.

cost-push (supply-side) inflation: A rise in prices driven by an increase in the cost of resources, such as labor or oil, which in turn pushes up the cost of everything else.

counterfeiting: Making false versions of a real currency.

craft union: A labor union comprising skilled crafters that seeks to unify workers in a particular craft industry.

credit: A person's ability to borrow someone else's money. Also, any deposit or addition made to an account.

credit cards: Plastic cards embedded with digital information that facilitates point-of-sale purchases based on the holder's ability to borrow (credit), typically offered by companies that receive a portion of each transaction in exchange for their risk.

credit freeze: The cessation of any accounts opening in a person's name.

credit history: Details about a person's financial history, ability to pay, and track record.

credit union: Commonly associated with unions, churches, and other social organizations, a financial institution whose members deposit their money in order to buy shares that pay an annual interest. Because they sometimes utilize volunteer labor and capital contributed by a sponsor organization, a credit union is able to loan out money to members at lower rates than those of commercial banks. Also, credit unions are not taxed on their income, while other depository institutions are.

creditors: Moneylenders.

crony capitalism: An economy in which success in business depends on close relationships between business owners and government officials.

crowdfunding: The process of selling products or offering special deals to the public in exchange for a special deal in the future. Some entrepreneurs sell shares in the business in order to get it started.

crowding out: This can occur when the government borrows too much of the country's money, drives the interest rates up, and forces consumers to stop buying durable goods and business to stop investing.

currency: Typically any type of non-electronic portable money like bills and coins. Bitcoin is considered a type of alternative, virtual currency.

cyclical unemployment: Unemployment that occurs when certain industries are hit hard by downturns in the economy. Companies will often lay off their workers to keep their prices stable.

deadweight loss: The loss of efficiency that occurs when the equilibrium for a product or service cannot be achieved.

debit: Money taken out of an account in the form of checks, cash withdrawals, paid bills, or fees.

deductible: The amount an insured person must pay out of pocket before the insurance company will cover costs.

deduction: Subtraction of some money from gross income on a paycheck or on a tax form.

default: The failure of a person to repay a debt.

deficit: The amount of spending that exceeds revenue.

defined contribution plan: A plan whereby an employer will match an employee's contribution to a retirement fund up to a certain amount.

deflation: A condition where the average price of goods and services falls throughout an economy.

delayed gratification: Putting off the temporary burst of satisfaction of ownership until a later date.

demand: The amount of a good or service that consumers are *willing* and *able* to buy at a given price.

demand deposits: Deposits that are payable on demand but otherwise are stored in a bank.

demand-pull inflation: Inflation that occurs when too many dollars chase too few goods. Producers cannot keep up with consumer demand and they raise the prices.

demand-side theory: Originating in the 1930s with the writings of John Maynard Keynes, this theory states that the government can stabilize the economy by stimulating aggregate demand with fiscal and monetary policy.

democratic socialism: A system in which people of a country retain the basic democratic rights of free speech and public elections while the government plays a key role in planning the economy.

demographics: Data about people in groups according to age, income, gender, location, and past behavior.

determinant of demand: Any action that moves an entire demand curve.

determinant of supply: An occurrence that moves a supply curve left or right.

developing world: Nations that have yet to experience a transforming industrial revolution, have low productivity, and whose populations disproportionately live in poverty.

direct deposit: A safe and secure electronic delivery system that allows money to move from bank to bank.

discount rate: The rate that banks in trouble pay when they borrow from the Fed.

discretionary spending: Governmental spending on programs with budgets that the president can adjust according to the politics of the day and the needs of the economy.

disincentive: A reason to work less and not more.

disinflation: A lowering of the rate of inflation over time.

diversify: To spread money around among multiple mutual funds, stocks, and bonds.

dividend: A share of the profits from a business.

dollar-cost averaging: The gradual accumulation of value through regular periodic investment in a commodity or security, generally designed to increase over the long term. The investor regularly deposits money into an account regardless of the short-term fluctuations, thereby lowering the risk of overinvesting when the investment is losing value and taking advantage of periods when the investment is increasing in value.

double coincidence of wants: The situation that occurs when one has what another wants and another has what one wants.

double taxation: The process by which a business is taxed on its profits before it pays the dividends to stockholders, after which the shareholders pay a tax on the dividends received.

downsizing: The elimination of jobs.

ease of production: How easily a good or service can be produced and provided.

economic system: An organized set of procedures and practices that a society follows in the production and distribution of goods and services.

economics: A social science and a professional practice that studies and analyzes the production, consumption, and distribution of a society's scarce resources.

economy: A system of consuming and producing.

economy of scale: The efficiency that comes with larger and more efficient production practices. Marked by decreasing long-term average costs.

elastic demand: A situation when a price only changes a little, and the quantity demanded changes to a greater degree.

elasticity: The degree of change in supply or demand if a market price changes.

elasticity of supply: The degree to which a product's supply is affected by price.

embargo: Cutting off trade to a country.

entitlements: Mandatory expenditures that citizens are entitled to receive by law. They can be changed only by Congress.

entrepreneur: A person who risks time and money to start a business.

Environmental Protection Agency (EPA): The EPA sets environmental standards for industry and oversees inspections of the fitness of the outdoors.

equilibrium: The state when the supply for a product matches the demand for a product.

equity: Another word for ownership. A synonym for a share of stock or any other value (assets minus liabilities) residing in a security or real estate.

estate tax: Sometimes called "inheritance tax" or the "death tax," a tax imposed when a person dies and leaves money or property to someone else.

excise tax: A tax on particular products or services.

exemption: A declaration that ensures that the government will take less money from each paycheck; however, people pay additional taxes at the time of filing for declaring exemptions.

expansionary fiscal policy: The method of managing the economy whereby the government lowers taxes and boosts spending on programs in order to ameliorate the worst impacts of a recession.

expenses: Money that a business or household must pay, such as invoices or bills.

export: A good or service that is sold to someone in another country.

externality: An external social cost. A cost of production that is not accounted for in a business's ledger while an individual outside of the firm incurs an expense.

factors of production: The resources needed to produce goods, such as labor, natural resources, and capital.

Fair Labor Standards Act: Passed in 1938, the law guaranteed workers a maximum eight-hour workday, a maximum 44-hour workweek, and a 25-cent-per-hour minimum wage. Since then the minimum wage has been periodically increased.

Federal Communications Commission (FCC): Established in 1934, the FCC issues licenses for the use of public airwaves and sets standards for all electronic communications.

Federal Deposit Insurance Corporation (FDIC): A corporation created by the US government in the 1930s that began to guarantee all deposits in banks across the United States. The FDIC insures bank deposits up to $250,000 and supervises banks to make sure they are financially secure.

Federal Election Commission (FEC): A group in charge of tracking compliance with existing campaign laws.

federal funds rate: The rate that banks pay other banks for overnight, short-term loans.

Federal Open Market Committee (FOMC): This board makes all major decisions for the money supply and interest rates.

Federal Reserve (Fed): Created by the Federal Reserve Act, this agency watches and protects the economy from the worst economic problems, inflation and recession. To do this, it tracks and supervises banks. It is the national bank of the United States.

Federal Reserve Act: Passed in 1913, it established the mechanism for the government to monitor our money supply and issue more money in times of financial strain.

federal savings bank: Organized under the Federal Home Owner's Loan Act, a type of bank that serves primarily as a mortgage lender. Federal savings banks are often not members of the Federal Reserve System.

Federal Trade Commission (FTC): An agency that investigates charges of unfair trade practices and violations of the law. It reports its findings to the Justice Department, which decides whether or not to go to court. Founded in 1914, the FTC works for the promotion of consumer protection and the elimination and prevention of anticompetitive business practices. It watches for violations of US antitrust law.

Federal Trade Commission Act: Passed in 1914, this law created the Federal Trade Commission.

federalism: The shared responsibility among city, county, state, and federal governments.

Federalists: Led by Alexander Hamilton, the political faction that held that the federal government, not the states, should monitor and engineer the growth of the economy.

feudalism: A social system in which lords who controlled the land allowed other people to work on it. The farmers kept some of the product, but the lords kept most of it. In exchange for their work, the farmers received protection from various outside invaders.

fiat money: Money whose value is granted by the decree of a government, not backed by precious metals.

FICA tax: *See* **Social Security tax**.

fiscal policy: The means by which a government adjusts its spending levels and tax rates to influence a nation's economy and social norms.

fixed costs: Budgetary expenses that do not change from one month to the next.

flexible spending account (FSA): This is money that you can set aside from your paycheck before taxes are taken out. These accounts are funded by employers and must be spent within a certain amount of time.

floating exchange rates: The state of currency markets around the world that fluctuate in value against one another.

Food and Drug Administration (FDA): Founded in 1906, the FDA, along with the Department of Agriculture, is responsible for the safety of the nation's food supply. This agency is also in charge of approving new drugs, food additives, and cosmetics for consumers.

foreclose: The action whereby a mortgagee (lender) takes back property on which a borrower has defaulted, including land, buildings, and homes.

foreign exchange rates: The conversion of currency across countries, in which some of the currency may gain or lose value in the transaction.

franchise: A business that comes from a parent company.

fraud alert: A warning notification placed on an account or credit report at the request of the owner who suspects that someone may be attempting to steal his or her identity. Action gives a person extra protection, while the credit agencies watch the person's data closely. This alert will also allow a person to get free copies of his or her credit reports all at once.

free enterprise: An economic system that has private property, freedom to choose, voluntary exchange of goods and services, competition, and consistent rule of law.

free market: A market that operates without interference, taxation, and regulation.

freelance worker: A person who is self-employed and does jobs for a business outside of its payroll for full-time employees.

frequency: The likelihood that somebody will make an insurance claim.

frictional unemployment: Unemployment that occurs when people are just entering the job market or when those who are employed decide to leave their current jobs to find "greener pastures."

frustrated workers: People who have stopped looking for employment.

full employment: The state of employment when the economy is operating at or near full capacity. In the United States, this means that the unemployment rate will drop below 5 percent or so.

future: A type of investment, the right to buy a contract to take shipment of a commodity not yet produced.

GDP composition: A percentage breakdown of where production occurs in an economy based on labor force participation in manufacturing, services, or agriculture.

geographic monopoly: A monopoly that results when a supplier is isolated and has little or no competition.

Gini coefficient: A calculation that is helpful in analyzing disparity of wealth. A more equal society will have a number closer to zero and a society with maximum inequality with have a Gini coefficient of one.

globalization: The increasing interconnectedness and integration among the people, companies, and governments of different nations.

going public: The process by which a corporation sells pieces of itself to the general public in order to raise money for expansion.

goods: Things that are produced for consumption.

government: A system by which public policy is determined and enforced. Laws are made and executed by the government.

government expenditures: The spending of money by the government.

governmental monopoly: Certain services have been determined to be best controlled by governments, such as the sewer service and highway maintenance.

Gresham's law: The tendency of bad and damaged money with less value to drive out good money in an economic system based on specie currency.

gross domestic product (GDP): The dollar value of what the citizens of a country produce within its borders.

growth stock: Stocks that give large capital appreciation.

health savings account (HSA): A tax-exempt account that employees can establish for health costs, usually used to help pay for a high-deductible medical plan. Anyone can contribute to a person's health savings account. Also, this fund can grow without limit and without any time restrictions.

hedger: A person who holds options for several months to secure a modest gain. Often, the person works for a firm that needs the commodity as an input.

horizontal combination merger: A merger of two companies that offer the same good or service.

Human Development Index (HDI): An index of life expectancy, education, and income used to rank countries into four tiers of human development.

hyperinflation: A runaway rise in prices such that currency loses its value at a very rapid rate; there is no absolute number, but 10 percent or more annually would be typical.

import: A good or service that is produced in another country and then brought to the United States.

impulse buy: Purchasing something without much thought.

income: The amount of money consumers make that they can possibly spend on products.

income stocks: Stocks from large companies with a long track record of paying dividends. Sometimes called blue-chip stocks, they are issued by prominent and notable companies.

income tax: The tax on one's wage or salary. The IRS and other agencies typically require employers to withhold money from each paycheck to cover this tax bill.

individual retirement account (IRA): An account designed to save money for an individual's retirement.

Industrial Workers of the World (IWW): A union founded in the early twentieth century. Led at times by firebrand "Big Bill" Haywood, many members of the IWW believed in the ideas of Karl Marx and saw poor working conditions in factories as a reason to organize marches, strikes, and sometimes violence.

industrialization: The application of machines and nonhuman power to the production of goods and services. This process drives down the price of products as more is produced. It may also drive down wages.

inelastic demand: A quantity demanded for a product that will not be affected greatly by a change in price.

inelastic supply: A situation in which the quantity supplied of a product does not change greatly with a change in price.

infant mortality rate: The number of babies per 1,000 citizens who die before reaching the age of twelve months.

inferior products: Products of lesser quality that people buy less of when their incomes rise.

inflation: The steady rise in prices across an entire economy.

Information Revolution: A time of rapidly advancing technology in which data, money, and knowledge move across the globe at the speed of light.

initial public offering (IPO): A company's first sale of stock to the general public on a public market.

injunction: An order that requires workers to go back to their place of employment. It is usually in the form of a court order.

inputs: Things that are physically necessary to produce your good, like wood in a furniture factory.

insurance agent: A person who sells coverage on behalf of an insurance company.

insurance policy: The contract that spells out what an insurance company will pay for should the insured suffer some financial loss.

interest: The cost of using someone else's money.

internal financing: A company's use of its profits to pay for new capital and develop new products.

Internal Revenue Service (IRS): This agency collects tax revenue on behalf of the US federal government.

Internet bank: A bank without branches that is accessible only on the Internet.

investment bankers: People who specialize in helping companies to raise capital.

investment grade bonds: Bonds that are issued by the federal government, local governments, or large corporations. They are low risk and low yield, and they are rated BBB and higher.

job security: The length of time that a worker can expect to have a specific job.

junk bonds: Risky bonds whose lenders (investors) bear a greater risk of losing their principal. They are rated BB and lower. They offer lenders a higher interest rate in exchange for the higher risk.

Keynesian economic theory: Created by John Maynard Keynes, these ideas offer an antidote to the boom and bust cycles that occur in unregulated economies. Keynesians advocate the use of government involvement to alleviate the unwelcome social and economic impacts of recessions.

kleptocracy: A government whose fundamental organizing principle is based on theft and graft.

Knights of Labor: Created in the late 1860s, it was the first union in US history to cater to unskilled workers. At its height, it had more than 1 million members, including minorities and women. By the late 1880s, however, it was in decline as the American Federation of Labor came into prominence.

labor: The application of human physical and mental talent to the production process.

labor force: All of the people in the country who are over the age of sixteen and who are working or looking for work.

labor union: An organization that seeks to unify workers in unskilled industries.

Laffer curve: Created by Arthur Laffer, a graph that shows that too much taxation will be a disincentive to work. Used by conservatives to argue for lower marginal tax rates.

lagging indicators: Indicators that typically take weeks to compile and therefore influence economists' analyses later and lead to reassessments of economic events.

law of demand: The principle that an increase in price will bring a decrease in quantity demanded, while a decrease in price will cause an increase in quantity demanded.

law of supply: The principle that an increase in price will result in an increase in the quantity supplied, while a decrease in price will cause a decrease in the amount supplied.

leading economic indicators: Economic indicators that may show the direction the economy will go in the next six to twelve months.

legal: The aspect of a business, such as contracts or deals, which requires the use of a lawyer.

legal tender: Money that may be used to settle any debts or transactions, public or private.

liabilities: Debts that a business or individual owes.

liability: Full financial responsibility for an investment. Also, the responsibility for the actions of an individual or a business.

liable: Responsible for actions by law.

liberal: A person who, economically, advocates for a stronger federal government, more stringent business regulations, and social programs that alleviate social problems.

life expectancy: The amount of time a person or people can expect to live.

liquidity: The capacity of a particular asset to be converted to cash; assets (such as cash in savings accounts) that can easily be converted to cash are said to be "liquid."

literacy rate: The percentage of people in a country who can read.

living wage: The minimum income a person needs to earn in order to afford basic needs like food, shelter, and medicine.

lobbyists: Professional advocates who try to influence elected representatives on behalf of a special interest.

local income tax: An income tax charged by some but not all local jurisdictions, such as a city in which you work.

loose-money policy: When the FOMC buys bonds from investors with cash from its own vaults. The money will end up in banks, which will then lend the money to producers and consumers. It is intended to bring interest rates down and encourage economic growth.

Lorenz curve: A graph that economists use to demonstrate the distribution of wealth in a society using four or five quintiles and percentages.

luxuries: Products people feel they do not need to survive, such as candy bars. When the economy worsens, people will buy fewer of these.

M1: Money in the form of currency, traveler's checks, and different types of checking accounts. It constitutes about 11 percent of the money supply.

M2: M1 plus any money that is kept in any short-term investment that allows a person quick access to that money. Mostly, this is in savings accounts.

M3: M2 plus money that includes types of bonds and certificates of deposit. M3 money is stored for extended period of time and is not liquid.

macroeconomics: The study of economics focusing on international trade issues and national topics.

management: The process of running a business through supervision of personnel.

marginal benefit: An additional benefit to be considered when making an economic decision.

marginal cost (MC): The cost of producing one additional unit or the additional cost of making any economic decision.

marginal propensity to consume (MPC): Given after tax income, this is the percentage of money that a typical consumer will spend. When added to MPS, the result is one.

marginal propensity to save (MPS): The percentage of after-tax income that the typical consumer will save. When added to MPC, the result is one.

market economy: An economy that relies on individuals to make all or most economic decisions. The government has little or no say in what is produced, sold, or consumed.

market failure: The failure of a market to be efficient.

market size: The number of consumers in a market.

marketing: The management of a product or service through advertisement, promotions, pricing, and distribution in which a business attracts customers and makes sales.

Marxism: A worldview and way of thinking that focuses on class relations as the major source of historical trends. It also stresses that the disproportionate distribution of wealth causes social strife.

Marxist economic theory: Attests that history is a story of class struggle between owners and laborers. Its creator, Karl Marx, wanted a worldwide revolution in which workers would distribute resources more equally.

mature: The state of a CD or bond at which a person can cash it in without penalty.

mediate: To settle disputes as an intermediary between parties.

medical insurance: Insurance people pay into that helps cover medical expenses like medicine and doctor visits.

tax: A flat 1.45 tax on your income (2.9 percent if you are self-employed) that funds the health care of retired Americans. There is no income cap on Medicare contributions.

medium of exchange: Money or anything that comes between the producer and the consumer in a financial transaction where goods or services are exchanged.

merger: The absorption of one company by another.

microeconomics: The study of economics on a smaller scale. Businesses, product markets, and consumer behavior are included.

microloans: Loans of a few hundred dollars or less.

mint: The place where coins are made; also the act of making a coin.

mixed economy: An economy that combines aspects of the market and command systems. Individuals own and control the resources, and the government does have some control of the economy through taxation and regulations.

moderate: A person whose political beliefs rest between liberal and conservative.

monetarists: People who believe that all the Fed should do is let the money supply grow slowly and not respond to the temporary fluctuations in the economy by altering interest rates.

monetary policy: Actions and rules made by the Federal Reserve primarily to manage interest rates and money supply.

money market account: An account that usually requires a large balance but offers an interest rate that is tied to other market rates. It is relatively liquid and money may be withdrawn without penalty.

monopolistic competition: A form of market competition in which many producers all produce slightly differentiated products. Producers try to stand out from their competitors and need to advertise heavily.

moral suasion: An appeal or statement to the public from the Federal Reserve that typically is made to signal a potential movement in base interest rates.

mortgage: A loan made to buy land or property.

multiplier effect: The amplified impact that a tax cut can have on an economy. In essence, more money given to a consumer will result in more consuming. When goods and services are sold, the business owner will then turn and spend that money. As the process continues, it has a larger impact on the economy than the amount of the initial tax cut.

municipal bonds: Sometimes called "munies," these are bonds offered by local governments that are exempt from federal taxation.

mutual fund: A pool of money that is invested by a manager in a specific type of security (stocks and bonds usually).

National Labor Relations Act (Wagner Act): Passed in 1935, a law that for the first time gave unions the right to collectively bargain. It also formed the National Labor Relations Board to mediate and arbitrate labor disputes.

natural monopoly: Circumstances in which it is impractical to start a business to compete in a particular market due to considerable start-up expenses. Utilities are often natural monopolies as a result of the massive amounts of money needed to enter the market.

natural resources: Resources that are harvested off the land or taken from the earth, including the land itself.

necessities: Products that are required for our survival and the demand for which tends not to change if the economy worsens.

needs: Things that are vital to life and necessary to our survival, such as food and shelter.

net migration: The positive or negative number of the population that indicate whether citizens are leaving.

network: The list of doctors and hospitals with which an insurance company has negotiated prices and whose services are covered by the insurance.

networking: Interacting with other people to exchange information, develop contacts, and further one's career.

nondiscretionary spending: Government spending on programs that cannot be changed without an act of Congress. Such spending may be forced to expand if the economy goes into recession.

nonprofit: A company that tries to serve a public need. Because the government wants certain services to be provided to citizens, nonprofits do *not* pay tax on their revenue.

normal goods: Products that people tend to buy more often as they make more money.

North American Free Trade Agreement (NAFTA): A treaty between Canada, Mexico, and the United States that agreed to do away with the economic barriers between these countries.

Occupational Safety and Health Administration (OSHA): Part of the Labor Department and established in 1970, OSHA inspects workplaces and sets standards for job safety.

oligopoly: A monopolistic domination of a market by only a few companies. These firms together behave like a monopoly in that they have great control over prices. There is little difference in their product, but they advertise heavily. Prices in this market from one company to the next do not differ all that much.

open market operation: An activity that contracts and expands the money supply by increasing or decreasing it through bond sales.

opportunity costs: The benefits a person gives up by making a decision.

paid sick days: Time a worker can use to visit physicians or recover from illness and still be paid for.

paid vacation time: Time a worker can take off and still be paid for.

partner: A person who owns a share of a business.

partnership: A business with two or more people sharing responsibility in the funding or operation of the business.

payroll tax: Regardless of income, all citizens who make money pay these taxes, which fund Social Security, Medicare, and other programs.

pension plans: Usually a perk offered by older companies and unions. The organization contributes money to a pension fund in the name of the employee. The money is pooled together and invested. Upon retirement, the worker will receive a predetermined amount of money each month.

per capita GDP: The number produced when dividing the GDP by population.

perfect competition: The most ideal market situation for consumers and the economy. There is a large number of buyers and sellers, each seller must account for only a small part of the market, firms accept whatever price the market consumers will pay, and there is easy entry and exit into and out of the market.

perfect monopoly: A monopoly that has total control over price and quantity in a market. A company chooses to produce where it maximizes profit, not its efficiency. There are no substitutes. Furthermore, because information is controlled by the monopoly, it can use advertising to mask the actual quantity of its product. A monopoly may cause great inefficiency in an economy.

personal funds: The financial assets of an individual.

picket line: A protest that occurs when workers march outside their place of employment with signs and try to draw public attention to their cause.

Pinkerton: A worker hired to infiltrate a union or simply use violence to break up picket lines. Pinkertons got their name from the famous Chicago detective agency that employed them.

pitch: A short, verbal presentation to convince people of one's idea.

political action committee (PAC): An organization created to support a political candidate by raising and spending funds, usually representing a particular interest group. In PACs, resources are pooled, and because there is no limit to the donation size a considerable amount of cash can be channeled to candidates through them.

pork-barrel spending: The act of allocating money from an act of Congress to the people and pet projects in a home district.

portfolio: A person's collection of various investments.

poverty: The state of being extremely poor.

preferred stock: Stock that gives the investor a fixed share of the profits before common shares.

premium: The cost consumers pay for an insurance policy.

price ceiling: A maximum price that certain producers cannot exceed.

price floor: A minimum price for a product.

price leadership: In an oligopoly, producers watch one another's prices closely and match raised or lowered prices.

price of related goods: The price of a comparable product.

price system: The means by which the price of a good or service is determined in a market economy.

primary market: The market where bonds are issued for the first time and which may offer more money on their return. This market is usually populated by large investment firms and pension funds.

prime rate: The rate that banks give to their best customers.

principal: An amount borrowed from bank or other lender.

private good: A good from which people can be excluded.

producer price index (PPI): A measure of the prices of producers' goods.

production possibilities frontier: A graph that demonstrates all the possible combinations between making one good or another. It demonstrates the opportunity cost incurred by shifting resources in a business or economy.

productivity: The act of producing a greater dollar amount of goods in the same time period. Also, the marginal revenue that one employee brings into a business. The efficiency with which a business or economy produces goods and services.

profit: The amount of money that a business owner can keep once all expenses are paid.

progressive tax: A tax based on income brackets; it increases the percentage of income as people make more money.

property tax: The tax that homeowners and businesses pay on houses, buildings, and land. These taxes vary from locale to locale. Tax is levied upon the estimated value of the property.

public good: A good that cannot be denied to anyone, whether or not they pay taxes.

Purchasing power parity (PPP): A calculation that analyzes the ability to buy goods in different nations by compensating by variations in the cost of living from one country to the next. It looks at baskets of specific goods and compares them across nations.

put: An option that gives the holder the right to make another party buy his or her holding.

real per capita GDP: The number produced when factoring in the decreasing value of the dollar when calculating GDP.

recession: A decrease in GDP for six straight months.

regressive tax: A type of tax that takes a higher percentage of people's income as they make less money.

regulation: A rule or restriction passed by local, state, or federal government that businesses must follow.

relative poverty: Poverty experienced in relation to the lifestyles of other people in the same country.

representative money: Money issued that represents precious metal in a central bank.

reserve: An amount of money held by the bank that must be kept even. Usually, it is formed by taking 10 percent of each individual deposit.

reserve requirement: An amount of money that Federal Reserve member banks are required to keep in reserve as cash.

resource prices: Also known as "input prices," the prices of things needed to make a product or provide a service.

retirement contributions: Any money an employer contributes to a worker's retirement fund.

return on investment (ROI): The amount of return (earnings) on an investment relative to its cost, determined by dividing the return by the cost to produce a percentage.

revenue: Money that is coming into a business or government.

revolving debt: Debt where the outstanding balance does not have to be paid in full every month but still accrues interest.

Roth IRA: An individual retirement account whose contributions are not tax deductible but whose distributions are tax exempt.

rule of law: A system of laws that is written down, consistently applied, and predictably enforced.

runaway shop: A business that moved to another area where the workforce was less organized.

salary: Employee compensation that is stated as one (usually annual) sum and divided into equal periodic (usually monthly or bimonthly) payments.

sales tax: The tax collected on particular sales of specific goods and services. Most states collect sales taxes. Some counties also collect them.

savings account: A bank account that may carry an interest rate higher than that of a checking account (if it requires the holder to maintain a higher balance) but still low relative to other investments, because the money is still very liquid.

savings bonds: Bonds that can be bought for as little as $50. They have maturities of ten to thirty years, and they are bought at a fraction of face value, which is paid at their date of maturity.

Say's law: A law that states that "supply creates its own demand."

scab labor: Workers hired by businesses to replace striking workers.

scarcity: Limitation of resources. It is the fundamental problem of economics.

seasonal unemployment: Unemployment created when services depend on the season, typically affecting workers such as landscapers, farmers, and hotel workers.

seat: The ability to trade on an exchange floor.

Secret Service: An agency of the federal government that investigates counterfeiting and recommends new security measures.

Securities and Exchange Commission (SEC): Founded in 1934 in response to the 1929 crash of the stock market, the SEC watches for insider trading and fraudulent activity in the bond, stock, and futures markets.

selling short: The practice of borrowing someone's stock for an agreed time period, paying a commission, and selling the shares immediately. This is usually done if a person believes stock is about to go down in value.

services: Actions or activities that are done for others for a fee.

Sherman Antitrust Act: Passed in 1890, it is the true cornerstone of US free trade legislation. It prohibits any contract, combination, or conspiracy in the "restraint of trade."

shortage: A situation where quantity demanded exceeds quantity supplied.

slowdown: A protest that occurs when workers slow or stall the pace of production.

Social Darwinism: The idea that people who succeed in life and business are genetically superior to others.

social mobility: The ability of someone to move from one social class to another.

Social Security tax: Also known as FICA tax (after the 1935 Federal Insurance Contributions Act), this money helps to support the Social Security programs that pay for retirement pensions, aid for the indigent, and survivor benefits for orphans.

sole proprietorship: A business owned and controlled by one person or family.

specialization: The process by which a worker becomes skilled at a more specific task.

specie: Coins made of gold or silver.

speculator: A person who buys and trades futures (or other investments), trying to make a quick profit in the short term.

stagflation: A high inflation rate that coexists with a high unemployment rate.

standard of living: The overall level of wealth, luxury, comfort, and well-being of a population.

standard of value: An agreed-upon value for a transaction in a country's medium of exchange.

stock option: A contract that conveys to its holder the right, but not the obligation, to buy or sell shares of stock at a specific price on or before a given date.

store of value: How long a currency will keep its value over the years.

strengthen: Used to characterize one country's currency, to gain value against another nation's currency.

strike: A protest that occurs when a firm's employees refuse to work.

structural unemployment: Unemployment that occurs because of a major change in an economy, such as when an industry or need for a labor force becomes obsolete with new technologies. Workers with outdated skills get laid off and must find new work, demand for which is reduced as a result of the structural change.

subsidy: A payment to a business to help them lower costs or develop new products.

subsistence agriculture: When people must eat what they grow to stay alive.

substitutes: When one good is used in place of another.

surplus: A situation where quantity supplied exceeds quantity demanded.

tariff: Taxes on imports.

tax: A required payment to state revenue, levied by the government on workers' incomes and businesses' profits.

tax return: The official form that documents a year's income and tax activity.

tax revenue: The amount of money that the government brings in every year in fees, charges, and taxes.

taxable income: Income after deductions are taken.

technological improvement: Upgrading or replacement of old with new technologies in order to increase efficiency.

technological monopoly: A patented monopoly on a particular invention that remains the property of the holder of the patent for a particular amount of time.

technology: Any process, machine, or application of scientific knowledge that increases productivity.

term life insurance: Insurance merely for the death benefit; it usually has time limitations.

tight-money policy: When the FOMC sells bonds from their vast holdings to the bond markets. This will draw money from banks' reserves, and thus there will be less money to lend to producers and consumers. This is usually used to slow down a potentially inflationary economy.

time deposit: An investment with a bank in which a person promises not to touch the money for an extended period of time. In return, the bank offers a higher interest rate. Certificates of deposit (CDs) are typical examples.

time lag: The slow reaction of a market to the Federal Reserve's open market operations.

total costs: The amount is calculated by adding variable costs and fixed costs together.

total fertility rate: The total number of pregnancies a woman will carry to term in a lifetime.

trade: A manual labor occupation that requires advanced or specialized skills.

trade deficit: When more goods are imported than exported.

trade sanction: Restrictions on particular markets or specific countries; used as a means of coercion by the international community.

trade surplus: When more goods are exported than imported.

trade war: When nations escalate their tariffs in order to restrict trade.

trade-off: A choice between two alternatives.

traditional economy: An economy that relies on customs and past practices to answer economic questions. Religion and culture aid in the passing of skills from parent to child. Change happens slowly because people are reluctant to move away from customary practices.

transfer payments: Sums moved from one place to another in a society by a government. They are used to socially engineer greater income equality.

Treasury bills: Bonds that require a minimum investment of $10,000. They are held for a range of three to twelve months.

Treasury bonds: Bonds whose minimum investment is $1,000. The average investment duration is five years.

Treasury notes: Notes whose minimum investment can range from $1,000 to $5,000. Maturity ranges from two to five years.

underdeveloped: The economic status of a country that lacks industry, infrastructure, and economic resources.

unemployment rate: The percentage of the labor force that is out of work but actively looking for a job.

universal life insurance: Life insurance that pays a person's beneficiary a set amount of money when that person dies. Payments into the policy in excess of that person's premium help build cash value. Upon retirement, a person can make withdrawals from the plan.

US Department of the Treasury: An agency that handles the money of the federal government.

utility: The perceived ability of something to satisfy our wants and needs.

variable costs: Expenses that can change from one month to the next.

venture capitalist: A person who lends money to help businesses get started.

vertical merger: A merger of two companies at different phases of the production of the same good or service.

veto: The refusal of a president, governor, or mayor to sign an act into law.

vision: The idea behind a business.

W-2: A statement that employers will send employees sometime in January. It is a declaration of all the money made and taxes paid in the previous year.

W-4: A form that must be filled in when a person gets a job. The employee gets some control over his or her withholding tax on this form.

wage: What a worker is paid by the hour.

wage-price spiral: The tendency for people to spend quickly when prices increase. Faster spending will prompt businesses to raise prices further, which in turn causes a demand for higher wages. With the higher wages, consumption escalates again, which raises prices again.

wants: Things that are not vital to life but that we desire, such as jewelry or a new dining room set.

weaken: Used to characterize one country's currency, to lose value against another nation's currency.

wealth: A person's total amount of accumulated assets.

white-collar jobs: Occupations that tend to be nonmanual and nonroutine jobs, like most office work.

yellow-dog contract: A contract businesses would make with potential employees that specifies that they will not strike.

yield: A return on deposited and invested money.

Bibliography

Arnold, Roger A. *Economics in Our Times.* St. Paul: West, 1945.

Board of Governors of the Federal Reserve System. "Regulations." http://www.federalreserve.gov/bankinforeg/reghist.htm#B.

Boris, Eileen, and Nelson Lichtenstein. *Major Problems in the History of American Workers: Documents and Essays.* Lexington, MA: D.C. Heath, 1991.

Brue, Stanley L., Campbell R. McConnell, and Sean M. Flynn. *Essentials of Economics.* 3rd ed. New York: McGraw-Hill/Irwin, 2014.

Butler, Eamonn. *Milton Friedman: A Guide to His Economic Thought.* New York: Universe, 1985.

Central Intelligence Agency. The World Factbook. https://www.cia.gov/library/publications/the-world-factbook/.

Congressional Budget Office. "Economy." https://www.cbo.gov/topics/economy.

Export.gov. "Information for Exporters of U.S. Goods and Services." http://export.gov/worldwide_us/index.asp.

Federal Reserve Bank of St. Louis. "FRED Economic Data." https://research.stlouisfed.org/fred2/.

Foner, Philip S. *History of the Labor Movement in the United States.* 10 vols. New York: International Publishers, 1947–1994.

Friedman, Milton, and Rose D. Friedman. *Free to Choose: A Personal Statement.* New York: Harcourt Brace Jovanovich, 1980.

Hailstones, Thomas J., and Frrank v. Mastrianna. *Basic Economics.* Cincinnati, OH: South-Western College, 1992.

Hayek, Friedrich A. *The Road to Serfdom: Text and Documents—The Definitive Edition.* Vol. 2 of *The Collected Works of F. A. Hayek,* edited by Bruce Caldwell. New York: Routledge, 2008.

International Trade Administration. "Trade Topics." http://www.trade.gov/trade-topics.asp.

Kurzweil, Ray. *The Singularity Is Near: When Humans Transcend Biology.* New York: Penguin, 2006.

Legal Information Institute. "Sherman Antitrust Act." https://www.law.cornell.edu/wex/sherman_antitrust_act.

Marx, Karl, and Friedrich Engels. *The Communist Manifesto.* Translated by Samuel Moore. Harmondsworth, UK: Penguin, 1967.

McConnell, Campbell R., Stanley L. Brue, and Sean Flynn. *Microeconomics: Principles, Problems, and Policies.* 19th ed. New York: McGraw-Hill Education, 2012.

Ray, Margaret, and David Anderson. *Krugman's Microeconomics for AP*. New York: Worth, 2012.

Ray, Margaret, David A. Anderson, and Paul R. Krugman. *Krugman's Macroeconomics for AP*. New York: Worth, 2011.

Smith, Adam. *The Wealth of Nations*. Books 1–5. Edited by Andrew S. Skinner. London: Penguin, 1999.

Starr, Isidore, Lewis Paul Todd, and Merle Curti, eds. *Living American Documents*. New York: Harcourt, 1961.

US Census Bureau. "Census Bureau Economic Statistics." https://www.census.gov/econ/index.html.

US Department of Commerce. Bureau of Economic Analysis. "U.S. Economic Accounts." http://www.bea.gov/.

US Department of Labor. Bureau of Labor Statistics. "Occupational Outlook Handbook." http://www.bls.gov/ooh/.

US Department of Labor. Occupational Safety and Health Administration. "Safety and Health Topics." https://www.osha.gov/SLTC/index.html.

US Government Accountability Office. "Fiscal Outlook and the Debt." http://www.gao.gov/fiscal_outlook/overview.

US Securities and Exchange Commission. "What We Do." http://www.sec.gov/about/whatwedo.shtml.

Image Credits

1.2 **Photo of Cruise Ship.** By iStock.com/ATGImages, Bridgetown, Barbados, 2013.

1.5 **Sphinx of Hatshepsut.** Unknown artist, circa 1479-1458 BCE, the Metropolitan Museum of Art Rogers Fund, 1931, 31.3.166

1.7 **Cornfield at Sunset.** By iStock.com/hansslegers.

2.1 **Photo of Chef.** By iStock.com/mangostock.

2.8 **Chicago Neighborhood.** By iStock.com/stevegeer, 2012, Chicago.

2.13 **Corn Harvest.** By iStock.com/fotokostic.

2.14 **Diamond Mine.** By iStock.com/alicenerr.

2.15 **Microsoft Sign.** By iStock.com/jhutchin, 2012, Redmond, WA.

2.21 **Girl in Cherryville Mill.** By Lewis Wickes Hine, 1908, Library of Congress Prints and Photographs Division, Washington, DC, LC-DIG-nclc-01357.

2.22 **Working on Pipe Connector.** By iStock.com/Sebastien_B.

2.23 **Photo of John L. Lewis.** By Harris & Ewing, 1936, Library of Congress, Prints and Photographs Division, Washington, DC, LC-DIG-hec-33497.

2.24 **Photo of Strike.** By iStock.com/casch, 2014, Roseville, CA.

2.25 **Chart.** By US Bureau of Economic Analysis and US Bureau of the Census, retrieved from FRED, Federal Reserve Bank of St. Louis.

2.26 **Photo of Tablet.** By iStock.com/Naphat_Jorjee.

CH3 **Photo of Federal Reserve Bank, Cleveland, Ohio.** By Carol Highsmith, 1946, Library of Congress, Prints and Photographs Division, Washington, DC, LD-DIG-highsm- 04395.

3.1 **Photo of Gold Bars.** By iStock.com/filmstroem.

3.2 **Gold Stater.** By unknown artist, circa 560-46 BCE, the Metropolitan Museum of Art, Gift of the American Society for the Excavation of Sardis, 1926, 26.56.4.

3.3 **Tobacco Currency.** By unknown artist, 1863, Library of Congress, Prints and Photographs Division, Washington, DC, LC-USZ62-51222.

3.5 **Paper Bill.** By the US government, US Currency Education Program.

3.6 **Currency Exchange Kiosk.** By iStock.com/tiri83, 2011, London.

3.7 **Graph.** Data source from Google Finance, "US Dollar ($) -> Chinese Yuan (CN¥)."

3.10 **Photo of Container Ship.** By iStock.com/Raghu_Ramaswamy, 2014.

3.13 **Graph.** By the US Bureau of Labor Statistics, "Civilian Unemployment Rate," by FRED, Federal Reserve Bank of St. Louis.

3.14 **Fisher Body Plant.** By iStock.com/searagen, 2015, Detroit.

3.18 **Chart.** By the US Bureau of Labor Statistics, "Consumer Price Index for All Urban Consumers: All Items," by FRED, Federal Reserve Bank of St. Louis.

3.20 **Before Pati's Ban[k], Elizabeth St.** By unknown artist, 1908, Library of Congress, Prints and Photographs Division, Washington, DC, LC-USZ62-94974.

3.21 **Map.** By Chris N. Houston; CC BY-SA 3.0.

3.22 **Photo of the Federal Reserve.** By iStock.com/gangliu10, Washington, DC.

3.23 **Effective Federal Funds Graph.** By the Board of Governors of the Federal Reserve System, "Effective Federal Funds Rate," from FRED, Federal Reserve Bank of St. Louis.

3.27 **Current and Former Chairs.** By unknown artist, courtesy of the Federal Reserve Board.

CH4 **Bonneville Power and Navigation Dam.** By unknown artist, 1936, US National Archives and Records Administration, Washington, DC, 195807.

4.1 **Illustration of Peasants.** By Queen Mary Master, 1310–1320 CE, in "Queen Mary Psalter," British Library, London, Royal MS 2 B0.vii

4.2 **Portrait of Thomas Jefferson.** By Rembrandt Peale, 1800, the White House Historical Association.

4.8 **Photo of Shell Station.** By iStock.com/picmov, 2011, Åkersberga, Sweden.

4.9 **Photo of 1040.** By iStock.com/Get Up Studio.

4.13 **Photo of National Mall.** By Emw; CC BY-SA 4.0, 3.0 Unported, 2.5, 2.0, 1.0.

4.17 **Photo of John Maynard Keynes.** By unknown artist, circa 1930, the Harvard University Library. **Photo of Friedrich Hayek.** By unknown artist, 1981, the British Library of Political and Economic Science, IMAGELIBRARY/1025.

4.18 **Total Deficits or Surpluses Graph.** By the Congressional Budget Office.

4.20 **The Consumer Financial Protection Bureau.** By unknown artist, courtesy of the Consumer Financial Protection Bureau.

4.21 **Photo of K Street.** By AgnosticPreachersKid, 2010, Washington, DC; CC BY-SA 3.0.

4.22 **Photo of the Supreme Court.** By iStock.com/pkujiahe, 2016, Washington, DC.

CH5 **Photo of Wall Street.** By iStock.com/khyim, New York City.

5.2 **Photo of Worker.** By iStock.com/deadandliving.

5.9 **Budget Plan.** By iStock.com/alexskopje.

5.12 **Online Banking.** By iStock.com/Spaceliner.

5.13 **Blank Check.** By iStock.com/rwarnick.

5.14 **Vault Door.** By Spamguy, 2006, Cleveland; CC BY-SA 3.0, 2.5.

5.17 **Nest Egg.** By iStock.com/randymir.

5.19 **Photo of Dow Jones 100 Year Historical Chart.** By Macrotrends and Dow Jones Yahoo Finance, courtesy of Macrotrends, http://www.macrotrends.net/1319/dow-jones-100-yearhistorical-chart.

5.20 **Photo of Bloomberg Terminal.** By Jm3, 2012, San Francisco; CC BY-SA 3.0.

5.23 **Print Specimen of Stock Certificate.** By Augustus Kollner, circa 1850, Library of Congress, Prints and Photographs Division, Washington, DC, LC-DIG-ppmsca-24846.

5.26 **Savings Bond.** By iStock.com/svanhorn.

5.28 **Credit Report.** By iStock.com/kchungtw.

5.30 **Car Loan Calculator.** By iStock.com/maxuser.

5.31 **Bankruptcy.** By iStock.com/woodsy007.

5.32 **Photo of Healthcare.gov Website.** Courtesy of Healthcare.gov.

5.33 **Photo of Healthcare.gov Logo.** Courtesy of Healthcare.gov.

5.34 **Health Benefits Claim Form.** By iStock.com/i_frontier.

5.36 **Identity Theft on Laptop Computer.** By iStock.com/blyjack.

CH6 **Container Ship.** By iStock.com/rramirez125.

6.1 **Photo of Shanghai.** By iStock.com/chuyu.

6.2 **Persia in Full Sail.** By iStock.com/HultonArchive.

6.3 **Fiber Optics.** By iStock.com/yurok.

6.4 **Photo of Vietnam.** By iStock.com/bluesky85, 2011, Hanoi.

6.6 **Kenyan Children**. Courtesy of US Navy, ID 080208-F-7577K-063.

6.7 **Photo of CIA World Factbook Website**. Courtesy of CIA.gov.

6.8 **Gandhi and Lawrence**. By anonymous, public domain.

6.11 **Photo of Muhammad Yunus.** By University of Salford Press Office, Salford; CC BY 2.0.

6.13 **Map of Free Trade Blocs.** By Nystrom Education, original by Alinor; CC BY 3.0.

6.15 **Principles of Free Trade.** By World Trade Organization. "Understanding the WTO: Basics; Principles of the trading system."

6.18 **Photo of Korea at Night.** By NASA and NOAA, 2012.

6.19 **Photo of Detroit Houses.** By iStock.com/imagixian.

6.20 **Rag Pickers of Calcutta.** By iStock.com/JeremyRichards, 2008, Kolkata (Calcutta).

6.21 **Graph.** By The World Bank staff, 2010.

6.22 **Rio de Janeiro Urban Contrast.** By iStock.com/dabldy, Rio de Janeiro.

6.25 **Photo of Ho Chi Minh City Building.** By iStock.com/Pil-Art, Ho Chi Minh City.

6.26 **Dubai Cityscape.** By iStock.com/serts, Dubai.

6.27 **Photo of Intel Chip.** By Konstantin Lanzet; CC BY 3.0